HANDS UP

OR,

THIRTY-FIVE YEARS

OF DETECTIVE LIFE

IN THE MOUNTAINS AND ON THE PLAINS

Reminiscences by

General D. J. Cook

Chief of the Rocky Mountain Detective Association.

Compiled by John W. Cook.

A Condensed Criminal History of the Far West.

1897

Contents

GENERAL D J. COOK.

This book consists of a series of reminiscences of Gen. D. J. Cook, chief of the Rocky Mountain Detective Association, which has been in existence for the past thirty-five years, during which time Gen. Cook has been continuously at its head. He organized it in the beginning and has remained with it from that time until his own name and that of the associations, have become almost synonymous terms in the entire Rocky Mountain country, where both are known and where both are respected and relied upon implicitly by honest people, nm; where both are proportionately feared by evil doers of all classes likely to "have business" with them. The stories told are all true records, but while their number is quite considerable they are only a portion of the thrilling experiences—whether his own or those of officers of his association—with which his mind is stored. Indeed, if Gen. Cook should attempt to even furnish a complete narrative of his own adventures, it would fill a volume much larger than this one, for his has been a life of excitement and adventure, of exposure and hardships, of heroic deeds and many narrow escapes. Beginning as the son of an Indiana farmer, Mr. Cook has by his own unaided exertions, placed himself at the head of the detective force of the West, and has in many ways made himself prominent as a useful citizen of a growing region.

David J. Cook was born August 12, 1810, in Laporte county, In., being a son of George Cook, a farmer and land speculator. Receiving a moderate education, he worked on farms in Indiana, Iowa and Kansas until 1859. His father settled in Iowa in 1853, on the present site of Laporte, now a thriving city', but then a how bug wilderness. Selling out to good advantage, the family moved to Jefferson county, Kansas in 1855, settling on a tract of land north of where the little city of Meriden now stands, on Rock creek. When the wave of excitement which swept the country on the discovery of gold at Pike's Peak came, it bore him to the Rocky Mountains, where he spent nearly two (years in mining in what is now called Gilpin county, Colorado. Returning to Kansas he bought a farm, but in the fall of 1861 he went to Holla, Mo., and engaged in running supply trains.

He was soon afterward transferred to the ordnance department of the Army of the Frontier, and early in 1863 came again to Colorado and established the association with which his name has since been connected, and which has so long been a terror to evil doers and a trusty guardian of the public safety.

Enlisting in the Colorado cavalry, he was in the spring of 1861 detailed by the quartermaster of the Denver post as government detective in Colorado, and served until the abandonment of the post in 1866. He next served three years as city marshal of Denver, and in the fall of 1869, was elected sheriff of Arapahoe County. So satisfactory to the people of the county, of both political parties, was his administration of the sheriff's office, that at the end of his term he was reelected without opposition, and served two years longer. From 1873 he gave his entire attention to the detective work, holding at the same time the position of deputy United States marshal until the fall of 1875, when he was again elected sheriff, and reelected at the end of two years, his last term expiring in January, 1880. In 1873 he was appointed by Gov. Elbert, and confirmed by the senate, major general of Colorado militia; was reappointed by Gov. Routt, and again by Gov. Pitkin, serving four years under each. He has served as major general for nine years, and has rendered efficient service in quelling riots throughout the state, as well as in recent Indian troubles. During the Leadville strike, which occurred in June, 1880, and in which Mooney was to that city what Dennis Kearney has been to San Francisco, Gen. Cook was sent by Gov. Pitkin as commander-in-chief of the state militia, and by his efficiency soon brought the rioters under subjection to the laws of the state. During what was known as the Chinese riot, which caused such disgrace to Denver on October 31, 1880, the mayor and sheriff called on Gen. Cook to quell the riot, after the authorities had failed to do so. Gen. Cook took charge of the police and twenty-five special police, nearly all of whom were trusted members of the Rocky Mountain Detective Association, that he swore into service and in a short time brought the rioters under subjection and caused them to disperse, after arresting the ringleaders and placing them in jail. The resignation of Mr. Hickey as chief of police caused a vacancy which the leading business men of Denver thought Gen. Cook the most fitting man to fill. Knowing the great desire manifested in regard to having an efficient chief of police, the city council confirmed Gen. Cook in that position.

In addition to the responsible position to which Gen. Cook was then elevated, he has also acted as deputy United States marshal for the district of Colorado, to which he was again appointed two years previous.

Gen. Cook is a born detective. When asked one day how he happened to follow this business, he replied: "It is natural. I can't help it; I like it." He never received a day's training from any other detective in his life, and yet from the very beginning he took rank with the best in the country. He stands today alongside of Mr. [Allan] Pinkerton. Indeed, many of his exploits have far exceeded those of that justly-renowned officer in thrilling detail and startling climax. A hundred times in his life Dave Cook has been placed in positions where another man, under the same circumstances, less shrewd or less courageous, would have been shot dead in his tracks or eternally disgraced. But he was ever the right man in the right place as a detective, and it is owing to this fact that he has passed thirty-five years of detective and official life on the frontier without being killed. He possesses the essential qualities of mind and body necessary to become a successful detective in a degree rarely equaled in one man. He is both brave and discreet. He is never afraid to strike. No position appalls him. Yet he is cool-headed and cautious and wastes no blows—ventures into no unnecessary danger, and knows how to reserve his strength until it is needed most. When the time comes to act he acts with decision and promptness, always accomplishes his purpose, no difference what the odds. He is an excellent judge of men. He knows how to select the best assistants, and he "spots" a criminal nine times out of ten. He knows when to talk and when to allow others to talk. He will listen half a day to a string of surmises entirely contrary to his own without interposing an objection, with the hope of getting a clue, where other men would spoil everything by airing their own opinions. His memory is excellent, his patience inexhaustible, his ability to put this and that together is unexcelled, his perception is sharp, his reasoning is clear, his courage is undoubted and his judgment is cool under all circumstances. Add to these faculties the fact that he always deals fairly with the public; that he never fails to protect his prisoners, and that he is a man of fine bearing, of splendid figure, a face of iron on which a smile appears at home, and you will discover the secret of Dave Cook's success as a detective and as an executive officer on the frontier in the Rocky Mountains.

It was when Cook was sixteen years of age that he went, with his father, to Leavenworth. He was a country boy, roughly clad and without experience in life. His father sent him forward to the hotel to engage rooms, he had never before had such a duty as this imposed upon him. When he went in there was no one behind the counter, but the seats outside were filled with the usual crowed of hotel loafers—voting fellows living in the city, who, seeing a country boy enter, concluded to "guy" him. Finding no one at the counter, he turned to the crowd and asked for the proprietor. The loafers were inclined to giggle, and as they pointed out one of their own crowd as the individual sought, the country boy thought he observed several sly winks and heard suppressed laughter. Turning to the man whom he was told was the party sought, he asked:

"Are you the proprietor?"

"I am," he replied, and he and all the rest laughed.

Then it was that Dave's insight into character and his ready ability to "say things that hurt" came to the surface at the right time.

"I just wanted to know," he replied, "for if you are I shall hunt another hotel."

The character of the laugh which accompanied the boy's walk to the door was quite different from that which had prevailed before.

Mr. Cook did his first detective work three years afterwards, and then discovered his ability in that line he left Kansas and came to the Rocky mountains in 1859, accompanied by a brother, their purpose being to seek their fortunes mining. They were operating in the placer diggings in Missouri Flat, between Black Hawk and Russell Gulch, and had accumulated $250 in gold-dust, which they discovered one morning to be missing. Mr. Cook remembered that a man, against whom no one had suspicions, however, had been around the camp until recently, but now found that he was gone. Contrary to the advice of all the "older heads," he decided this to be the man he wanted, and concluded to follow him. He overtook the fellow near Golden and made him disgorge, and, besides, pay all the expenses which Cook had incurred in his pursuit. This man was one of the very few criminals whom Cook has allowed to escape without placing them in the hands of the authorities. But in this case the offense was against Cook himself, and he was his own officer. The law of the miners of that day inflicted the death penalty for stealing only $5 worth of any article from a miner. Cook knew what the result would be if he took the man back to camp, and he allowed the promptings of humanity to prevail and permitted the fellow to go free, much to the man's relief, who also knew the laws of the pioneer gold hunters to be more severe than those of the Medes and Persians.

It was not, however, until Cook returned to Colorado, in 1863, that he really began his detective career in earnest. He was engaged at first as an assistant detective for the quartermaster's department in the district composed of the camps at Denver, Fort Collins, Boonesville, on the Arkansas, and Julesburg. But he soon became chief of the department for the district, a position which he held for three years, resigning at the end of that time to be elected city marshal of Denver. During the three years of his service as government detective he saved the country over $100,000* worth of property, such as horses, mules, provisions and feed which would otherwise have been lost, and was the means of exposing the tricks of many who were high in authority.

*More than $1,800,000 in 2015.—Ed. 2016

His first exploit of note was the breaking up of a gang of horse thieves, who were plundering both the army and the citizens, and by both of which pa ties he was engaged to perform the service. Being allotted to this special work, he went to Chase & Healey's gambling hall, on Blake street, then a noted gambling establishment, and took a table and began to deal Spanish monte between two then notorious characters, who afterwards met death at the hands of vigilance committees, called respectively "Goggle-Eyed Ed" and "Smiley," whom he suspected of being at the head of the thieves. In less than ten days he was in possession of their secrets, and was able to "spot" their assistants, to arrest several aids and to recover some twenty horses, besides a vast deal of other property, worth in the aggregate $10,000. He discovered, among other things, that some of the soldiers were in the habit of selling army horses to a certain saloonkeeper. Ten horses had disappeared, but they could not be traced. He procured an assistant in the person of a soldier, who succeeded in negotiating the sale of a horse to this purchaser for a mere song, and was requested to deliver him at midnight at the saloon. Stationing himself at a convenient point with a companion, Cook saw an assistant of the purchaser mounted upon the horse which the soldier detective had turned over to him, and start off at a brisk gallop towards the north. Cook and his man followed at a safe distance behind, through the darkness, over the plains and into the mountains and out again, down to a secure hiding place on the St. Vrain, where the rider stopped, after a fifteen hours' gallop, quite unconscious that he had been pursued. Coming upon him Cook captured the rider and twelve head of army horses, which were grazing nearby. The details of other captures made at this time are just as thrilling as this, but this will serve as a specimen, and will help to explain the popularity which Mr. Kook soon attained as an efficient officer—a popularity which a few years afterwards elected him to the city marshalship in the face of vigorous opposition by numerous contestants for the prize.

A strong point with Gen. Cook has ever been his splendid capacity for organization and controlling men. This faculty makes him one of the most capable as well as one of the most popular commanders of our militia, and it has also aided him in making the Rocky Mountain Detective Agency, of which he was the originator, one of the most efficient of the kind in the world. It covers Colorado, Kansas, Nebraska, New Mexico, Utah, Texas, Wyoming, Arizona and California, the entire country north of Mexico and between the Missouri river and the Pacific, besides having agents in all the principal cities of the United States, and is perfectly organized, every detail being understood and superintended by Mr. Cook. Its operations have been very extensive and its "'dead certainty" has made it a terror to evil-doers. Cook has held his place at its head by the undisputed right of superiority. As good a detective as the best of his aides, he is a better commander and organizer than any of them. He is versatile and quick to see a point, and just as quick in adapting himself to circumstances. He knows when to smile, when to frown. He can drive steers, play faro or become a lawyer when circumstances demand.

As an officer, Mr. Cook's career has been quite remarkable. He has almost continuously since 1860 held some office besides that of superintendent of detectives, which has placed him in positions of danger. Beginning as city marshal, he held that place for years, and was afterwards deputy United States marshal, sheriff of Arapahoe County eight years and also chief of police. It is doubted whether there is a parallel case in the country, especially in this far western country* where men are more often desperate than elsewhere. During his experience he has arrested over three thousand men, fully fifty of whom have been the most desperate murderers, whom he has often taken at great disadvantage to himself. Of all these three thousand he never allowed one to seriously hurt him, no one of them to get away when taken, and not one to be violently dealt with when in his hands as an officer. His remarkable success he attributes to the observance of the following rules which he here prints for the benefit of young officers:

I. Never hit a prisoner over the head with your pistol, because you may afterwards want to use your weapon and find it disabled. Criminals often conceal weapons and sometimes draw one when they are supposed to have been disarmed.

II. Never attempt to make an arrest without being sure of your authority. Either have a warrant or satisfy yourself thoroughly that the man whom you seek to arrest has committed an offense.

III. When you attempt to make an arrest be on your guard. Give your man no opportunity to draw a pistol. If the man is supposed to be a desperado, have your pistol in your hand or be ready to draw when you make yourself known. If he makes no resistance there will be no harm done by your precaution. My motto has always been "It is better to kill two men than to allow one to kill you."

IV. After your prisoner is arrested and disarmed treat him as a prisoner should be treated—as kindly as his conduct will permit. You will find that if you do not protect your prisoners when they are in your possession, those whom you afterwards attempt to arrest will resist you more fiercely, and if they think they will be badly dealt with after arrest, will be inclined to sell their lives as dearly as possible.

V. Never trust much to the honor of prisoners. Give them no liberties which might endanger your own safety or afford them an opportunity to escape. Nine out of ten of them have no honor.

It will not be out of place to remark in closing, that Gen. Cook has never violated a confidence and never failed to satisfy those by whom he was engaged—whether private individuals, corporations, the army officials or the public at large. Gen. Upton, who was the author of *Upton's Tactics*, was in command in this district while Mr. Cook was chief detective, he wrote of him on a certain occasion: "Mr. Cook is a reliable and an experienced detective."

See A Genius for War: Emory Upton in the Civil War *for more on this fine soldier.—Ed. 2016*

The *Tribune* said of him when he was a candidate for sheriff in 1875:

"He is admirably adapted to the office to which he has been nominated. This combination of good politics and exact fitness is the source of a great deal of satisfaction to all genuine and steadfast republicans. No one presumes to question D. J. Cookes [*sic*] official fidelity and efficiency. The common verdict is that he has made the best sheriff Arapahoe county has ever had. And the people in supporting him in the canvass, and voting for him at the polls, support him and vote for him for sheriff. He will be elected to discharge the duties of that office, and for nothing else. And the people all have the certain assurance that he will discharge those duties ably, faithfully, promptly and honestly; that he will surely arrest criminals, and as surely keep them after arrest; that he will effectively aid in the maintenance of peace and order in the community, and that he will afford much sure protection to the persons and property of the citizens."

He was elected sheriff in the contest above referred to, and after the term of office had expired the *Rocky Mountain News* summed up the results of his term of office as follows:

"Money and property worth $80,000 was recovered and transferred to the lawful owners. The press of the city was often placed under obligations for valuable and timely information. Four gangs of railroad thieves were effectively broken up in different parts of the state, and riot prevented on several occasions. Three of the apprehended criminals were hanged after transfer to the local authorities: Robert Shamle, in Georgetown, and Woodruff and Seminole, in Golden. The beginning of the term was marked by the arrest of the Italian murderers, nine in all, and its close by the chase and capture of the Hayward murderers. During the four years ending at noon today, Sheriff Cook and his deputies conveyed 121 prisoners to the penitentiary at Cañon, and lost none by the way. There was no jail delivery in Arapahoe county, nor was the board of commissioners at any time asked to offer one cent as reward for the return of fugitives. During the term three men were killed while resisting arrest, under orders of Sheriff Cook. They were Doan, at Cheyenne; W. T. McLaughlin, at Garland, and George Wilson, in Arizona. The sheriff and his force, during the term under notice, recovered 315 head of stolen cattle and sent seven of the thieves to cañon. Also, fifty stolen horses, sending nine of the thieves to cañon. Of the cattle mentioned, Arapahoe, county lost not a hoof during the last eighteen months."

Indeed, during his entire career he has received many words of praise from press and public, and has seldom been criticized for any other than political reasons or because of personal spite which was the result of treading upon tender corns in the discharge of official duty.

A HIDDEN TREASURE

"It's no use, pard; the jig is up, and I'm goin' across the range mighty shortly." The speaker was John Reynolds—miner, gambler, rebel guerrilla, stage robber and cut-throat—as reckless a daredevil as ever met his just deserts in the whole West The person addressed was his partner in crime, Albert Brown, a desperado like himself, a man hardened to scenes of bloodshed and death, yet he brushed a tear from his eye as he turned to get a drink of water for the dying man.

"If we could only have got to Denver, we'd have been all right," continued Reynolds. "I've got over $60,000 buried not fifty miles from there in the mountains, and I could go right to the spot where Jim and me buried it in 1864. But there's no use in me wastin' breath, for I'm to the end of my rope now, an' I'll tell you just where it is, so that you can go an' get it after you've planted me deep enough so the coyotes won't dig me up an' gnaw my bones."

The dying man was sinking rapidly, but he went on: "Jim an' me buried it the morning before the fight at the grove on Geneva guide You go up above there a little ways and find where one of our horses mired down in a swamp. On up at the head of the gulch we turned to the right and followed the mountain around a little farther, an' just above the head of Deer creek we found an old prospect hole at about timber line. There was $40,000 in greenbacks, wrapped in silk oil cloth, an' three cans of gold dust. We filled the mouth of the hole up with stunns, an" ten steps below there stuck a butcher knife into a tree about four feet from the ground an' broke the handle off, an' left it pointing to the mouth of the hole."

Reynolds fell back exhausted, and asked Brown for a pencil, so that he could draw him a map. Brown had no pencil, but breaking open a cartridge he mixed the powder with some water, and as soon as Reynolds had revived a little he drew a rude map of the locality on the back of an old letter. Cautioning Brown to remember his directions, he fell back upon his rude couch, and in a few minutes was dead.

Brown set to work to digging a grave in the dirt floor of the dugout, and having no tools but a sharp stick, spent two days at the work. He placed Reynolds' body in the shallow grave, covering it up carefully, then carried stones and put over it in accordance with his agreement. As soon as Brown completed his task, he secured his horses and started for Denver. While he is on his way thither, we will improve the opportunity to relate the history of the boldest band of robbers, and indeed, the only party of rebel guerrillas that ever invaded Colorado, of which John Reynolds, whose death we have just chronicled, was the last surviving member. Before beginning the recital of our story proper, it might be well to give a hasty sketch of the conditions prevailing in Colorado at the time our story opens.

The population of Denver in 1861 was decidedly cosmopolitan. The mining excitement had attracted hither men of almost every nationality, profession and occupation on the globe. On the question of secession, then the theme on every tongue, the people seemed pretty evenly divided. The Unionists, however, seized upon the opportunity, and enlisting several companies of militia, were soon masters of the situation. All suspects were then called up to take the oath of allegiance.* Those who refused to do this were thrown into jam. Among those arrested were two brothers, James and John Reynolds. They belonged to a large class of men just upon the borderland of crime, working in the mines, driving bull teams, steering for gambling houses, in fact, turning their hands to whatever offered. Jack Robinson, a guard at the jail, was a fitting companion for them, although he had not fallen under suspicion.

The Oath of Allegiance, also called a Loyalty Oath, was a document signed by persons during and after the Civil War to pledge loyalty and allegiance to the Union.—Ed. 2016

One night while he was on guard, a large party of suspects, known as the McKee party, broke jail and made their escape, probably through the connivance of Robinson. At any rate he carried food and supplies to them while they were concealed about the city, and when they went south to join the rebel army, Robinson went with them.

Early in 1864, James Reynolds, who was beginning to tire of the restraints of military life, little irksome as they were among the irregulars under the Confederate flag in Northern Texas, found himself at the head of a company of fifty men, among whom were his brother, John, and Jack Robinson. Then, too, Reynolds had an ambition to be a second Quantrell [sic], to be a freebooter, going where he pleased and plundering all who were not strong enough to resist.

William Clarke Quantrill (1837 – 1865) was a Confederate guerrilla leader during the Civil War. His band was called Quantrill's Raiders.—Ed. 2016

He believed that with his company he could imitate Quantrell's famous raid on Lawrence, overrun all Southern Colorado and burn and sack the city of Denver, where he had been imprisoned. The majority of his men were Texans, and they did not relish the idea of a 500-mile raid through a hostile country, so that when he got ready to start, in April, 1864, he found that but twenty-two of his men would stay with him. Nothing daunted, he resolved to push forward with this small band, fully believing that he could get plenty of recruits in the mines, where rebel sympathizers had been plentiful enough a few years before. In this, as we shall learn later, he was badly disappointed, never securing a single recruit. His friend, Col. McKee, gave them a pass through to Belknap, and taking only a few rations they pushed on through the Confederate lines. Once through the lines they rode swiftly westward toward the Spanish peaks—grim beacons in an ocean of sand. When they ran out of food they killed their pack animals, and thus managed to subsist until they struck the Santa Fe trail.

They encountered a band of hostile Indians, but defeated them without loss. A little further along the trail they met a wagon train which Reynolds decided was too strong to toe attacked, so he traded a horse for some provisions. A few miles further up the trail they struck a Mexican train, which they attacked and captured. Here they made a rich haul, securing $40,000 in currency, $6,000 in drafts and about $2,000 in coin. Taking arms, ammunition, provisions and such mules as they wanted, they proceeded northward, leaving the Mexicans to get along as best they could. A great deal of dissatisfaction had arisen among the members of the band on account of Jim Reynolds taking possession of most of the money himself. A portion of the gang sided in with Reynolds' theory that the captain should have charge of the surplus funds, since he proposed to arm and equip recruits as soon as they reached Colorado. Accordingly fourteen of the party quit the gang and rode back toward Texas.

The little party now consisted of but nine men: James Reynolds, John Reynolds, Jack Robinson, Tom Knight, Owen Singletary, John Babbitt, Jake Stowe, John Andrews and Tom Halliman. That night they held a council of war. It was decided to push on to Pueblo, then up the Arkansas into the rich placer mining districts of the South park. Here they felt confident of securing not only much plunder, but enough recruits to swoop down on Denver. They cached a lot of their heavy plunder, consisting of extra guns, ammunition and several hundred dollars of silver coin, which was too heavy to be carried easily. Resting their horses, they moved, on toward Pueblo. Crossing the Arkansas at that place they rode on up the river to where Cañon City now stands, where they went into camp. A man named Bradley kept a store where the city now stands, and Reynolds dispatched several of the gang with plenty of money to purchase clothing, provisions and whisky, he did not go near Bradley himself, as he feared that gentleman would recognize him, and Reynolds was not yet ready for trouble. After having secured their supplies they pushed on to Current creek. Finding there plenty of grass and water for their horses, they decided to camp several days for rest and recuperation.

After holding another council they decided it: would be better to push on to California gulch (the present site of Leadville) in small squads so as not to excite suspicion. After looking over the gulch for a day or two they decided that the Buckskin and Mosquito camps offered better opportunities for plunder. Accordingly the band reunited and came back down, the Arkansas, entering South park below Fairplay. They stopped for the night at Guireaud's ranch, and Capt. Reynolds had a long talk with Guireaud, with whom he seemed to be acquainted. He wrote several letters to friends at Fairplay, and the next morning inquired of Guireaud what time the coach left Buckskin, as he wanted to beat it to McLaughlin's Q ranch to mail his letters. They at once set out for the ranch, which is ten miles from Fairplay. On the road, Capt. Reynolds halted his men and informed them that he proposed to rob the coach at McLaughlin's. When they reached the creek below the ranch, they met McLaughlin and Maj. Demere, and took them prisoners. McLaughlin was riding a very fine horse, and Capt. Reynolds at once suggested that they swap. McLaughlin demurred, but got down when Reynolds and several other members of the party drew their guns. Reaching the ranch the party dismounted and put out a picket. McLaughlin treated the men to some whisky and ordered his wife to prepare dinner for the gang.

When the coach drew up, Reynolds stepped out and commanded the driver, Abe Williamson, and Billy McClelland, the superintendent of the stage line, who occupied the seat with the driver, to throw up their hands, one of his men stepping in front of the horses at the same time. Their hands went up promptly, and after being disarmed by another of the gang, Reynolds ordered them to get down, at the same time demanding their money. Williamson resented the idea of his having any money, saying that it was the first time in all his travels that a stage driver had ever been accused of having any of the long and needful green about his person. But his talk didn't go with the bandits, and after searching him carefully they found fifteen cents, which they took. Williamson s eyes scowled hatred, and as will be learned later, he finally took an awful revenge for the outrage. They "shook down" McClellan with much better results, securing $400 in money and a valuable chronometer balance gold watch. They then turned their attention to the express trunk, there being no passengers on this trip. Halliman secured an axe to break if open, when McClellan offered him the key. Reynolds refused the key, venturing the opinion that they could soon get into it without the key. Breaking it open they took out $6,000 worth of gold dust and $2,000 worth of gold amalgam That John W. Smith was sending to the East, it being the first taken from the Orphan Boy mine, as well as the first run from the stamp mill erected in Mosquito gulch. Capt. Reynolds then ordered Halliman to cut open the mail hags, passing him his dirk for the purpose. They tore open the letters, faking what money they contained, which was considerable, as nearly all the letters contained ten and twenty-dollar bills, which the miners were sending back to their friends in the East. The haul amounted to $10,000 in all, a much smaller sum than the coach usually carried out.

After having secured all the valuables, Capt. Reynolds ordered his men to destroy the coach, saying that he wanted to damage the United Suites government as much as possible. His men at once went to work to chopping the spokes out of' the wheels. They ate the dinner prepared by Mrs. McLaughlin, and Capt. Reynolds then announced his determination to go on to the Michigan ranch and secure the stage stock which were kept there. Before leaving, he said to McClellan and the other captives, that if they attempted to follow the bandits they would be killed, and that the best thing they could do-would be to remain quietly at the ranch for a day or two, adding that they were only the advance guard of 1,500 Texas rangers who were raiding up the park, saying also that 2,500 more Confederate troops were on their way north and had probably reached Denver by that time.

BROUGHT TO DENVER AND SENTENCED FOR LIFE

They then rode away, leaving the settlers dumbfounded by the news. There had long been rumors of such a raid, and there being neither telegraph nor railroad, they had no means of verifying the reports. McClellan at once announced his determination to alarm the mining camps of their danger, and although his friends endeavored to dissuade him from his hazardous trip, he mounted a mule and followed the robbers, he rode through Hamilton, Tarryall and Fairplay, spreading the news and warning out citizens and miners, arriving in due time at Buckskin. From there he sent runners to California Grilled and other camps. McClellan himself stayed in the saddle almost night and day for over a week, and in that time had the whole country aroused. His energy and determined fearlessness probably saved many lives and thousands of dollars' worth of property.

Active measures were now taken for the capture of the guerrillas. Armed bodies of miners and ranchmen started on their trail. Col. Chivington sent troops from Denver to guard coaches and to assist in the capture. Gen. Cook, at that time chief of government detectives for the department of Colorado, accompanied the troops, and was soon on the trail of the marauders. The news that a band of armed guerrillas was scouring the country was dispatched by courier to Central City, and all the camps in that vicinity were notified. Even south of the divide, at Pueblo and cañon, companies were organized, and it was but a question of a few days at least when the band would be wiped out. Indeed, if there had been 4,000 of them as Reynolds had reported, instead of a little band of nine, they would have been gobbled up in short order.

Reaching the Michigan house the guerrillas took the stage horses and robbed the men who kept the station. Going on they passed the Kenosha house, stopping at various ranches and taking whatever they wanted, and robbing everybody they met. Passing Parmelee's and Haight's, they camped near the deserted St. Louis house, and at daybreak moved on to the Omaha house for breakfast. Besides refusing to pay for their meal, they robbed all the travelers camped

16

around the station except an Irishman hauling freight to Georgia gulch. He gave them the pass word and grips of the Knights of the Golden Circle, and was allowed to go on unmolested. While here they found out that large bodies of citizens were in pursuit, and they decided to move off the main road; so after leaving the Omaha house they turned off and went up Deer creek to the range. Just after they had gotten off the road into the timber a posse of twenty-two mounted men passed up the road toward the Omaha house. After awhile they saw another party evidently following their trail. Capt. Reynolds took a spyglass, and finding that there were but eighteen of them decided to fight He strung his men out in single file in order to make a plain trail, and after going about a mile, doubled back and ambushed his men at the side of the trail. Fortunately for the pursuing party, they turned back before they were in gunshot of the guerrillas. Whether they scented danger, or were tired of following what they thought was a cold trail, is not known, but it was probably the latter, as the Reynolds gang was not molested that day nor the next, although with the aid of his glass Reynolds saw scouting parties scouring the mountains in every direction. He saw that they wore likely to be captured and resolved to scatter the band in order to escape, hoping to be able, to rendezvous away down near the Greenhorn.

Capt. Reynolds decided that it would be prudent to conceal the greater portion of their spoils until the excitement had died down somewhat. Calling his brother, John, they passed up the little creek that ran by their camp until they reached its head. Elk creek also heads near there. They found a prospect hole which they thought would answer their purpose. Capt. Reynolds took from his saddle-hags $40,000 in currency and three cans full of gold dust, about $63,000 in all, leaving one large can of gold dust and considerable currency to be divided among the band before separating. They wrapped the currency up in a piece of silk oil cloth and put it and the cans back in the hole about the length of a man's body. Re-turning to the camp, Capt. Reynolds told his men that there were no pursuers in sight, and announced his determination to disperse the band temporarily, as he believed there was no chance of escape if they remained together he described the place of rendezvous mentioned, and told them that it would be safe to move on down to a grove of large trees on Geneva gulch, a short distance below, and camp for dinner, as there was no one in sight. They went on down and camped, and turned their horses loose to graze while dinner was being gotten.

Two of the men were getting dinner, and the others were gathered around Capt. Reynolds, who was busily dividing the remaining money and gold dust among them, when suddenly a dozen guns cracked from behind some large rocks about 220 yards from the outlaws' camp. Owen Singletary fell dead, and Capt. Reynolds, who was at that moment dipping gold dust from a can with a spoon, was wounded in the arm. The outlaws at once broke for the brush, a few even leaving their horses.

The attacking party, which consisted of twelve or fifteen men from Gold Run under the leadership of Jack Sparks, had crawled around the mountain unobserved until they reached the rocks, and then fired a volley into the robber band. When the robbers took to the brush, they went down to their camp and secured several horses, the can of gold dust, the amalgam that was taken from the coach at McLaughlin's, Billy McClellan's watch, and a lot of arms etc. It weds coming on night, and after searching the gulches for a while in vain, they cut off Singletary's head, which they took to Fairplay as a trophy of the fight. This was July 31, 1864.

The next day Halliman was captured at the Nineteen mile ranch, and they kept picking up the guerrillas one or two at a time until the Thirty-nine-mile ranch was reached. John Reynolds and Jake Stowe, who were traveling together, were pursued clear across the Arkansas river, but they finally escaped, although Stowe was severely wounded.

The remainder of the party were brought from Fairplay to Denver under a heavy guard and placed in jail. They were given a sham trial, and as it could not be proven that they had taken life they were sentenced to imprisonment for life, although a great many of the citizens thought they richly deserved hanging. While the party were in jail in Denver, Gen. Cook had a long talk with Jim Reynolds, the captain, and tried to find out from him what disposition had been made of all the money and valuables the robbers were known to have captured, knowing that they must have concealed it somewhere, since they had but little when captured. Reynolds refused to tell, saying that it was "safe enough," and afterwards adding they had "sent it home."

THE GANG FINALLY WIPED OUT

About the first week in September the Third Colorado cavalry, commanded by Col. Chivington, was ordered out against the Indians. Capt. Cree, of Company A, was directed to take the six prisoners from the county jail to Fort Lyon for "safe keeping" and to shoot every one of them if "they made any attempt to escape." The prisoners knew that they would be shot if the soldiers could find the slightest pretext for so doing. The troop was composed of citizens of Denver and vicinity, some of whom had suffered from the depredations of the gang. One man they particularly feared was Sergt. Abe Williamson, who, it will be remembered, drove the coach which they robbed at McLaughlin's. As they left the jail, Jim Reynolds called out to Gen. Cook, who stood near watching the procession start, "Goodbye, Dave; this is the end of us." He did not know how soon his prediction was to be fulfilled.

The first night out they camped eight miles from Denver, on Cherry creek. The prisoners were given an opportunity to escape, but they knew better than to try it. The next day the troops moved on to Russellville, where they camped for the night. Again the prisoners were given a chance to escape, but were afraid to try it.

The next morning they were turned over to a new guard, under command of Sergt. Williamson. They were marched about five miles from camp, and halted near an abandoned log cabin. Williamson now told the prisoners that they were to be shot; that they had violated not only the civil but the military law, and that he had orders for their execution. Capt. Reynolds pleaded with him to spare their lives, reminding him of the time when the rubbers had him in their power and let him unharmed. Williamson's only reply was the brutal retort that they "had better use what little time they still had on earth to make their peace with their Maker." They were then blindfolded, the soldiers stepped back ten paces, and Sergt. Williamson gave the order, "Make ready!" "Ready!" "Aim!" "Fire!" The sight of , six unarmed, blindfolded, manacled prisoners being stood up in a row to be shot down like dogs unnerved the soldiers, and at the command to fire they raised their pieces and fired over the prisoners, so that but one man was killed, Capt. Reynolds, and he was at the head of the line opposite Williamson. Williamson remarked that they were "mighty poor shots," and ordered them to reload. Then several of the men flatly announced that they would not be parties to any such cold-blooded murder, and threw down their guns, while two or three fired over their heads again at the second fire, but Williamson killed his second man. Seeing that he had to do all the killing himself, Williamson began cursing the cowardice of his men, and taking a gun from one of them, shot his third man. At this juncture, one of his men spoke up and said he would help Williamson finish the sickening job. Suiting the action to the word, he raised his gun and fired, and the fourth man fell dead. Then he weakened, and Williamson was obliged to finish the other two with his revolver. The irons were then removed from the prisoners, and their bodies were left on the prairie to be devoured by the coyotes. Williamson and his men rejoined their command and proceeded on to Fort Lyon, with Williamson evidently rejoicing in the consciousness of duty well done.

Several hours afterward one of the prisoners, John Andrews, recovered consciousness. Although shot through the breast, he managed to crawl to the cabin and dress his wound as best he could. He found a quantity of dried buffalo meat, left there by the former occupants, upon which he managed to subsist for several days, crawling to a spring nearby for water. About a week later, Andrews, who had recovered wonderfully, hailed a horseman who was passing, and asked him to carry a note to a friend in the suburbs of Denver. The stranger agreed to do this, and Andrews eagerly awaited the coming of his friend, taking the precaution, however, to secrete himself near the cabin for fear the stranger might betray him. On the third day a covered wagon drove up to the cabin, and he was delighted to hear the voice of his friend calling him. His friend, who was J. N. Cochran, concealed him in the wagon, and taking him home, secured medical attendance, and by careful nursing soon had him restored to health and his wounds entirely healed. While staying with Cochran, Andrews related to him the history of the guerrilla band as it is given here, with the exception of the story of the buried treasure, which neither he nor any of the other members of the band, except Jim and John Reynolds, knew anything about.

When he had fully recovered, Andrews decided to make an effort to find John Reynolds and Stowe, who, he thought, had probably gone south to Santa Fe. Cochran gave him a horse, and leaving Denver under cover of darkness, he rode southward. Reaching Santa Fe, he soon found Reynolds and Stowe, and the three survivors decided to go up on the Cimarron, where they had cached a lot of silver and other plunder taken from the Mexican wagon train on the way out from Texas. Their horses giving out, they attacked a Mexican ranch to get fresh ones. During the fight Stowe was killed, but Reynolds and Andrews succeeded in getting a couple of fresh horses and making their escape. They rode on to the Cimarron, and found the stuff they had hidden, and then started back over the old trail for Texas. The second day out, they were overtaken by a posse of Mexicans from the ranch where they had stolen the horses, and after a running fight of two or three miles, Andrews was killed. Reynolds escaped down the dry bed of a small arroyo, and finally succeeded in eluding his pursuers. Returning to Santa Fe, he changed his name to Will Wallace, and lived there and in small towns in that vicinity for several years, making a living as a gambler. Tiring of the monotony of this kind of a life, Reynolds formed a partnership with another desperado by the name of Albert Brown, and again started out in the hold-up business. They soon made that country too hot to hold them, and in October, 1871, they started toward Denver.

When near the Mexican town of Taos, they attempted to steal fresh horses from a ranch one night, and Reynolds was mortally wounded by two Mexicans, who were guarding the corral Brown killed both of them, and throwing Reynolds across his horse, carried him for several miles. At length he found an abandoned dugout near a little stream. Leaving his wounded comrade there, he set out to conceal their horses after having made Reynolds as comfortable as possible. He found a little valley where there was plenty of grass and water, about two miles up the cañon. Leaving his horses there, he hastened back to the dugout, where he found Reynolds in a dying condition, and the conversation related in the first chapter of this story took place.

Brown pushed on northward to Pueblo, intending to push his way along the Arkansas on up into the park, but found that the snow was already too deep. Returning to Pueblo, he pushed on to Denver. He stayed there all winter, selling his horses and living upon the proceeds. When spring came he was broke, but had by chance made the acquaintance of J. N. Cochran, who had befriended John Andrews, one of the gang, years before.

Finding that Cochran already knew a great deal about the gang, and needing someone who had money enough to prosecute the search, he decided to take Cochran into his confidence. Cochran was an old '58 pioneer, and had been all over the region where the treasure was hidden, and knowing that Brown, who had never been in Colorado before, could not possibly have made so accurate a map of the locality himself, agreed to fit out an outfit to search for the treasure. They took the map drawn by Ret molds while dying, and followed the directions very carefully, going into the park by the stage road over Kenosha hill, then following the road down the South Platte to Geneva gulch, a small stream flowing into the Platte. Pursuing their way up the gulch, they were surprised at the absence of timber, except young groves of "quaking asp," which had apparently grown up within a few wears. They soon found that a terrible forest fire had swept over the entire region only a short time after the outlaws were captured, destroying all landmarks so far as timber was concerned.

They searched for several days, finding an old white hat supposed to be Singletary's, near where they' supposed the battle to have taken place, and above there some distance a swamp, in which the bones of a horse were found, but they could not find any signs of a cave. Running out of provisions they' returned to Denver, and after outfitting once more returned to the search, this time going in by way of Hepburn's ranch. They found the skeleton of a man, minus the head (which is preserved in a jar of alcohol at Fairplay), supposed to be the remains of Owen Singletary. They searched carefully over all the territory shown on the map, but failed to find the treasure cave. Cochran finally gave up the search, and he and Brown returned again to Denver.

Brown afterward induced two other men to go with him on a third expedition, which proved as fruitless as the other two trips. On their return, Brown and his companions, one of whom was named Bevens and the other an unknown man, held up the coach near Morrison and secured about 13,000. Brown loafed around Denver until his money was all gone, when he stole a team of mules from a man in West Denver, and skipped out, but was captured with the mules in Jefferson county by Marshal Hopkins. Brown was brought to Denver and put in jail, while Gen. Cook was serving his second term as sheriff.

When Sheriff Willoughby took charge in 1873, Brown slipped away from the jailer and concealed himself until he had an opportunity to escape. He went to Cheyenne, and from there to Laramie City, where he was killed in a drunken row.

Gen. Cook secured Brown's map, and a full account of the outlaws career substantially as given here, and although he has had many opportunities to sell it to parties who wished to hunt for the treasure, he declined all of them, preferring rather to wait for the publication of this work. There is no question but that the treasure is still hidden in the mountain, and, although the topography of the country has been changed somewhat in the last thirty-three years by forest fires, floods and snow-slides, someone may yet be fortunate enough to find it.

CAPTURE OF THE ALLISON GANG

Frank A. Hyatt, of Alamosa, Colo., assistant superintendent of the Rocky Mountain Detective Association for the district embracing Arizona, New Mexico and southern Colorado, has a greater string of captures of criminals and desperadoes to his credit than any other, officer in that section. He served three years as city marshal of Alamosa, when that town was accounted one of the toughest places in the Southwest, and has been for twenty years deputy sheriff of Conejos county, Colorado. The people of that section have learned to appreciate his worth, and when desperate criminals are to be taken Frank Hyatt is the first man called upon. Plain, modest and unassuming, Mr. Hyatt does not pose as a man-killer, although he has more than once taken his life in his hands in desperate encounters with criminals, and has been compelled to take human life to save his own. His rule has been to capture his men by strategy, leaving the law to deal justice to them, rather than to kill them in trying to make arrests. He is still deputy sheriff of Conejos county, and his name is as much of a terror to evil-doers as of old, although he does not employ as much of his time in hunting bad men as he did in the early '80's. In fact, the bad men have learned to shun his section pretty carefully.

Mr. Hyatt is engaged in the manufacture and sale of a patent handcuff, the best thing of the kind made, of which he is also the inventor. It is known as the "Dead Cinch," and once it is snapped on a prisoner he cannot escape. Give him the key and he cannot unlock it; still his hands have more freedom than with the old-style handcuff. One hand can be loosened to allow the prisoner to feed himself, while the other is held fast in its grip. It is almost indispensable to officers, who have charge of desperadoes, or even of the insane, as hundreds of sheriffs, policemen and other officers scattered over Colorado, New Mexico, Arizona and Utah can attest.

One of Mr. Hyatt's greatest exploits was the capture of the Allison gang of stage robbers in 1881, shortly after he became a member of the association. This gang was composed of Charles Allison, Lewis Perkins and Henry Watts. Allison was a Nevada horse thief, who had escaped from Sheriff Mat. Kyle, of Virginia City, while that officer was conveying him to the state penitentiary at Carson City, after his conviction and sentence for ten years, in 1878, by jumping from the train, he made his escape and came to Colorado. In some way he ingratiated himself into the good opinion of Sheriff Joe Smith, of Conejos county, and was made a deputy sheriff. For a time he performed the duties of his position very satisfactorily, but he finally drifted into the holdup business, while still a deputy sheriff, with Perkins and Watts as his partners.

Alamosa, in the spring of 1881, was the terminus of the Denver and Rio Grande railroad, and stages ran from there in nearly every direction. This afforded a fruitful field for the robbers and in less than a month they had robbed five coaches, securing plunder worth several thousand dollars. Emboldened by their successes, they decided to operate on a larger scale, and riding into Chama, N. M., they terrorized the inhabitants by firing off their revolvers. When most of the inhabitants had sought places of safety, they went through the stores at their leisure, taking all the money they could find and what other stuff they wanted. A few days later they repeated the experiment at Pagosa Springs, Colo., and were again successful.

By this time the people were thoroughly aroused. Gov. Pitkin offered $1,000 reward for the capture of Allison, and $250 each for the other two and the stage company offered an additional $250, which last, we may remark parenthetically, was never paid. Notwithstanding the heavy rewards offered, no one seemed to fare about hunting up the outlaws. They were know n to be well-armed and equipped, and it was thought that as they would in all probability be lynched if caught, they would not surrender, preferring rather to die fighting. Judge Hayt, now chief justice of the state supreme court, was at that time district attorney for the twelfth district, with headquarters at Alamosa. He sent for Hyatt and asked him if he would not go after the robbers if he would issue a warrant. He replied that while everybody thought they couldn't be taken, and that he was only a young and inexperienced officer, he would do his best.

Hayt issued the warrant, and Hyatt secured the services of Hank Dorris, an old ranchman, on whom he could rely; Miles Blaine, an Alamosa saloon keeper, and Cy. Afton, a painter, and at once started after the gang. It was soon learned that they had gone almost due south from Chania, and Hyatt divined immediately that they had gone to Albuquerque, N. M. Putting his men on the train, they all rode to Espanola, the end of the road, and from there they went by stage on to Santa Re, and then took the train for Albuquerque. Hyatt felt sure that the robbers would cross the Rio Grande at that pointy so he put his men to guarding the bridge, while he inquired about town to learn whether they had already passed through or not. He could find no traces of them, so he concluded that they had not yet reached the city. After waiting all day' and all night, Hyatt decided to leave his men there, and go back up the road himself to Bernalillo, eighteen miles above, to look for them there.

Hyatt got off the train at Bernalillo and went into a restaurant to get breakfast, and while he was eating who should walk in but the very men he was after! They set their three Winchesters by the door, and as they seated themselves at the cable Allison drew his two revolvers from his belt and laid them on his lap.

It was a trying moment. Allison had been slightly acquainted with Hyatt, while they were both serving as deputy sheriffs of Conejos county, and had the detective given a sign of recognition would have shot him dead before he could reach a gun. Hyatt's face remained as immovable as that of the Sphinx. He simply looked up, said "Good morning, gentlemen," and went on nonchalantly eating his breakfast.

His conduct disarmed the suspicions of the men, and when he had finished his meal he walked out as unconcernedly as if there were no stage robbers within a thousand miles. He went to the depot, where he could watch their movements, and when they had come out and rode off southward sent a dispatch to his assistants at Albuquerque to meet them on their way, and telling them that he would follow on horseback. Then he went to looking for a horse. There was none to be had. Finally an old Mexican drove in with two fine horses hitched to a wagon. After some parley, he agreed to furnish a horse and go with Hyatt for $100. They set out and followed the robbers, keeping within sight of them, until they stopped about two miles from Albuquerque.

Meanwhile they had seen no signs of Dorris, Blaine and Afton, who should have met them before this. Hyatt and the Mexican cut across toward town and found their men just saddling up to start, having only just then received the telegram. The robbers had camped within sight of town, and Hyatt thought they might be decoyed into town and taken without bloodshed. He knew that somebody would be killed if they attempted to capture them in their camp.

At this juncture, Jeff Grant, a liveryman, volunteered to go out to the robbers' camp and try to bring them in. He got on a bareback horse, and pretended to be looking for horses that had strayed off. He went up to the camp, inquiring about horses, and finally struck up a conversation with them. Allison told him they were on their way to Lincoln county, N. M. Grant fell in with the idea at once, and told Allison that he wanted to go down there himself about the 19th of June (this was Saturday the 17th), and would like to have them wait and go with him. They claimed they were short of funds, but Grant told them that he owned a livery stable, and that it should not cost them anything to stay over a couple of days and rest up. He added that the reason he wanted them to go with him was that he was going to take down a string of race horses and quite a sum of money to back them with, and as the country was infested with thieves and desperadoes, he did not like to go alone.

This decided the robbers. Here was a good chance to rest of their jaded animals at someone else's expense, and also a prospect of some very good picking afterward. Of course, they would wait and go along with him if that was the case.

Pretty soon Hyatt and his men saw the four men come riding into town. They hastily concealed themselves in the barn, Hyatt climbing into the hay mow, and the others getting back in the mangers. They had but a minute to wait. The men rode into the barn, dismounted, and Grant led the horses back.

The three men stood close together. "Throw up your hands!" commanded Hyatt. They hesitated a moment, but when they caught the gleam of a Winchester only a few feet from their heads, three pairs of hands shot up instanter. They were disarmed and put in chains in a few moments, and telegrams were sent out announcing their capture.

Some of the local authorities were disposed to interfere in the case, and to avoid any trouble in getting a requisition, Hyatt agreed to turn over the 500 reward offered by Gov. Shelton of New Mexico to them. It was a cowardly holdup, but Hyatt couldn't well help himself, as the big end of the reward was offered by Gov. Pitkin, and he had to get the prisoners to Colorado in order to get it.

They were allowed to depart with their prisoners, and in due time reached Alamosa without further incident. They placed them in jail, and Hyatt, almost worn out with loss of sleep, went home and went to bed. In a few minutes he was awakened by a messenger from Mayor Broadwell saving that a mob was being formed to take the prisoners from the jail and lynch them. Hyatt at once gathered a crowd of his friends, among whom were Judge Hayt, Mayor Broadwell, Hon. Alva Adams, now governor of Colorado, and a number of others, and took the prisoners from the jail, put them in a caboose with an engine attached, which the mob had provided to take them outside of town before stringing them up, and signaled to the engineer to pull out, with an angry mob of several hundred following.

They escaped from the mob, and the next day the three prisoners were placed behind the bars of the Arapahoe county jail at Denver. Gov. Pitkin promptly paid Mr. Hyatt the $1,500 reward, and gave him $50 out of his own pocket.

When the excitement had partially subsided the three men were taken back to Conejos, the county seat, tried, convicted, and sentenced to the pen for thirty-seven years each.

Perkins was pardoned out after having served eight years, and is now running a big saloon and gambling hall at Trinidad, and is supposed to be worth at least $25,000. Allison was pardoned after having served ten years, and is now tending bar in a Butte City, Mont., saloon under an assumed name. Watts, the third member of the gang, was pardoned out at the same time Allison was let out, and afterward joined a band of train robbers and was killed in Arizona about two years ago.

A COWBOY'S SAD FATE

Johnny Van Pelt, a cowboy, who used to make his headquarters at Alamosa, was as reckless a lad as ever punched cattle in southern Colorado, a region particularly known for its tough characters, and while there was nothing exceptionally bad in his makeup, his recklessness and his desire to help a friend out of trouble cost him his life, and very nearly resulted in the death of two brave officers.

William Morgan, an old acquaintance of Van Pelt's, was in jail in Buena Vista, charged with the murder of his father-in-law. He managed to get word to Van Pelt in some way that he was in jail, asking him to assist him in escaping. Van Pelt at once quit work, and getting a couple of saddle horses, he helped Morgan to break jail, and the precious pair rode southward, intending to go to Old Mexico. They traveled on down the valley until they reached Hank Dorris' ranch, fourteen miles above Alamosa. Dorris had known Van Pelt, and their idea in stopping there was to borrow some money. He was not at home, and they stayed around two or three days waiting for his return, sending word by one of his friends that they were there waiting to see him. Shortly after their arrival at the ranch, Marshal Prank Hyatt, of Alamosa, received a telegram from Sheriff J. J. Salla, of Buena Vista, offering $30 reward for the capture of Morgan and Van Pelt. He kept a close lookout for a day or two, when he happened to run across his old friend, Dorris, of whom he made inquiries as to whether anyone answering their description had been seen up the valley. Dorris was surprised to learn that Van Pelt was a fugitive from justice, and telling

Marshal Hyatt that he had just received word from his ranch that they were there waiting for him, volunteered to go out and help the officer get them. Dorris was sitting on his horse and Marshal Hyatt was just going after his own animal when Van Pelt rode up and tied his horse in front of the post office. He spoke pleasantly to the two officers, and when he had tied his horse, stepped up and shook hands with the marshal. As he did so the marshal said, "Johnny, I guess I will have to hold you awhile." Van Pelt jumped back, and drawing a revolver from each overcoat pocket leveled them at the marshal's breast.

Although the desperado had the drop on him, the brave officer never flinched. He dared not attempt to draw a gun so he decided to talk Van Pelt out of shooting. Looking him straight in the eye, he said: "Don't shoot, Johnny; you haven't done anything to shoot me for." Van Pelt, his eyes still glaring with savage hate, evidently decided not to add cold-blooded murder to his crimes, but keeping the officer covered, commenced backing away to where his horse was tied. Just then Dorris, who had slipped off his horse while the parley was going on, grabbed Van Pelt from behind. The desperado jerked loose from Dorris, and, whirling around, fired at him, the ball cutting through his coat and vest and cutting a cigar in his vest pocket in two, but doing no serious damage. He then turned and fired at Marshal Hyatt, who had torn his overcoat open and gotten his own gun by this time. Then began a three-cornered battle—Van Pelt retreating toward his horse, and firing as he went, with the two officers following closely, and keeping up a fusillade of bullets.

When Van Pelt reached the telegraph pole where his horse was tied, he took shelter behind it, and commenced to untie his horse with his left hand, while he kept shooting with his right. Just as he got his horse untied, Hyatt and Dorris both fired, and both shots took effect, one entering the breast and the other smashing his thigh. He dropped his remaining gun, let go his horse, and still holding to the pole, sank slowly to the earth, saying "I'm killed." In twenty minutes he was dead.

Leaving the coroner to take charge of Van Pelt, Hyatt and Dorris hurriedly mounted their horses and started for the latter's ranch to secure Morgan. Arriving at the ranch, they found Morgan busy getting supper, haring unbuckled his belt containing his revolvers and thrown it on a lounge. At Hyatt's command, he put up his hands with alacrity. It was but the work of a few minutes to tie him securely, and Marshal Hyatt was soon on his way back to Alamosa with the fugitive.

But little else remains to be told. The verdict of the coroner's jury was that the officers had killed Van Pelt while in the discharge of their duty. Thomas O'Connor, a shoemaker, who stuck his head out of the shop door when the shooting began, was struck in the cheek by a glancing bullet, but was not seriously injured. Morgan, the man who caused all the trouble, was taken up to Buena Vista, tried for the murder of his father-in-law, convicted, and sentenced to the penitentiary for eight years. People generally thought he should have been hung, as he was the cause of at least three deaths. After her husband's murder, his mother-in-law died of grief, and Van Pelt, as has been related, was killed while trying to help the murderer escape.

DENVER'S LAST LEGAL HANGING

The murder of Street Car Driver Joseph C. Whitnah by the two negroes, Green and Withers, is noted not only for the coldblooded nature of the crime, but for the swift retribution which followed.

Oddly, the Rocky Mountain News *of the day spells the deceased's name both Whitney and Whitnah in the same article. It is spelled Whitnah on his gravestone in Denver's Riverside Cemetery. Whitnah was born on December 27, 1854. His gravestone is rather impressive.—Ed. 2016*

Whitnah was shot dead by Andy Green, a negro tough, on the night of May 19, 1886, in the boot of his car, at the Gallup turntable at Alameda avenue, on Broadway street, in Denver. Green and an accomplice named John Withers, generally known as "Kansas" by his associates, were bent on robbery. Denver did not then have her splendid system of cable and electric cars, but the old-fashioned horse cars in a measure filled their place. These cars carried no conductor, the passenger simply depositing his fare in a little box in the front of the car in sight of the driver, who also carried a box containing change for the accommodation of such passengers as might not have the requisite nickel. Sometimes the driver would have as much as $20 or $25 in his possession—scarcely enough to tempt the average highwayman.

About 10 o'clock on the night of the murder, several parties living in the vicinity of the turn-table heard a shot, then a scream, and then another shot. A number of men ran to the scene of the shooting, but Whitnah, the driver, was dead when they reached him. One or two of them had seen a man running from the scene immediately after the shooting, but whether he was white or black they could not tell.

The police soon arrived, but not a single clue to the perpetrators of the dastardly crime could be obtained. What made the case all the more difficult was the total absence of any apparent motive for the crime. The money box had not been touched, and the young; man, who was popular and well-liked by everyone, was not known to have an enemy in the world. Another thing which greatly complicated the case was the number of robberies and holdups that occurred the

34

same night, and the officers vainly tried to connect this crime with some of the others.

Since there was apparently no attempt at robbery, many people believed that there was a woman in the case, and. Sheriff Cramer and his deputies went so far as to assert they had positive evidence that the crime had been committed by one of the men who was first on the scene, a blacksmith by the name of F. O. Peterson. He was held by the coroner's jury for several days—long enough for the actual murderers to have escaped had they chosen to do so—but was finally discharged, there being not a particle of evidence against him.

Mrs. Peterson was called to testify at the inquest and was a difficult witness. Apparently the newspapers had played rather fast with rumors about a possible connection between her and Whitnah romantically. (Rocky Mountain News, May 22, 1886)—Ed. 2016

Gen. Cook had taken a great deal of interest in the case from the start. Whitnah had formerly been employed by him on his ranch near Denver, and as he was an honest, industrious and inoffensive young man, Gen. Cook was very anxious to have his murderer caught and punished. Although not conceded with either the sheriff's office or the police department at the time, Gen. Cook had gone quietly to work making inquiries on his own account, having confidence in the old adage, "Murder will out." He soon learned that a negro named Larry Foutz who hung out at a very disreputable Larimer street saloon, had been dropping a hint or two to his associates that he could tell a whole lot about the mysterious murder if he chose, and at once had him brought to the office of the Rocky Mountain Detective Association. Foutz did not deny having knowledge of the crime, but wanted to be assured by Gov. Eaton personally that he would receive the $500 reward which had been offered for the arrest of the murderer in case he gave information that would lead to the arrest of the guilty parties. Gen. Cook at once took him to the governor, who gave him the assurance asked for, and Foutz immediately put Gen. Cook into possession of the principal facts in the case, and enabled hint to arrest the murderers within a very few minutes.

Fouts did, in fact, later receive the $500 reward from the governor. The Street Car company paid $500 to Chief Hogle.—Ed. 2016

Foutz's story was to the effect that he had talked to Green that evening at the saloon, and that Green had proposed that Foutz and "Kansas" Withers should go out with him and rob a street car driver. Foutz seemed to consider the proposition very favorably, but got very drunk before they got ready to start and was left behind. He talked to Green the day after the killing, and Green told him that the reason they killed Whitnah was that he did not throw up his hands when commanded, as he was turning his car. Green fired a shot to scare him, and he gave a couple of loud screams. Green then stepped closer and shot him through the body, and he immediately fell back dead. Withers was to have secured the money box, but when the shooting occurred he ran like a deer. Green heard a man coming and he followed Withers.

Gen. Cook lost no time in arresting the two men. He went to Chief of Police Hogle and found that Green, who had been arrested and fined for carrying concealed weapons a few days before, was still on the chain gang in North Denver. The patrol wagon was secured, and in less than an hour Green was in jail. Withers was carrying a hod on a new building going up on Arapahoe street. He was at once taken into custody, and confessed his share in the crime before the jail was reached. His confession did not differ materially from the story already related by Foutz, except that he insisted that he was not a party to the killing, having told Green that he would not go along if there was to be any shooting.

Green was much more reticent and could not be induced to talk for a long time. Being told that Withers had already confessed he at length decided to tell his side of the case. He had nothing new to tell as the detectives already knew he was the man who had committed the cruel murder. He denied that he had gone out there with any intention of killing the driver, but simply fired the first shot to scare him, and as the ball was afterward found lodged in the top of the car, his story was undoubtedly true. He said that Whitnah screams scared him, and he made another step or two towards him and then fired to kill him as he said, "To stop that d—d racket." He then ran after Withers. They then went to their homes and went to bed, and had it not been for Foutz s talk might never have been suspicioned of the crime.

A local shoe store manager placed a case in the window of his store and for thirty days, after any pair of shoes was sold, he deposited a nickel in the case. In this way he raised money for Whitnah's widow.—Ed. 2016

A mob of several hundred men and boys was formed the night after their capture, to break into the jail and hang the two negroes, but lacking leadership it was soon dispersed by the police.

Public excitement and the danger of lynching induced the calling of a special grand jury, the indictment of Green and Withers and a speedy trial. They were tried separately. On the 22d of June the trial of Green opened. Two days were spent empaneling a jury, and on June 25 he was convicted of murder in the first degree, and sentenced to be hanged on July 27. Withers was allowed to plead guilty to murder in the second degree, and was sentenced to the state penitentiary at Cañon City for life, where he is now serving his time, having made two or three ineffectual attempts to secure a pardon.

The efforts of Green's attorneys to secure a new trial were unsuccessful, and he was executed on the day set by Judge Elliott, July 27. The scaffold, which was a very simple affair of the "twitch up" variety, was erected in the bend of Cherry creek, directly east of the Smith chapel, West Denver, and about midway between Broadway and Colfax Avenue bridges. The execution was public and free to everybody, and the crowd was estimated at 15,000. Green stepped upon the low scaffold in an easy, careless manner, fully conscious of the fact that he was entertaining the crowd of his life, and deriving no small amount of satisfaction therefrom. He was permitted by Sheriff Cramer to deliver a long rambling speech, in the course of which he advised everybody to beware of drink and gambling halls, which he said had led to his ruin. At the conclusion of his speech the black cap was adjusted, and at 2:20 Sheriff Cramer cut the rope. Green's body rose slowly into the air and his limbs twitched convulsively for several minutes. At the end of twenty-live minutes he was pronounced dead, and his body was taken down and delivered to the undertakers. The autopsy disclosed the fact that his neck was not broken.

Thus ended the career of as depraved a wretch as ever existed. According to the story of his life, written by him for a local paper [*Rocky Mountain News*], his thieving propensities were early developed, as was his disregard for human life.

Green, 24 years old, was articulate, thoughtful about his end, and faced the inevitable rather bravely.—Ed. 2016

At the age of fourteen he had shot his father while the latter was chastising him for a theft, inflicting a severe wound. After that he had served sentences in innumerable jails and workhouses for various crimes, principally stealing. He had also served a five-year term in the Missouri penitentiary for a burglary committed at Lexington, a little town near which he was born. The trial and execution of Green scared hundreds of petty crooks away from Denver, and for a long time afterward the city was almost entirely free from holdups and burglaries.

THE ITALIAN MURDERS

One of the most horrible crimes that ever cast a silhouette athwart the darkened pages of criminal history was revealed to the startled citizens of Denver on the 21st day or October, 1875, consisting in the discovery of what afterwards became known throughout the state as the Italian murders. The revelation of the crime, the obscurity of the victims, the length of time elapsing between the perpetration and the discovery, the mystery enveloping the deed with an apparently impregnable mantle, and the swift following detection and apprehension of the perpetrators, all combine to form the basis for one of the most interesting narratives ever found in criminal or detective literature.

For several days prior to the finding of the bodies of the victims, those residing in the vicinity of No. 2334 Lawrence street had detected the presence of a stench, faint at first, but: daily increasing, leading to a suspicion that the body of some animal had been permitted to remain there long after life was extinct. The smell from this supposed carcass becoming more obnoxious, the investigation which eventually revealed the crime, that all were surprised to find had been committed, was instituted.

Accompanied by an officer, persons residing in the neighborhood began a search, and their attention was directed to an unoccupied frame building, where countless flies swarmed around the windows, causing a suspicion that within the portals of the house reposed the object sought.

The building contained three rooms, the front and larger one communicating with those in the rear by a hall, while a rude, unfinished cellar had been excavated below. The door was unlocked, and pushing it open, the room was gained, when it became apparent that crime and not carelessness would be revealed.

Evidences of a sanguinary encounter were but too plainly visible. There was blood on the floor, and a dozen pools were yet bright and crimson. On the walls were great splotches of blood, and in the hall leading to the kitchen the tell-tale imprints of bloody hands seemed to point with grim and ghastly fingers the way to the crime.

The house was destitute of furniture, but in the middle apartment stood a scissor-grinding machine, over which had been thrown a torn and soiled blanket, revealing the occupation of some of the late inmates. Following along the hall, where a crimson trail proved that some heavy and bleeding object had been dragged, the kitchen was reached. This room was very dirty, and contained a broken stove, a wash boiler, a box, a dilapidated valise and some fragments of food. Here a trapdoor was found, and when it was opened a rush of effluvia nearly overpowered those present. A rickety stair led to the dark hole beneath. A candle was procured, and its fitful flame exposed a sight that passes all description.

Under the stairs, in a dark, filthy corner, lay four decaying human bodies, piled two on two, with all four heads touching the walk Over them had been thrown some dirty mattresses and blankets, and on these a miscellaneous assortment of traps piled on as weights. At the feet of the bodies lay three large harps, two violins, a scissor-grinding machine, a hatchet, a hammer and several dirks. The edge of the hatchet was besmeared with blood, while to the handle still clung a tuft of hair, showing that the tool had been used in the bloody murder. The dirks were blood-covered from point to hilt. On the harp-strings and on the violins and also on the stairs, the life-tide of the victims had left its gory stain, while the mattresses and blankets were saturated with it.

The clothing, down to the bloody shirts, had been stripped from the bodies of the victims, while those of the others were a slit and rent where the cruel knives had torn their way to the vitals.

But greater horrors and more ghastly sights than these were there. The four throats had been cut from ear to ear, and the sickening wounds gaped wide, like the mouth of some huge fish. The abdomens, the arms and the hands of the bodies had been cut and mangled, while the blackened faces scarcely any trace of humanity wore.

The coroner was soon on the scene, and while the undertaker was transferring the bodies to coffins, a crowd of morbid sightseers assembled. The news of the discovery spread with marvelous rapidity, and the throng grew larger and larger, until the streets, the neighboring yards and even the adjacent: housetops were packed with people. Men, women and children fairly trampled each other in their wild desire to view the bodies, and the officers were powerless be preserve anything approaching decorum.

The wildest and most exaggerated stories were circulated. It was evident to all that a quadruple murder had been committed, but no one knew the authors of the crime or its inspiration; for while it was known that a party of Italians had occupied the house, no one could be found who had seen anyone enter or emerge since the preceding Sunday. One body was identified by a colored shoemaker, who had repaired the shoes still on its feet, but aside from the fact that one of the victims was an old Italian called "Uncle Joe," and that the others were three boys, two of whom had passed as his sons, and the other as his nephew, little could be gleaned from the excited crowd.

The four bodies were taken away in an express wagon and buried in the Potter's field. Still the object of the crime and by whom committed were things wrapped in mystery so profound that it seemed as though the final day alone would reveal the awful secret.

But all are not gifted with that insight into the ways of crime that comes only from long experience in hunting it out, and is often so marvelous that it takes the aspect of instinct. Gen. D. J. Cook, chief of the Rocky Mountain Association, and then sheriff of Arapahoe county, without waiting for any offer of reward, took the case in hand even before the coroner's jury had completed its task. With a shrewdness almost without parallel he had comprehended a theory of the murders, and had his vigilant detectives on the track of the murderers.

The inquest developed but few facts, and these strengthened the theory the keen chief had entertained. Persons were found who identified the remains as those of Guiseppe Peccora, his two sons, Giovanni and Guiseppe, and a nephew called Luigi, and the fact was

41

also elicited that Filomeno Gallotti, Michiele Ballotti and one or more unknown confederates had been their former associates.

Little was known of the class to which the victims belonged, for by occupation they were itinerant musicians and scissor-grinders, and were constantly wandering from place to place. No. 2334 Lawrence street had been a lounging place for some eight or ten of this class.

Putting this and that together, Gen. Cook formed the theory that the old man and three boys had been murdered by the visitors for their money, although many entertained the idea that a free fight had culminated in the death of the weaker ones, and that the visitors had hastily concealed the bodies and fled. Suspicion pointed to a gang of Italians headed by Gallotti, who had occupied a shanty on lower Fifteenth street, and Cook soon ascertained that some nine or ten made that a stopping place, as shown by the registry lists of the ward in which the building stood. The boss of the gang was this Filomeno Gallotti, a man possessing some means, and the owner of a tin shop at that place. Antonio Dertiro, a good looking, fair haired boy, claimed to be his apprentice at the munificent salary of $150 a year [about $3,200 in 2015], and the wily detective learned that on the Thursday or Friday preceding the discovery of the bodies this youth had disappeared. The following day Gallotti also took his departure. It was learned that he claimed that the boy had stolen some money, and that he professed to be following him—all of which Gen. Cook pronounced "too thin." The tools, traps and miscellaneous plunder had disappeared from the shop and none of the gang had been seen after Saturday night.

While the coroner jury was pursuing its investigations. Cook and his men were at work on their own clues. They had already become thoroughly convinced that Gallotti and his satellites were responsible for the murder, and determined to waste no time in waiting upon the verdict of the inquisition. They set to work to discover the extent of the conspiracy, which to their minds had resulted in the wholesale murder; to determine upon the participants in the first place, and in the next to obtain clues by which they might be hunted down. They had disappeared; that was a point beyond peradventure. But wither had they gone? This was more important to those who were anxious that justice should be meted out to the wretches responsible for the crime, the horrible evidences of which confronted the community. It had become quite evident that Gallotti had been engaged in the murder, and Gen. Cook was also convinced that he had had accomplices, but who they were and what marks of identification they bore were among the facts which were not known, but which detective skill was expected to bring to light. There was evidently much work to be done. All were crying for the apprehension of the criminals—the state, the county, the city, the people. But no one offered a reward. Calling his associates together, Gen. Cook spoke briefly to the point, without any flourish of rhetoric or waste of words. "Boys," he said, "you know there has been a great crime committed here. The murderers are hardly known; of their whereabouts we are utterly ignorant. They must be brought to justice, and that is our work. There is no reward offered, but at this time we will not wait to ask for pay. Hunt the scoundrels down at any cost, and I will see that your bills are met. Do your duty." After a brief comparison of notes the men were off, this one going here and that one there, as Gen. Cook might direct.

It was not long until the discovery was made that Gallotti had been assisted in his work of murder by several others— perhaps half a dozen. A clue found here and another there gradually disclosed to the detectives the work before them. In prosecuting their investigations they learned something of tin-character of Gallotti himself. His history had been one of thrilling and romantic interest—fitting him especially for the role he had assumed as leader of the murderous band of this city. Back in Italy he had been a member of a band of outlaws, which for a score of years had been the terror of travelers and residents of the district in which it operated. Stolen from his home as a boy by these banditti, Gallotti grew up with them, soon became one of them, and gradually advanced in his accomplishments until he became one of the most renowned of the gang. He was cold-blooded, cunning, self-possessed and daring when necessary. To him no man's life was sacred. Murder was regarded only as a part of the work necessary to secure booty. Gallotti never shirked his "duty" when assassination was a part of it. Ultimately he was elected chief of the band of which he had long been virtually leader, but soon afterwards was compelled to flee the country. He came to America and ultimately landed in Denver, where he became acquainted with Michele Ballotti and others of his nationality, including "Old Joe" and his boys. It was further learned that the children who called Pecorra "father" and "uncle" were not united to him by any tie of kindred, but that he was merely an old padrone* who had stolen the boys and was compelling them to work and earn money for him. He worked himself as a scissor grinder and sent the boys out as musicians, and compelled them at times to beg for money. When they came home at the end of the day, with scant earnings, he beat and abused them; so that they worked hard and brought many a coin to the old man. Pecorra was supposed by Gallotti to be rich, and adding this point to the knowledge which he possessed of the outlaws character, Gen. Cook had no difficulty in fixing upon him as the leader of the murderous gang.

Another point of more immediate interest was soon brought to light. In looking about, Gen. Cook learned of numerous purchases that had been made by Italians. Many such articles as agricultural implements and guns had been purchased by the men whom he had come to suspect as the murderers. He was thus led to infer that it was the intention of the murderers to go into farming somewhere. He concluded that they would not risk their lives by remaining near Denver. If they had been going East they would not have bought these articles in Denver. He took the precaution to telegraph to all the important European seaports to have the men apprehended in case they should land, spending no small amount of money for cablegrams. But he was really convinced from the first that the men whom he sought had not gone across the plains, and that they did not intend to cross them. Putting this and that together he reached the conclusion in an instant that the men would make an effort to escape by going south to Mexico. He also learned that three men, who Mere described as Italians or Mexicans, had boarded a south-bound train at Littleton a few days previous. He concluded that these were the men, or some of the men, that he wanted. Selecting the late W. Frank Smith and R. Y. Force, as two of the most efficient of his officers, he started them south in pursuit of the culprits.

PURSUIT OF THE ITALIAN MURDERERS

Meantime the coroner's jury continued its work. A verdict was rendered in accordance with the facts gleaned concerning the murders as related in the previous chapter, but beyond these nothing was known. The suspected men had disappeared, and it was shown that the crime had been committed nearly a week before it was discovered. Public indignation ran high, and it was feared that, should the murderers be captured, the enraged people would not brook the necessary delay incident to the legal trial of the fiends. This feeling culminated in the firing of the house on Lawrence street a few nights after the discovery of the crime. The firemen confined their attention to the preservation of the adjoining buildings, and by one accord public sentiment allowed the building to be entirely consumed.

The details of the pursuit and capture of the criminals, with the trials and adventures of the detectives, form a most interesting and thrilling narrative, and give an insight into the ways adopted by those keen men who render crime doubly dangerous by making the punishment of the offenders approximately inevitable.

The manner in which the perilous and responsible duty of tracking the murderers was performed proves the chief's sagacity in selecting Smith and Force for the work. For twenty-one days and nights they tracked the villains. Scarcely sleeping, alike regardless of hot suns, cold rains or chilling snows, through cañons, over plains, wandering through the slums and by-ways, these men of iron nerve and tireless constitution pursued their object until they met with the reward due their skill and perseverance.

Pursuant to the instructions of Chief Cook the detectives started south on Saturday morning after the discovery of the crime. At Pueblo they separated, Force remaining there, while Smith proceeded to Cañon City. The air was full of rumors, many wild and without foundation, while others possessed the element of plausibility. It was no easy task to arrive at anything like a correct opinion by giving credence to any rumor, but after infinite difficulty a trail was discovered at Pueblo leading toward Trinidad. This Mr.

Smith was averse to taking, and so telegraphed Gen. Cook, but the latter replied: "Go ahead; the money is mine." Smith and Force at once joined at Pueblo and hastened to Trinidad. Arriving there they went to a saloon frequented by Italians, and there found some of the very men for whom they were searching, namely, Michiele Ballotti, Silvestro Campagne and Leonardo Allesandri, against whom there were strong suspicions, who were making music for the saloon loafers with all their might. After looking on for a moment to make sure of their game, the officers approached the startled musicians with drawn guns and demanded a surrender, which was sullenly acceded to. Detective Smith at once asked Ballotti when he came to Trinidad. Ballotti answered quite coolly to the effect that he had been there about two weeks, but Silvestro trembled visibly, and seemed to realize that they were about to get into trouble. Being confident that these were the men they sought, the detectives took them in charge and placed them in jail.

Up to the present time it will be borne in mind that there had as yet been no definite clue obtained as to the identity of the murderers. It is true that strong suspicion had been aroused, but, after all, suspicion is no proof. It remained for these three men to "give the whole thing dead away." When they were taken to jail and searched some of the money taken from old Pecorra's house was found upon the persons of the men, and when they were stripped the most convincing proofs of their guilt stared the officers in the face. The undershirts which they wore were still saturated with blood—blood which they confessed had flown from the veins of their victims, the padrone and his little boy slaves.

The fact of the crime being once acknowledged, the men were very free to talk, and they not only confessed their own crime, but revealed the names of others engaged with them, and poured into the ears of the detectives the bloody story of the murder which they had committed a few days before in Denver. The same stories were afterwards repeated in Denver, and will be told in their proper place. The names of the murderous band, including their own, as revealed by this delectable trio, were: Filomeno Gallotti, Henry Fernandez, John Anatta, Frank Valentine, Michiele Ballotti, Silvestro

Campagne, Leonardo Allesandri, Guiseppe Pinachio and Leonardo Deodotta, all of them being Italians except Fernandez, who was a Mexican.

They also told a story which confirmed Cook's theory that the band intended to flee to Mexico, and informed the officers where proof could be obtained of the facts in the case. They stated that not only agricultural implements had been secured, but guns and ammunition as well. The party had intended to select as a hiding place some quite, secluded valley, where they could make their headquarters, and whence they, as a band of brigands of the old Italian model, could make their forays upon the traveling and civilized world. They stated further that Gallotti and some of his men had fled from Denver, but that they had left confederates in the persons of Deodotta and old Joe Pinachio, living quietly near Sloan's lake, who, they said, knew of the whereabouts not only of the implements and munitions to be sent to Gallotti in Mexico, but also of the place at which was hidden away the bulk of the money taken from old Pecorra's house after the murder, as well. These facts were, of course, promptly telegraphed to Gen. Cook, who acted upon them, as shall be detailed in the proper place.

Within two hours the prisoners were securely ironed, and the next morning they commenced the journey that would terminate in the city where they had committed the terrible crimes, and where the news of their capture was, even then, creating wild excitement.

By 5 o'clock on the afternoon of their arrival a crowd began to gather at the depot. The afternoon was dark and lowering, and a fitful fall of snow chilled the air. But the impatient crowds surged and stamped around in a vain effort to keep warm, determined to suffer rather than to let the prisoners arrive without their knowledge. Day was fading to chill and cheerless night when the train drew up at the platform. A wild rush ensued, but the police kept a passageway open, and the prisoners were soon landed in an omnibus that had been secured for the purpose, officers mounted the top and with Gen. Cook and his assistant detectives inside and an officer on the step, the omnibus started for the jail. Scarcely had the wheels revolved, ere the crow d by one great common impulse made a rush for the vehicle with cries of "a rope!" "a rope!" "hang them!" which were caught up and repeated until the vast array seemed turned into a mighty mob bent on avenging the death of the old man and the boys, determined on a sudden and swift execution of the human birds of prey, and it seemed as though the officers would be powerless to protect the ironed ingrates who trembled as they beheld the wrath of the populace. Chief Cook was there, and his cool and steady eye had watched the pulsations of the throng, and just as the vehicle was fairly surrounded he drew his revolver and ordered the leaders of the mob back. Detective Smith was ordered to present his Winchester, which he did, and the officer on the steps also covered those nearest him. The crowd fell back and the driver lashed his horses into a run, ploughing through the crowd. Numbers followed, intent on overtaking the omnibus and capturing the criminals, while others rushed on to see the results. The tide swept down Blake street in a wild disordered procession. The driver was instructed to push the horses, and in a few moments the prisoners were securely locked in the jail, to their great relief, and to the disappointment of the crowd that had followed, hoping to see them dangle from the limb of some tree or suspended from a telegraph pole.

Great satisfaction was felt that these wretches had been secured, and the public sentiment, which always sooner or later arrives at correct conclusions, could find no praise too flattering for the able superintendent and his worthy assistants.

After hearing the news from Trinidad, and especially that which told of the presence of some of those who had been implicated in the murders near Denver, Gen. Cook was not idle but he went to work to make investigations here. He began by arresting an Italian known as "Old Joe," who lived on the ranch near Sloane's lake, with Deodotta. Joe was placed in jail for a day or so. He was a half-crazy creature, and it was believed that he could be made to tell whatever he might know of the facts in the case. He was consequently informed by Cook chat he must either divulge his secrets or submit to sudden annihilation. He promised to reveal everything, but when taken by Gen. Cook out to the place where the treasure was supposed to be buried, he failed to find the spot, either because of ignorance or craftiness.

Better success was had with Deodotta. He was also placed under arrest, and after being told that he must die or tell where the money taken from old Pecorra's house had been buried, he promised to do all in his power to find it. He was accordingly taken from the jail one morning before sunrise and driven out to his house and told to find the treasure, no one accompanying the detective and his prisoner except the driver of the express wagon. Arriving at the place, Deodotta made a last effort to conceal the whereabouts of the money, and when his protestations were doubted he crossed his breast and prayed with fervor. When Cook swore at him, he crawled on his knees and cried before him like a sniveling cur. After digging in one or two places for the money and failing to find it, Cook leveled his gun at the old sinner's head and said to him:

"Now find that money in just one minute or I'll kill you where you stand."

There was no foolishness now. Quick as thought Deodotta jumped to a spot where lay a bone and where a weed was standing with the top end stuck in the ground, and with two or three strokes of the pick, brought the treasure to light. It consisted of a package of money amounting to $350 which had belonged to the murdered man, and which was picked up and brought back to town by Gen. Cook, and Deodotta once more lodged in jail. This was a very essential part of the work performed with but little ostentation and no blow in the newspapers.

THE MURDERERS RUN DOWN

It must not be supposed that Gen. Cook had been devoting his entire attention to either the men who had been captured at Trinidad or those taken near Denver. He had now learned enough to know that. Gallotti had been the organizer and head executor of the quadruple murder, and him he wanted more than any other of the gang of cut-throats. He had been seeking anxiously for some clue that would reveal the whereabouts of this wretch and lead to his capture. The most assiduous attention and the most arduous labor seemed at first likely to prove barren of results. At last one night, however, Gen. Cook was summoned to a dark side of the street by an individual, who poured into the general's anxious ear the story of the flight of the chief of the band and three of his accomplices. This man was a friend of the Spaniard, Fernandez, and to convince the detective that he spoke the truth he pulled a letter from his pocket, from Fernandez, bearing the post mark of Fort Garland, in San Luis park. This letter was turned over to Gen. Cook, and being read revealed the welcome news that Gallotti and Fernandez and Anatta were then in San Luis park, making their way to Mexico by going down the Rio Grande river. The letter told further that they were traveling by slow stages, that because Gallotti had sent Valentine back to Denver on horseback to carry certain instructions to Deodotta and to bring the money deposited near Sloan's lake to him.

This was about as good a thing as Cook wanted. He slept but little that night, but devoted himself with all the intensity of his nature to maturing plans for the pursuit and capture of the outlaws. He decided to put the pursuing expedition in charge of Smith, who should be accompanied by an Italian who had taken the American name of James Lewis, and who, by the way, afterwards became the notorious Arizona Bill. This man knew Gallotti and besides spoke English as well as Italian. He was known to be faithful and was considered "a happy hit."

The two men were off early the next, morning, bound for the southward, Smith carrying a letter from Cook to Maj. Horace Jewett, who was then in command at Fort Garland, informing the major of the mission of the detectives and requesting him to furnish them with whatever facilities might be required for the prosecution of their work. They were told to obtain army horses and to dress as soldiers, for Americans other than "blue-coats" were then scarce in San Luis, and likely to create suspicion. Armed with these and other instructions from their chief, the men departed upon their mission, going as far as they could in the cars, the Denver and Rio Grande railroad then being completed only to Walsenburg. Leaving the railroad they turned their faces westward, towards San Luis park.

After walking a few miles they secured a team of horses from a ranchman, with which they expected to continue the journey. The horses unfortunately were affected with the epizootic, then raging, and proved a source of inconvenience and annoyance. From one place to another through the San Luis valley the trail was steadily followed. At Fort Garland, Maj. Jewett received the officers cordially and entered heartily into the plan suggested by Gen. Cook, giving Smith and Lewis soldiers' uniforms and a pair of government mules branded "U. S." Assuming the role of government officers in search of deserters, the pursuers continued their journey to Culabra, where it was hoped to intercept the criminals. But in this hope the officers were disappointed, for upon arriving there it was discovered that the men sought had gone further southward. But a point was gained in learning that they were on the trail.

It was ascertained that while in Culabra, the fugitives had stopped at the house of a Frenchman. The Frenchman was ready to render any assistance in his power, and to this end informed the detective that the men had gone on foot about fourteen miles down Culabra creek. By a little sharp practice it was discovered that the Frenchman was endeavoring to aid the criminals and had himself lent them horses and accompanied them on the road towards Taos, N. M.

Detective Smith here suddenly conceived a violent passion for the sheep business. His suit of blue was changed for a brand new one corresponding with his newly assumed avocation, and a broad-brimmed hat and a glittering array of jewelry completed the make-up of as perfect a stock king as ever proudly paced the soil of New

Mexico. A gentleman named Thaw, who had formerly been a policeman in Denver, and who was now living in San Luis, was called upon, and the detective's wand also transformed him into a sheep buyer, and he was at once admitted as a partner in the imaginary firm. The interpreter, Lewis, was also given a new role, or rather a double character. He was to ride along the road and inquire for his "partners," describing the other Italians whom they were pursuing, and at various places he would also claim to be connected with the firm of sheep purchasers as an assistant. At Sierra de Guadaloupe they passed one night, and Lewis lost no time in spreading the news that the detective and his partner were men of means, traveling through the country for the purpose of buying sheep. The entire population turned out to see them, and by cautious inquiries they learned that the murderers had undoubtedly gone toward Taos.

Before daylight the officers were on the road again, and by rapid driving reached Taos during the afternoon. Repairing to the only hotel in the place, the detective again "talked sheep," and soon gathered around a good share of the population, nearly all of whom had sheep to exchange for the ducats the detective was supposed to possess. Here it was learned that there were only about thirty-five Americans in the county, the balance of the population consisting of Mexicans and Pueblo Indians, and all the officers being Mexicans, which was a point against the detectives. They kept a vigilant outlook for Lew is, and ere long that individual was observed approaching, mounted on his mule, wearing a most abject mien. Turning at once to Thaw, Smith exclaimed in a loud voice: "Here comes that damned greaser, looking for his partners." The remark attracted attention, and as Lewis dismounted the crowd went to the door.

Lewis commenced inquiries for his "partners" and as he talked Spanish fluently, he soon discovered that three men answering the description given were then in the town. Bidding the interpreter to remain at the hotel, the detectives at once went to a store kept by two Americans named Miller and Clothier. Here they ascertained that Filomeno Gallotti had borrowed a gun and that he had left five $20 gold pieces to sell.

Being satisfied that they had the criminals almost within their grasp, Mr. Smith cast about for some plan whereby they could entrap them. To that end he sent for Thaw and Lewis, and Gallotti was then sought out and brought to the store under the pretext that Clothier desired to sell more gold for him. Although a wily and cunning brute, Gallotti suspected nothing, and almost immediately presented himself in front of the store, where he met Lewis, who, in a surprised and highly delighted manner; grasped Gallotti by the hand. That grasp was not one easily to be shaken off, however, for fingers of iron held the criminal's hand as in a vise of steel. A moment later Smith came up from behind and seized Gallotti's left hand, as if also to shake hands, and turning he gazed into the muzzle of a cocked revolver.

Gallotti realized instantly that he had been entrapped, and that resistance would be worse than useless, and begged piteously for his life. He was disarmed and handcuffed, and the leader of the band of murderers was in the clutch of the law.

But how were the others to be secured? Fate made this easy of accomplishment, for hardly had the handcuffs clicked around the wrists of the prisoner than another Italian entered the store. He was promptly seized, but proved to be a resident of the place. He was badly frightened, however, and seeing this the detective told him he would be allowed his freedom provided he would bring Fernandez and Anatta to them. To this demand he gladly acceded, and soon returned with John Anatta, who was at once overpowered and placed in irons.

One other of the men for whom the officers were searching was still unsecured. By judicious inquiry it was learned that this one was Henry Fernandez, the Mexican, the knowledge of whose connection with the crime had led Gen. Cook to infer so correctly that the criminals had gone south. It was ascertained that he had gone that morning in the direction of Red river. The Mexican officials of the county insisted upon a requisition being shown before they would consent to see the officers depart with their men, but their qualms of conscience were eased by the presentation of a purse of $100, and the captors and captives were allowed to depart. The detectives at once gave chase to Fernandez, and reached Red river at night. Here they discovered the house in which Fernandez was sleeping, and soon had secured him.

Having three of the fugitives for whom they had been in pursuit, the detectives pushed on rapidly to Fort Garland, and thence to Pueblo. After an uneventful journey the railroad was reached, and the second trio of prisoners were soon en route for Denver.

The fact that the capture had been accomplished was kept comparatively quiet, the previous lesson having been sufficient for the officers. But a large crowd was present when they landed at the depot. The manacled murderers were lifted bodily from the cars and placed in an omnibus. A few policemen rode on the top, Gen. Cook being inside with Smith and the prisoners, having joined them down the road. Aside from the presence of the officers there was nothing in the appearance of the party to attract attention. The crowd followed the vehicle out of curiosity, manifesting no especial feeling, probably remembering the prompt rebuff they had met on the previous occasion.

After Gallotti and his crowd were placed in jail they were seated for a few moments in a row along the wall, while reporters, officers and others passed around, eager to scan the faces and to discuss the relative depravity of the interesting trio.

Thus were eight of the monstrous butchers pursued and captured. But one other was yet at large, and Superintendent Cook considered his task incomplete while any of the death-dealing demons were free to enjoy the fruits of their awful crime. Frank Valentine was the only one of the number now at liberty. He had returned to Denver, but found his accomplices locked up, and had wisely taken his departure to return to Gallotti. Valentine had been a companion and associate of the gang at the tin-shop, but aside from the fact that he bore the title of "The Miner," and that he had come on this mission for the chief murderer, but little was known concerning him.

Superintendent Cook silently commenced a series of close investigations, and finally concluded that this man was at least an accessory. That brutal instinct given vent when the crime was committed was still apparent in those already secured in the jail, and they seemed anxious that Valentine should be captured, and from hints let drop by them Cook was enabled to trace the fellow back towards New Mexico.

All of the members of the detective association had been instructed by the chief to keep a sharp lookout for him, and one day it was learned that he was in the vicinity of McCorkle's ranch, in Costilla county. Thomas T. Bartlett was then sheriff in Costilla county and a member of the detective association, and he was soon on Valentine's trail. One day the officer found himself near the ranch about the hour of noon. Feeling hungry and fatigued, he determined to visit the house and obtain refreshments for the inner man. While seated at the table a rap was heard on the outer door, and in obedience to the summons "Come in," who should enter but the very man for whom the officer was in search. The assassin asked for something to eat, and while he was dispatching his dinner the detective engaged him in conversation, and carelessly asked him if he had a pistol. He replied in the affirmative and handed it over for examination. The officer informed him that it was a fine pistol—a very fine pistol, and that he wanted it. Suddenly changing his manner, he added that he also wanted the owner of the weapon.

The startled Italian gazed alternately into the muzzle of the presented revolver and the cool eye of the officer, and saw that the man was terribly in earnest. Realizing that escape was impossible, he surrendered, and while denying Mat he took any active part in the assassination, he admitted that he was a spectator to that horrible slaughter. He was brought to Denver, where Superintendent Cook met him at the depot, and soon he was behind the bars of the county jail.

MURDERERS TELL THE STORY OF THE CRIME

So prompt had been the retribution overtaking the band that the popular desire for revenge was in a measure appeased, and all seemed to be confident that the law would effectually dispose of the bloody crew. Before showing how the people were disappointed in this, and prior to relating the means by which these villains escaped the gallows, it would be interesting to visit the jail and, by conversing separately with the prisoners, ascertain so far as possible the manner by which the four victims came to their death. With the exception of Gallotti, they were all willing to talk of the affair.

The jailer leads the way to his cell. A dark-eyed man with the keen, cool, deadly look which only a murderer by birth and education could possess, rises to see who comes as the iron door swings open. He is rather a small man, but has a well-knit, compact frame, and evidently possesses considerable muscular activity and strength. His eyes are small and piercing and have a serpentine look. In this look can be found one of the reasons why he was able to absolutely control the band, to whom He was more than king or czar. Possessing some education, with an unbending will, a heart devoid of pity, a conscience knowing no regret and with those glittering eyes, transfixing the one who had dared to displease him, he was just what his ambition desired—the chief of a desperate band of banditti, whose pastimes were the cutting of throats and whose revels were in scenes of blood. He would not talk at length, but when it was suggested to him that "It is said that you were the leading spirit in that affair," replied: "I am not. The others did the murder, and now are trying to drag me into it."

So Gallotti will not talk. Let us visit Allessandri and get ids story. This boy (for he is scarcely more than a boy) was the first to make any statement to the officers, and he can think or talk of nothing but the crime. He looks up as his cell is entered and readily answers all questions.

His story as he relates it, with great rapidity and constant gesticulation is as follows: "The band consisted of Gallotti, Anatta, Ballotti, Campagne and a miner. I was forced to join them against my will but was powerless to resist Gallotti. The killing commenced Friday, October 15, at half-past one o'clock p m. I was playing a harp in the front room. The old man, called Joe in English, the biggest boy and one or two others were playing cards in the front room. The cards lay on a box and the players were seated around in a circle. Ballotti, Campagne and The miner were playing, too. Gallotti, the boss tinker, was standing up and watching the game. Suddenly Gallotti reached under his coat, drew a knife, seized the old man by the hair, drew his head back and with one powerful stroke cut his throat from ear to ear. The blood flew upon the cards and into the faces of the other players. Not yet content, Gallotti stabbed the old man in several places and releasing his hold, he let the lifeless body fall on the floor. At the same time the others seized the big boy who was sitting at my side playing the harp, but he made a desperate resistance and tried to fight them off.

"Seeing that the others were not very successful, Gallotti left old Joe's body and, grabbing the boy, cut his throat, crying to me, 'Play louder!' In the struggle they all used knives, and Anatta cut his lingers so badly that when they ceased bleeding he could not close them.

"I kept on playing the harp, for I did not dare stop, and I was so frightened that I trembled violently. Once I stopped playing, but Gallotti shook me and, drawing his knife across my throat, told me he would cut my damned head off if I did not play on. So I started up again.

"They let the bodies lay where they had fallen, and someone threw blankets over them. In about half an hour the other two came into the yard, carrying their harps. Gallotti watched the front door and Ballotti stood guard at the rear one. The smaller one came in first, carrying his violin under his arm. Gallotti seized him and, driving a knife to the hilt just under his right ear, cut the boy's throat. The little boy who played the harp came up to the door and, catching a glimpse of the blood, attempted to retreat, but Silvestro seized him and dragged him into the house. As Silvestro did not succeed in cutting his throat very quickly, Anatta went to his aid. But the boy escaped them and ran, bleeding and crying, into the front room, where Gallotti caught him around the neck with one hand and, with the boy's head under his arm, cut his throat from ear to ear.

"I was still playing on the harp, but the sight of dead bodies and the blood running on the floor made me sick. Filomeno made me lick his knife and ordered me to drink some of the blood. He scraped up a handful of blood running from the big boy's throat and drank it, the others doing likewise, as a pledge of fidelity. They then threw the bodies into the cellar and commanded me to continue playing, as the music deadened the noise and would divert any suspicion that might be entertained. Some of the bodies they dragged and some they carried to the trap-door, where they threw them into the cellar. Filomeno or someone else then went into the cellar and secured the money. I don't know how much was obtained, but he gave Ballotti $140, another $40 and handed me $20.

"After everybody had washed their hands and taken off their bloody shirts, which were thrown into the cellar, we took four revolvers, locked the doors and went to the tin-shop on Fifteenth street. About 9 o'clock that night Filomeno, Deodotta, Ballotti, Valentine, Guiseppe and the light-haired tinker went back to the house. I did not go, but went to sleep between two tinkers, who, I think, knew all about the murder, for Filomeno told them to watch me, and also told me that if I said anything about the murder, or attempted to run away, he would kill me. That night Ballotti, Campagne and I walked to Littleton, where we slept near the depot until a freight train arrived, which we boarded and rode on to Pueblo.

"I came from Central City about three weeks before the murder, and Filomeno told me he should kill the old man and the boys. I was afraid to tell anyone, fearing that he would kill me, too, and the gang never allowed me out of their sight, day or night. Filomeno told us he was going to Mexico, and would write to us."

As the musician who played the harp as an accompaniment while the throat-cutting was in progress has talked so plainly, let us visit Ballotti and, if possible, obtain from him an account of the crime. Entering the cell, a rather good-looking young man, of a compact frame and with the dark skin of an Italian, comes forward to greet us. He commences his story as follows:

"When I came here some months ago, Filomeno Gallotti assisted me in many ways, and placed his house and his purse at my disposal. He finally told me that he intended to kill the old man and the boys, and I endeavored to obtain funds sufficient to go to Cheyenne and get away, but in this I was unsuccessful, and I told Deodotta, together with another man at Sloan s lake, what plans had been made. Filomeno told us to go to the house on Lawrence street and pretend to teach the boys music, and we were thus engaged for three days prior to the murder. After Filomeno cut the old man's throat, he gave me a knife and told me to help the others. I did not wish to kill them, but, fearing Filomeno, I drew the back of the knife across the big boy's throat, but did not hurt him. When the last two came Filomeno stood behind the door and, as the little one entered, carrying his harp, he said, holding up a fancy article he had purchased, 'Look here. I have, bought you something nice today,' and just then he seized the poor boy, pulled him down upon the floor and, putting his knee on his head, said, in Italian: 'Ah, my boy, I've got you now.' With that he thrust his knife up to the hilt back of the ear and gashed the throat wide open. When the other entered, Filomeno, the miner and the tall tinker cut him all to pieces. He held on to his harp and ran around the room with his throat cut, the blood pouring from the wounds in a torrent, and Filomeno pursuing and stabbing him. Finally he succumbed and fell with the harp on top of him. The old man wore a belt filled with gold, and Filomeno divided it around. In all I suppose the belt contained about $1,400."

From this point on the story contained only unimportant details.

Says John Anatta, and their of the murderers, when talked to: "I cannot sleep, for "Old Joe's' spirit haunts my dreams, and when he approaches me I seem to be cutting his throat, Rut no sooner have I done so than a brand new one takes its place, and I awake horrified. It was awful, but I could not help it, and I did not do any of the cutting. I hit one of the boys on the head, but the knife bent and cut my hand, and that was all I did."

Let us again visit Gallotti, and after we have told him what the others say, perhaps he will be induced to give some account of the horrible butchery in which it is claimed he took such a prominent part. A dark scowl again greets us, but he is in better humor—just in trim to cut throats were the occasion propitious.

"Now, see here, Gallotti, the others have told us all about this affair, and you might as well say something, too."

"Well, you see, I commenced the job at the card table, by catching 'Old Joe' by the hair and sawing my knife across his throat until he was quite dead. I helped to kill one of the boys, as the others were making a bad job of it. I then put up my knife and watched Anatta, Ballotti and Guiseppe cut the other two. I secured $800 in gold and $377 in currency, but I gave the most of it to the others. I conceived the idea of the murder some time ago, and when I broached the subject to the others individually and at different times, they all were eager to engage in the scheme. My reason for killing the old man was this: Several years ago I lived in New Orleans and, being successful in business, my countrymen often deposited their savings with me. The sum thus entrusted to me increased until I had about six thousand dollars of other people's money. Thinking it proper to invest this, I loaned it to a fruit dealer, who promised to pay a fair rate of interest on the amount advanced. Subsequently, and as I afterwards learned, by 'Old Joe's' advice, the fruit dealer decamped with the money. I followed him all over the country, but finally my means became exhausted and I came to Denver, where I settled down at my trade. One day I was asked to write a letter for the man on Lawrence street, and when the address was signed, I learned for the first time that 'Old Joe' was the one who advised the fruit dealer to abscond with the six thousand dollars. I kept this to myself, but continued to watch him, and finally was satisfied that he was the identical 'Joe' who had been in New Orleans. Then I determined to kill him, and enlisted the others in the plot. They are as guilty as I, and deserve as severe a punishment."

This being all Ballotti has to say, we are forced to withdraw.

TRIALS OF THE ITALIANS

It would seem from the evidence and their own confessions that this band would surely be hung. But such a fate was not in store for them. On Saturday, December 4, 1875, the preliminary examination was had before Justices Whittemore and Sayer. Gallotti and Ballotti pleaded guilty, and, together John Anatta, Leonardo Allessandri, Guiseppe Campagne, Leonardo Deodotta, Frank Valentine, Guiseppe Pinachio and Henry Fernandez, they were bound over to the district court for trial on the 26th day of the following January. John Anatta and Allessandri, the young harpist, turned state's evidence before the grand jury and indictments were returned against the entire band. On the 30th of January the accused were brought into court and counsel was assigned them.

February 8 they were arraigned, pleaded not guilty, and their cases were set for trial during the April term. May 20 Gallotti was before the court and pleaded guilty. Great excitement was occasioned when it became known that under a section of the statutes he could not be hung, a life sentence being the utmost penalty in cases when the accused entered a plea of guilty. The next day Ballotti was arraigned and endeavored to withdraw his plea of not guilty. The motion, for reasons not clearly apparent, was overruled and his case was set for trial on the following day. The evidence in the trial of Ballotti was simply a repetition of the facts already known to the reader, and a verdict of murder in the first degree was rendered.

It was decided that under the law Gallotti could be tried in spite of his plea. When arraigned Gallotti again entered the plea of guilty, and it was considered proper to carry his case to the supreme court as a test of the loose law then in force. The same proceedings were had in the case of Frank Valentine. Campagne also pleaded guilty, and Anatta and Allessandri entered special pleas of voluntary manslaughter. Deodotta was acquitted on the charge of being accessory, and the following sentences were meted out to the bloodiest band that ever went unhung: Gallotti, Valentine, Campagne and Ballotti were sentenced for life; Anatta and Allessandri received each ten years while the others went scot free.

Gallotti, the leader of the cut-throat band, was pardoned out in 1885, leaving immediately for his native land, Italy, but, according to reports, never reaching it, but dying on his journey. Ballotti, the best one of the lot, died in the prison at cañon, December 20, 1887. Campagne was pardoned out June 29, 1888, and Valentine, the other life man, was restored to liberty by Gov. Waite on August 5, 1895.

MUSGROVE AND HIS GANG

For a few years previous to 1868 Denver was a paradise of quiet and repose. The mining excitement, v hick had attracted so many people to this region a few years before, had subsided to a great extent. The settlers were becoming accustomed to a residence in this region. The novelty of the life in the Far West had died out. There were few mining "booms," if any, and the "hard cases" which invariably follow in the wake of mining discoveries of importance had become disgusted with the slow life in this section, and had folded their tents and quietly departed for more inviting and, to them, more congenial fields. Of course, the good people had no fault with this state of affairs. They went on following their customary avocations, delving steadily for the precious metals, tilling the soil and building up town and country. In a word, Denver seemed, within a remarkably short period, to have settled down into the perfect repose, so far as crime was concerned, of the New England village.

But with the approach of railroads there came a change—a radical and important change. The building of a new railroad in any section always introduces a large element of irresponsible and vicious people. In the West the percentage of this element is larger than in the East. But as the Union Pacific was the pioneer railroad line built across the plains, and as the country was new and inviting to men of adventurous spirit, its construction was probably accompanied by a greater number of arrivals than that of any other line built since in this region. There were gamblers of all degrees, sneak thieves, burglars, highwaymen, horse thieves, murderers, fugitives from justice and amateurs in crime. In many places along the line of the road it was "quite the thing" to be a bad man, and honesty and civility were at a serious discount. Yet in places the better element would ultimately gain the ascendancy. In many cases the contest was close and often there was doubt as to whether the good or the bad would triumph. As a rule, however, respectability asserted itself, although frequently not until much blood had been shed and the most heroic measures resorted to, to rid the various communities affected of these human pests. There were vigilance committees at

Cheyenne, Laramie City and other places along the line of the Union Pacific [Railroad], which, after months of endurance of the most terrible outrages, took the law into their own hands. The results were numerous warnings to offenders to leave these places, and many "neck-tie parties" as well, at which no "duly elected" judge sat for days in weighing the evidence, but where justice was seldom, as in other courts, blind. The action of these vigilance committees was so energetic and efficient that many of those of the worst classes were compelled to get away from the railroad camps, and large numbers of them poured into the Colorado towns.

Of such were Sanford S. C. Duggan and Edward Franklin, whose tragic fate, as well as that of L. H. Musgrove, it is the purpose of this and succeeding chapters to treat.

Musgrove was one of the marked villains of the pioneer days of Colorado, and as cool a character as it was ever the fortune of a detective or criminal officer to fall in with. He was a man of large stature, of shapely physique, piercing eye and steady nerve, who might have stood as the original for the heavy villain of the best story of a master in romance literature. He was a man of daring, inured to danger, calm at the most critical times—a commander whose orders must be obeyed, who planned with wisdom and who executed with precision and dispatch. He was the leader of an organized band of horse thieves, highwaymen and murderers, who infested the western plains, with Denver as general headquarters, during the years 1867-'"68. They made the railroad tow us a convenience in disposing of their booty, but did not spend time in loafing about these places when there was other and more profitable business to attend to in other places. Mus- grove was a southern man by birth, being a native of Como Depot, Miss. He had gone to California during the days of the gold excitement on the coast, and had located in Napa valley. His sympathies were with the South in the rebellion, and he quarreled with a Napa man about the merits of the conflict, which quarrel resulted in his coolly shooting the other party down. He was compelled to leave the place, and afterwards stopped in Nevada, where he killed two men before being driven from that then territory. Leaving Nevada, he came to Cheyenne, and from Cheyenne to Denver. He was at first, after cross mg the mountains, engaged as an Indian trader about old Fort Halleck, until a half-breed Indian had the temerity, half in sport, one day to call him a liar, when Musgrove calmly pulled his revolver from his pocket, and, taking deliberate aim, planted a bullet square in the middle of the Indian's forehead.

This transaction served to put an end to Musgrove's Indian trading, for he was compelled to leave the Indian region on very short notice. After this little affair he organized a band of horse thieves, which operated throughout the entire plains country, and which was one of the most formidable bands of desperadoes known to frontier history. Musgrove was a perfect organizer. He had his operators in Colorado, Wyoming, New Mexico, Texas, Nebraska, Kansas and others of the western states and territories, and carried on a regular business of stealing and selling stock. They would drive off entire droves of horses from one section and sell them in another five hundred miles away, and would steal another drove in the neighborhood of the late sale and drive it for sale back to the place at which they had made the previous raid.

Musgrove's band was broken up by degrees. As early as the spring of 1868 Gen. Cook, accompanied by Col. Egbert Johnson and one or two others, tracked four of them down after a two days' march, and captured them a t the point of Winchester rifles in a cabin near the city. Col. Johnson proved of invaluable service in this work in tracking the scamps, as he had had much experience in the mountains. In doing this work he had to even wade through a lake of water. Later he went to Georgetown after another of them, and capturing him there brought him to Denver alone. They were compelled to stay in a hotel at Idaho Springs all night, and both slept in the same room, Johnson setting his gun by the side of his bed and telling the desperado that if he made a move during the entire night he would blow his brains out. The fellow was as quiet as a mouse, and was afraid to get up when morning came, so thoroughly was he convinced that Johnson would put his threat into execution.

Musgrove was himself hunted down in Wyoming, and captured and brought to Denver. He was saucy to the last. Just a few days before his capture he took shelter in an invulnerable place on the Poudre, and sent a flag of truce to the pursuing officer, telling him that he could come in and pick out any stock that he could recognize; that he could have that and no more. Mr. Haskell, the then United States marshal, was in command of the pursuing party. He accepted the conditions laid down, as there was no alternative, and in doing so found the outlaw so barricaded, and his drove of stolen horses and mules so securely arranged, that he made no effort to dislodge him.

The arrest was finally affected by a bit of detective strategy, and the people throughout the entire western country rejoiced when it was announced.

Among Musgrove's outlaws there was none more daring and heartless than Ed. Franklin, who had been with his chief in many close places and who really seemed to cherish a great fondness for Musgrove. They had in their days of intimacy on the plains sworn eternal fidelity to each other and had taken a vow, with others of the party, to come at all times to the assistance of each other in times of danger. Hence, when Musgrove, the chief of the gang, found himself in the clutches of the law in Denver, he contrived to notify his followers and to ask their assistance. It was a fact well-known at the time to Gen. Cook that no less than twenty of these scoundrels responded to the call, which had been sent over the country. He was confident as to their character and their mission. He knew that they had come to Denver intending to effect Musgrove's escape. He was confident that such was their purpose, but he could, of course, make no arrests, as he would have been without proofs. He could only remain perfectly quiet and wait for the desperadoes to signalize their presence in some way, as he well knew they soon would. He was not compelled to wait long to have his opinion of the men verified and to find occasion for making arrests. He was at that time not only chief of the Rocky Mountain Detective Association, but also city marshal of Denver, and as such was the chief of the police of the city. It may not be out of place to remark that while Cook was marshal, and by virtue of this position chief of police, Mr. Frank Smith, who has already been mentioned frequently in this book, was one of his subordinate officers. Smith was one of Cook's most trusted men. The two learned to appreciate the striking qualities of manhood and bravery thus discovered in each other in those trying days, and became so thoroughly attached to each other that they never separated as long as Smith lived, which was until 1881.

Ed. Franklin, to whom reference has been made as one of Musgrove's most trusted lieutenants, responded with alacrity to the call to come to the rescue of his chief; and without intending to forestall the story so far as to mar it, it may be stated that the expedition proved fatally disastrous to him. Franklin was accompanied to Denver by Sanford Duggan. They were both bullies and desperadoes—not only bold brigandish boys, but that and villains of a lower order, men who did not hesitate to stoop to little meannesses when to do so suited their purposes. They came to Denver with records, and they had been in this city but a very short while before they began to look about for an opportunity to add to their "laurels."

It does not appear that Duggan had ever been a member of Musgrove's band, but he had led a career that would have entitled him to hold a place of distinction in that scoundrel's organization. Coming to Colorado in 1861, from Fayette county, Pa., when he was only sixteen years of age, he had lived for seven years in the company of low characters. At the age of eighteen he picked up a quarrel with a man named Curtis, in Black Hawk, and shot him down in a cold-blooded and merciless manner. For this offense he had been imprisoned for a short while, and then allowed to escape. Leaving Black Hawk after this experience, he came to Denver, where he became the associate of a prostitute, one Kitty Wells, who sold herself to obtain money for him to live on. He lived with her but a short while, when they quarreled one night and he struck her across the head with a pistol, wen nigh killing her he was then arrested by Gen. Cook while threatening to kill him. He was jailed, but escaped justice in some way. We next find him in the Black Hills, near Laramie City [now Wyoming], in company with a man named Al

Howard. Soon there is news of another murder, and Duggan is arrested on suspicion and taken to Yankton, Dakota, for trial, but the proof is insufficient to establish his guilt and he is allowed to go to prey upon the community. He returns to the line of the Union Pacific extension and to Laramie City, where he for a while acts as city marshal. Discovering the true character of the man the good citizens compel him to resign—not only force him to resign, but give him a set number of hours in which to get out of town. He takes the hint, and decides upon coming to Denver.

A few days out from Cheyenne Duggan falls in with Franklin, who has just passed through an experience which is worth relating, as it goes to show the character of the man with whom we are soon to deal. He had stolen a bunch of mules from Fort Saunders, and had succeeded in carrying them several miles to a place on the plains where the soldiers who were pursuing came up with him. There were seventeen of them in the pursuing party. It was no longer sensible for him to continue his flight, as he would, at best, be completely overtaken in a few miles. Most men, even desperadoes, would have surrendered without parley to such odds in numbers, but Franklin's motto was: "Die, but never surrender." He determined to fight. Dismounting from the animal which he rode, he hastily scraped a pile of sand up and threw" himself behind it. The soldiers came up and Franklin opened fire. They returned the salute, and for over an hour the entire seventeen poured their leaden balls in the direction of the horse thief. He retaliated as fast as he could, and during the entire hour held the whole party at bay. At last, however, he was struck in the breast with a ball and was compelled from weakness to cease shooting. He was taken at last, nearer dead than alive. Being removed to Fort Saunders [sic; Sanders], he recovered rapidly, and had no sooner regained his strength than he made his escape. Once out of prison he soon hears of Musgrove's predicament and starts to his chief's rescue, where he meets Duggan, and they journey on together. Of course, they prove congenial spirits.

They do not ride boldly into Denver, but decide to stop near the city on Clear creek, until night shall come on with its friendly cloak, for Duggan, it must be remembered, is known to Chief Cook and his police force.

The night, however, is not far advanced when they make their appearance upon the streets. That the original intention of the men in coming to Denver was to liberate Musgrove could not be doubted, but they did not propose to waste time, and hence determined to earn a few dollars by the simple "holdup" process in case opportunity should offer. Hence they sauntered out Blake street in quest of game. The first man they met was Mr. James Torrence, who was compelled to stand and deliver. They procured $22 from him and allowed him to pass on, soon afterwards meeting Mr. Alex DeLap, who is now a well-known and wealthy citizen of the state, who was halted, and who would have been robbed had he not taken the precaution before leaving home to divest himself of his valuables.

The thieves soon find themselves on Lawrence street, and discover Hon. Orson Brooks, then a justice of the peace and police magistrate for Denver, wending his way homeward. They followed him to a deserted place on the street, about the site of the Markham house (the old Grand Central hotel), where he was accosted by them with a polite request to hold up his hands. Possessing no means of defense and finding a pair of ugly revolvers staring him in the face, the judge was compelled to stand and allow himself to be robbed of $125. Judge Brooks had sat in the trial of Duggan for the assault upon the woman Kittie Wells and recognized him while the search was in process. He gave some intimation of this fact, and the knowledge came near costing him his life. In response to a sally from him came the cheerful proposition from Duggan to Franklin: "Let's plant the damned old snoozer—what d'ye say?" Franklin was quite willing, and the chances are that, had Judge Brooks not been able to laugh off the matter as he did, his body would have been made the sheath of a keen-pointed and silent dagger. But he succeeded in convincing the men that he had been mistaken when he supposed he recognized one of them, and after treating him to a maximum dose of profanity, they allowed him to depart.

THE OUTLAWS OVERTAKEN

The robbery of Judge Brooks was the event which sealed the fate of both these desperate characters, and probably indirectly also that of Musgrove. The event occurred on the night of Friday, November 20, 1868. Judge Brooks was a prominent and much-esteemed citizen. The whole town was indignant. There were demands on every hand to have the highwaymen hunted down. Denver had aroused from stupor to an active appreciation of the state of affairs. An outrage had been committed, and justice must be done. The guilty parties must be found and punished. To whom should this work be entrusted? The public of Denver had already learned to appreciate "Dave" Cook. He was now town marshal, and had already organized his detective association. The case was put in his hands. He had one clue. Judge Brooks remembered that he had on his person before he was robbed a $20 bill, which had been torn and which he had mended with a piece of official paper about his office. Mr. Cook naturally concluded that there were not apt to be two bills so torn and so mended. Hence he went to work to find the man who should offer to spend this piece of money. He notified not only the officers of Denver, but those of surrounding towns as well.

The robberies had been committed on Friday. On Sunday a messenger arrived from Sheriff John Keith, of Jefferson county, saying that the men that were wanted in Denver were to be found in Golden. It was stated that they had gone to that place on Saturday; that they had been drinking and swaggering about the streets, loaded down with revolvers and defying all the officers of Christendom. It was supposed that they were desperadoes, but they were not identified until Sunday morning, when the $20 bill was tendered to someone by Duggan. This fact had no sooner become known to Sheriff Keith than he dispatched a notification to Marshal Cook. The messenger arrived late in the afternoon, so that it was dusk before the marshal and his posse were off for Golden, eighteen miles distant. There was no Colorado Central railroad between Denver and Golden in those days to pick people up in one place and set them down in another within half an hour, as there now is. But there was a splendid dirt road, and over this the horses flew, their

71

hoofs beating melodiously on the frozen soil, as Cook and his men marched off towards the foot-hill metropolis in the pursuit of their business. The pursuing party was composed of the following named persons: D. J. Cook, W. Frank Smith, D. W. Mays, Eugene Goff, H. B. Haskell and Andy Allen. They were all mounted well and were armed very thoroughly.

Golden was reached about 9 o'clock in the evening of Sunday, November 23. The party stopped in the outskirts of the city for a few minutes, until Keith could be communicated with. Being found, he informed the Denver officers where their men were located. Franklin, he said, had been drinking heavily during the day and had retired to bed early at the Overland house. Duggan was at that moment at a saloon kept by Dan Hill. It was resolved to take Duggan first, and the officers, reinforced by Keith, started in the direction of the saloon indicated. While on their way to this point they met two men, one of whom said to the other as they passed: "What do these sons of bitches of officers want? That's Dave Cook, from Denver. I left one of my pistols at your saloon." This remark was overheard by Cook and Keith, and the latter whispered to the Denver marshal the fact that the speaker, of whom Cook had not had a fair view, was Duggan. The other man, he also told Cook, was Miles Hill, brother of the proprietor of the saloon. Immediately the two men were seen to turn and cross a vacant lot of ground to the rear of Hill's saloon. The officers stopped for a minute to arrange plan*: Cook directing Smith, with Keith and others of the squad, to proceed to the front of the saloon, while he, with Goff, would go to the rear. "In case there should be shooting, boys, do not hit Miles Hill," said Sheriff Keith, and taking up the sentence, Cook gave an order to his men to be very careful not to hurt any citizen of Golden.

The officers closed in upon the place with the greatest celerity. Smith and his force found all dark in front, but Cook and Goff discovered a small and glaring light near the door of the saloon as they came around the corner. It was evidently from the burning end of a cigar in a man's mouth. Soon the door of the saloon opened, shedding a light upon the man with the cigar in his mouth and revealing in him the fugitive Duggan. A man came out at the door and proved to be Hill. The friends of Hill assert that he only brought Duggan's pistol to him, but the officers say, be that as it may, he seemed to present the pistol at them, intentionally or accidentally, at which time Duggan fired on Cook and Goff, the ball flying by them and nipping a bit out of the blue soldier overcoat which Cook wore. Notwithstanding the officers carried cocked revolvers in their hands and were fearful that they would have trouble, they were considerably surprised, it was a moment before they collected themselves, and before they were entirely at themselves another ball came whizzing by them in dangerous proximity to their vitals. They were not more than ten feet from the men who held pistols in their hands. There was no time to hesitate or parley. A moment's delay might mean death to both of them. With that calm and commanding way, that cool and deliberate manner which has ever characterized Dave Cook in time of danger and placed him above other men, he raised his pistol with his left hand—he always holds his pistol in his left hand when he shoots—and taking aim, fired, telling Goff also to fire. One man fell to the ground, and the other started away on a full run, firing a parting salute as he left. The flash of the pistol revealed the fact that Duggan was the man who was making an effort to escape, and he was pursued by some of the members of the party. However, the man jumped a fence, and by so doing found a hiding place in a dense undergrowth, so that extensive pursuit of him that evening could not be otherwise than unavailing.

When the officers returned they found that the man who had been shot was Miles Hill. The ball had entered his left side and ranged downward through the abdomen and lodged in the opposite side of the man's body. It was evident that he could not live. He was found lying in the street with a cocked revolver near him. He demanded plaintively to know why he had been shot, and when told the circumstances of the case, apparently recognized the justice of his fate.

Hill seems to have been a thoroughly good fellow, and his kindness of disposition probably led him to the point of helping Duggan out of a bad scrape. What representation he had made to Hill was not revealed by him, and will now, of course, never be known. But that Hill was influenced to aid the disreputable man into whose company he had been so unfortunate as to fall can hardly be doubted. He died about twelve hours after the shooting, and was sincerely mourned by the citizens of Golden, who permitted their friendly feeling for and acquaintance with the social qualities of the man, for the time, to influence their judgment of the killing, and, what a few days afterwards was recognized as a necessary precaution by the officers in the protection of their own lives and in the discharge of their duty in attempting to arrest Duggan, was at first criticized as "haste and negligence." Cook and Goff either had to kill or be killed. They preferred the former alternative, repulsive as it was to them.

But there was then little time to linger over the man whose life blood was oozing gradually out as a consequence of his attempt to defend a criminal from arrest. There was other work than indulging in vain regrets to be accomplished. Duggan had escaped, but Franklin was still in town, and his whereabouts were known. He must be captured at all hazards. To allow him to escape was not a part of the programme of the officers. They had been notified by Sheriff Keith that Franklin had taken a room at the Overland house, then standing where it now does, and thitherward they wended their way, fully armed, and equipped with a strong pair of handcuffs with which they proposed to secure Franklin, and thus render his return to Denver quite beyond question when once he should be in their power.

Mr. Cook's associates in making this arrest were Frank Smith and Mr. Keith, they volunteering from the entire company to go with him. The hotel proprietor did not hesitate to inform the officers where Franklin was to be found, and they were soon in his room after starting in the search. They did not seek ad mission by knocking at the door, which was found unlocked. Although soaked with liquor when he retired, Franklin had left everything in perfect order for his defense in case he should be set upon suddenly, showing himself to be a criminal who was used to being hunted, and who never forgot his caution even when apparently "too far gone to know anything." His empty pistol scabbard hung on the bed-post, while underneath his pillow lay a large revolver, loaded, cocked and ready for use at a moment's warning. The officers stole in with quiet tread, Cook leading the van, with his fingers on his lips, and the others following as noiselessly as if treading upon velvet, although the floor was bare. Mr. Keith carried a candle, and as he came up to the bed with it, so that the light fell upon Franklin's eyes, he turned over with a groan. He lay stretched at full length—a man of brawny muscle and splendidly developed physique. His breast being partially bared, revealed the gunshot wound which was the memento he carried of his late exploit in standing off seventeen of Uncle Sam's soldiers near Fort Saunders, and which had yet scarcely thoroughly healed. As he turned in the bed his eyes opened. At that moment Mr. Cook laid a heavy hand upon the arm of the man, saying:

"Franklin, we want you."

The fellow was awake in a moment.

"The hell you do!" he exclaimed, showing that he took in the situation at a glance.

"Yes, come on quietly."

"Quietly, be damned! Where's my gun? No damned officer from Denver can arrest me. I'm not that sort of stuff. You can make up your mind to that."

By this time he was fully aroused. He was standing on his knees, his eyes flashing fire, and striking sledge-hammer blows at any of the officers who attempted to lay hands upon him. He would listen to no entreaty, but answered all appeals with derision. At last Mr. Cook produced the handcuffs, and made a move towards Franklin with them.

"Oh, it's irons you have, is it?" he exclaimed, as he lunged at the party. "If that's what you're up to, I have some myself."

And with this speech he turned to his pillow in the act of pulling his revolver from its hiding-place.

At that moment one of Cook's assistants, considering that Franklin was preparing to shoot, struck him on the head and knocked him to the other side of the bed. He was up in a minute and more furious than ever. He had well-nigh torn his underclothes from his body, and the blood was running from the fresh wound in his head. He was furious with rage, and snorted and roared and tore about like a wild animal brought to bay, exclaiming, "Come on, all of you!" as he rose to his feet. "I suppose you can kill me, but you cannot arrest me. I will not go with you. If you want to shoot, put it there—there!" And he slapped his hand violently two or three times upon his heart. The scene was extremely tragic.

Up to this time no one had intended to shoot, and Franklin was told so. "Damn you, if you don't shoot, I will," he exclaimed again. "I will fight your whole gang, if you will give me a fair show. I won't be arrested, I won't go; I'll die first—but I'll die hard. One or two of you will go with me if I go. Ed. Franklin does not sell out for a song." At this he made a lunge for a cocked revolver which Cook had laid on a table nearby. But the keen-eyed officers were too quick for him. They had detected the purpose of the move and were ready. They did not propose to stand up to allow another professional murderer and desperado to shoot at them. They were not betting blood on even terms with outlaws. Cook caught his pistol with his left hand, and even while Franklin was fighting his way to it like a mad man, sent a ball whizzing through his very heart. Smith's firing followed so soon as to cause what seemed little different from one report. With hardly a groan Franklin tumbled over on the blood-stained bed, a dead and harmless man. He had sowed the wild oats of a reckless and useless life, and he had reaped the full harvest.

So ended the last of the tragedies of Golden's night of horrors, November 22, 1868.

Of course the entire town had been aroused by this time. It was getting well along in the night, yet no one seemed to have retired. On the contrary, everybody appeared to be upon the streets. Hardly anyone understood the cause of the It Muffle or the crimes that had been committed. There were reports that a dozen men had been killed, and that a mob had taken possession of the town. The people flew here and there like mad. It was, indeed, a wild Sabbath night for Golden—ordinarily then, as now, a very quiet and orderly town.

Coroner's investigations of both killings, those of Miles Hill and Ed. Franklin, were ordered, and inquests were held. It was found that a ball had struck Hill in the left arm, entering his left side and passing through his abdomen, while two bullets had entered Franklin's breast, hardly an inch apart, and both passing through the heart. In the case of Hill, local prejudice was allowed to control the deliberations of the coroner's jury, the members of which were not in possession of all the facts in the case, and in the verdict the officers—who, the reader will bear in mind, were only returning the fire of Duggan—were slightly censured for "carelessness in the discharge of their duty." The verdict was signed by George B. Allen, W. M. B. Sarell, J. M. Johnson, Jr., Arthur C. Harris, P. B. Cheney and J. Pipe, either one of whom would doubtless, under the same circumstances, have acted just as the officers did—if they had not depended upon their heels instead of their pistols for protection.

The verdict in the case of Franklin stood as follows: Territory of Colorado, County of Jefferson:

An inquest, holden [*sic*] in Golden City, Jefferson county, Colorado territory, on the 22d day of November, A. D. 1868, before J. B. Cass, a justice of the peace, upon the dead body of Ed. Franklin, alias Charles Myers, lying at the Overland house, in Golden City, Colorado territory, dead, by the jurors whose names are hereto subscribed. The said jurors, upon their oaths, do say that the said Ed. Franklin, alias Charles Myers, came to his death by the shots of pistols in the hands of D. J. Cook and Win. F. Smith, officers, who were trying to arrest him; and that the deceased was shot because he refused to be arrested, and the officers shot him in the discharge of their duty, on the evening of the 22d of November, 1868.

D. C. CRAWFORD.
H. M. HOWELL. JAMES GOTT. JOSEPH CASTO.
H. R. KING.
WM. MARTIN.

Thus ended this series of tragedies, so far as Golden was involved. The officers, before returning to Denver, scoured the town of Golden and the surrounding country in search of Duggan, but failed to find him. Indeed, they soon became convinced that he had lost no time in leaving the place, and as there were then few residences either in the mountains or on the plains, there was little hope of overtaking him if pursuit should be decided upon. Consequently Gen. Cook decided to return to Denver with his men, and to send out information in all directions to his assistants of the detective association concerning the escape of the desperado, paying $50 to the landlord of the Overland house before leaving for damages done to the bed in which Franklin lay. The man who shared Franklin's bed was found to be a deserter from the army and was turned over to the military authorities.

AN ILLEGAL HANGING IN BROAD DAYLIGHT

The night was well advanced when the officers, who had gone to Golden, returned to Denver. Indeed, the morning was coming on, so that they were late in reaching their homes. Being well worn with the night's excitement and fatigue, they slept late on Monday morning. When they came out they found Denver in a state of general excitement. The story of the resistance which the officers had met with from the desperadoes in attempting to make the arrests in Golden had been generally circulated. The people were just then beginning to appreciate for the first time the real character of the outlaws who had so recently been in their midst. They had never before dreamed that these highwaymen would be guilty of outright murder. Their eyes were opened for the first time. Evidence had accumulated of Franklin's having been a partner of Musgrove. Even after the bold robberies of the preceding Friday night, Franklin had had the assurance to go to the jail where Musgrove was confined and ask for a conference with that individual. After this interview Musgrove made general announcement of the fact that his escape was planned for an early day, on such a perfect scale that it would not be within the power of the authorities to prevent it. It was also generally understood that there were many other desperadoes in the city, who, it was believed, had come to Denver for the purpose of assisting Musgrove to throw oil" his prison shackles. At any rate, the town was known to be full of bad characters, and the number was increasing every day. It was generally agreed that something must be done to teach these ruffians that Denver was no place for them. The laws were imperfect; it was difficult to convict witnesses, and the prisons were mere pens, out of which criminals could escape with small effort. There was but little for them to fear from the due process of law. Some more speedy remedy for the evil existing was needed. The community was sick and must be cured. A limb had been fractured, and amputation was necessary. Heroic remedies were demanded.

So the people were beginning to talk about noon of Monday, November 23. Someone suggested that the proper and salutary thing to do would be to hang Musgrove. The idea was wildfire in a dry prairie. It passed from one to another, and all the good people declared that Musgrove should be hanged by the people in the interest of the people—without technical warrant of law, but for the same purpose as that for which legal executions are intended, namely, to punish crime and to furnish a warning to evildoers wherever found. On general principles Musgrove deserved hanging. The West is a region which believes in giving every man his deserts. So Musgrove must hang. This was the verdict of the town.

Up to 3 o'clock there had been no organized meeting, notwithstanding the talk of lynching had been general, and almost everybody had come to understand that a tragedy of this kind might be expected at any moment. By 3 the people began to gather on Larimer street. A few minutes later found them marching by the score, as if by common consent, towards the county jail, in which Musgrove was confined. There were hundreds in the procession when the prison was reached. There was no general expression to denote the intention of the mob, but all understood its purpose. There were no masks worn or disguises adopted. It was broad daylight. The best men hi the town were in that procession—lawyers, doctors, and probably ministers, business and professional men. No officer dared stand in the way of that gathering. It was the people about to do the people's will.

Arrived in front of the jail a halt was called. Someone mounted an elevation. There was no disorder. "The question before you," rang out the voice of the speaker, "is, shall Musgrove be taken out of jail?"

There was a unanimous "Yes!"

"The next question is, shall he be hanged when taken out?"

The same unbroken "Yes" was the response.

There were none to object.

The jail was promptly entered. No obstacles were thrown in the way by the officials. Musgrove had himself been an auditor of the proceedings which had just been conducted on the outside of his prison house. But he had not been dumbfounded by the revelations made to him of his approaching fate. He met the mob with a bold face. "Come on!" he exclaimed, defiantly, "I am ready for you."

He was found to be armed with a heavy pine knot with which someone had provided him. This he hurled defiantly in the air. None cared to approach him while he held this formidable weapon. Hence the stratagem of firing two or three shots over his head was resorted to. This policy brought the desperado to terms. Musgrove agreed to surrender peaceably on condition that he be not shot down. He was consequently taken out of jail.

Once on the street the procession made towards the Larimer street bridge across Cherry creek. Musgrove was fairly pushed forward by the pressure from the crowd which followed behind. He walked onward in a sullen and uncommunicative mood, glancing to one side and then the other as if looking for assistance. But none came. When he reached the bridge he apparently lost all hope. He never once asked for mercy or made a single plea for his life.

"If you are bent upon murdering me," he said at last, "you will at least be men enough to permit me to write to my friends and tell them the shameful story of your conduct towards me." No one objected, and when the middle of the bridge was reached a halt was called and Musgrove was furnished with paper and pencil. Bending over the railing of the bridge he scratched off two brief notes, one to a brother and the other to his wife, the first being directed to Como Depot, Miss., and the second to Cheyenne. The poor criminal grasped the pencil with firmness and apparently wrote without a tremor, notwithstanding he was closely surrounded by armed men who were soon to be his executioners. He was an illiterate man, and wrote and spelled badly. Fortunately Gen. Cook preserved verbatim copies of the letters, which were as follows:

Denver November 23d, 1868

My Dear Brother

I am to be hung today on false charges by a mob my children is in Napa Valley Cal—will you go and get them & take caree of them for me godd Knows that I am innocent pray for me but I was here when the mob took me. Brother good by for Ever take care of my pore little children I remain your unfortunate Brother

good by

L. H. MUSGROVE,

Denver C. T.

My Dear Wife—Before this reaches you I will be no more Marv I am as you know innocent of the charges made against me I do not know what they are agoing to hang me for unless it is because I am acquainted with Ed Franklin—godd will protect you I hope Good by for ever as ever yours sell what I have and keep it. L. H. MUSGBOVE.

While he was still writing, some of the men had tied Mus-grove's legs together, and a wagon was procured, which he was told to mount, Placing his hands upon the seat in front, he sprang into the vehicle as nimbly as a cat, and the driver, who was George Hopkins of the present police force, was ordered to proceed. The procession then took its way to the west end of the bridge, reaching which, it passed down the bank of the creek to the dry and sandy bed of the stream, returning to a place under the middle span, whence a hangman's rope dangled, with the noose already prepared for service. Driving up under this cord. Musgrove was told that he could have an opportunity to make whatever preparation he should see proper for the end which was approaching.

His only reply was: "Go on with your work."

He was ordered to stand up, and mounted the seat of the wagon, surveying the crow d with his usual sullen and calm face. The rope was being tied about his neck, when Capt. Scudder, then a well-known and respected citizen, standing on the bridge above, began to address the crowd upon the illegality of the proceedings. Musgrove's countenance did not change. He coolly took a piece of paper from one vest pocket, and fumbled in the other vest pocket for some tobacco crumbs, which he took out, rolled in the paper, made a cigarette, turned the ends with care, placed it in his mouth, requested a match from the driver, struck it, lighted his cigarette and smoked it with as much composure as a Mexican ranchero sitting in his plaza on a summer evening, while Capt. Scudder continued his harangue.

This talk was not heeded. The crowd began to jeer, and to cry: "Drive on!" Someone hallooed to Musgrove and inquired: "'Where are the rest of your gang?"

"I am sure I don't know," came the reply, "unless you are one of them."

Those were among the man's last words. His hat was pulled down over his eyes. Musgrove threw his cigarette from his mouth, and feeling the wagon starting, stooped and sprang into the air.

The wagon was moving but slowly from under the man and he came down on the floor of the wagon bed. With an expression of great disappointment and disgust he made another determined leap which should almost, beyond peradventure, land him in the great beyond. The wagon had moved out this timer and Musgrove threw his entire weight upon the rope. His neck was broken by the fall, and death ensued instantly. There were a few shrugs of the shoulder and all was over. The hat which had played the part of a hangman's cap was removed before the crowd dispersed and the countenance was found to have changed but little. It was still sullen and devoid of any expression of fear. Musgrove had died as he had lived—coldly defiant of the world.

Referring to the matter at the time a local print said: "The people who assembled were good men, if we have any good men in the city. They were quiet and orderly, no shouting, no commotion—waiting to see the law executed upon one who had outraged them. They comprised a large part of the men of the city, and were not a crowd or a mob, but an assemblage of the people."

THE LAST OF THE MUSGROVE GANG

Duggan, it will be remembered, had escaped from the officers at Golden, but he was not allowed to get away. The descriptions which Gen. Cook had sent out had been received at Port Russell, near Cheyenne, and the agents of the Rocky Mountain Detective Association at that point were on the lookout for him. They did not wait long. He was picked up in company with a deserter, riding a stolen horse near Natural Fort, sixteen miles from Cheyenne, making his way eastward.

Chief Cook hearing of the arrest of Duggan, had himself gone to Cheyenne after the fugitive. He was satisfied from what he knew of the awakened spirit of the people of Denver that if they should get an opportunity they would lynch Duggan, but he was determined that such a fate should not befall the man while in his custody. In fact, it may be mentioned now, that Gen. Cook has ever made it a point to see that no prisoner should be taken from his hands by a mob, and none has ever been. He knew that he would be expected to get in at a certain time, and thought it more than probable that a mob would be organized by that time, for the purpose of taking Duggan from the officers and hanging him. To avert this fate Cook had caused the stage driver to double his speed and to come into Denver twelve hours ahead of time. It was fortunate that this precaution had been taken, for the people had already decided to make another example of Duggan by hanging him. They were terribly excited, and the watchword of the town was "Let no villain escape." Duggan must follow in the footsteps of Musgrove.

Rut Cook took the town by surprise in his early arrival with the culprit. They were not organized or ready to make a light for the man, as they had determined that they would be by the regular stage arrival time. However, the approach of the coach was discovered, as the Carr house on Fifteenth street was passed, by someone who cried out: "Here, boys, come; here's Cook with Duggan; let's take him!" There was a rush from the hotel, but Gen. Cook ordered the driver to travel for his life. The horses were whipped into a dead run, which was kept up until the Larimer street prison was gained.

Notwithstanding this great haste a mob of 500 people had gathered at the jail when it was reached and the driver had almost to plow through it with his team. The door was reached at last, however, and the prisoner, trembling like a leaf in a breeze, was pushed into the jail and turned over to the county authorities.

But that Duggan's life was not safe even now, all understood perfectly. It was generally believed that he would be lynched. The impression had gotten out that the jail would be assailed sometime during the afternoon, and the prisoner taken therefrom and executed, and in consequence of the rumor, about 4 o'clock a crowd of men, women and children lined the sidewalk along both sides of Larimer street from Fifteenth street, even on to the bridge, which was occupied by children principally. They held their position until nearly or quite dark, when thinking that the expected exhibition had been indefinitely postponed, they retired to their homes. They were mistaken in their surmises, as it appears.

It became known in some May that Duggan would be removed from the Larimer street prison to the city jail on Front street sometime during the evening, and the mob had concluded to improve the occasion by taking him from the officers and executing him. About 6 o'clock he was taken in an express wagon for the purpose of the proposed transfer. As the wagon left the west end of the bridge a whistle was sounded and immediately answered from the direction of the calaboose. Soon after the wagon crossed the bridge it was surrounded by ninety or a hundred armed men, who demanded a halt, and the surrender of the prisoner, and he was turned over to them without a struggle. Having him in possession they retraced their steps and turned west, to what was then Cherry street, to a point on that street where there stood two or three cottonwood trees, and under one of which the procession halted. The express wagon, which had been taken possession of, was brought to the front, and placed directly under a limb of the tree. In a moment a rope was thrown over the limb, and in another moment Duggan was standing in the wagon immediately under the fatal noose. Someone then told him if he had any remarks to make, to make them, for his time among the living was short. He commenced by asking them to send for a Catholic priest. "I killed a man in the mountains, but it was in self-defense," he said: "I did not kill the man in the Black Hills; 'twas another fellow that did it." To the question about having assisted in garroting Squire Brooks, he first said, "I didn't do it. I have never hurt anybody or stole anything. I have been a bad man, but I am not guilty of anything deserving of hanging." He frequently asked that a minister should be sent for. "One called this afternoon, but hadn't time to stay then, but wanted me to send for him if anything happened."

Again he was warned that his moments "were numbered, and again asked to confess, if he had any confession to make. "I killed the man in the mountains in self-defense and have been tried and acquitted. The man in the Black Hills was killed by another fellow. I never stole anything from anybody. I did assist in robbing Squire Brooks, but I was nearly out of money and had to do it or starve. I only had six or seven dollars, and could not get any, any other way. I had to do it or die. I have been a very bad man, but have done nothing to be hanged for. Spare my life; any other punishment. Oh, my poor mother! it will kill her. Don't let it get to her; send for a Catholic minister."

His confession or remarks were constantly interrupted by his cries. In fact, in the trying moment he was completely unmanned, crying and sobbing like a baby, and uttering prayers for mercy from Him whose laws he had frequently and repeatedly outraged—a spectacle quite different from that presented by Musgrove. After he had said all that he had to say, the order was heard, "Drive on," and the wagon which had served as his frail bulwark between life and eternity, moved from under, and the spirit of Sanford S. C. Duggan took its flight to the presence of Him who shall judge us all according to the deeds done in this world. The fall, about eighteen inches, broke his neck. He was a man six feet two or three inches in height and weighed 205 pounds. After the body was cut down it was given in charge of the coroner.

Thus ended the terrible series of tragedies which began with the shooting of Miles Hill at Golden on the night of the 22d of November. That the killings were justified no man who has ever lived on the frontier at such times as those were will deny. In all these affairs Gen. Cook and his officers were more or less concerned, but at all times doing all in their power both to bring offenders against the law to justice, and then to see that the laws were not violated when they were once secured. The lynchings they would gladly have prevented, but it was useless for them to fly in the face of an entire community", which had been outraged and which was aroused, not so much to vengeance as to the necessity of protecting itself against the rough element of the plains. The pictures drawn are not pleasant ones, but they are a part of the history of Denver, and have been given as such without any attempt at exaggeration or undue coloring.

THE EXCHANGE BANK ROBBERY

May 12, 1879, Cole's circus struck its tent in Denver and prepared to give one of the very creditable performances which generally characterize this "monster aggregation." The circus had bur recently returned to America from Australia and was passing through the country with considerable prestige. Being the means of getting large crowds of people together, it was naturally followed up or accompanied by as depraved a set of sneak thieves and pickpockets as ever traveled in the shadow of any circus. The day of the beginning of the series of performances given in this city was marked by an occurrence which will ever serve to call the date to mind. On that day a robbery was committed in Denver, which will long be remembered for the shrewdness with which it was planned, the expediency with which it was executed, and also for the speedy overtaking of the thieves and the restoration of the stolen property to its owners. The robbery took place at the Exchange Bank, then located on the corner of Fifteenth and Blake streets, about I o'clock in the afternoon, while the circus procession was passing and while the streets in front of the building were thronged with people, including those engaged in the parade and those who were looking on as it moved by.

About I o'clock the head of the procession began to move up Blake street from the depot. The cashier of the bank, Mr. J. M. Strickler, was at his desk. Mr. A. J. Williams, then the vice-president and now the president of the institution, was in the private office in the rear, and other attaches of the bank were behind the iron railing. There was a temporary lull in the task of receiving deposits, and the bank officers, with the exception of Mr. Strickler, stepped out to the door to see the procession go by. This left no one behind the counter except Mr. Strickler, who was running over some deposits that had been made by patrons of the bank, and talking with a stranger. A few moments later Hon. J. P. Welborn stepped into the bank and asked Mr. Williams to come out to the front, as he desired to speak to him a few moments on business. Mr. Williams joined Judge Welborn at one of the large windows fronting on Blake street, and they stood there chatting until after the procession had gone by. The other bank officers returned to their desks, and Mr. Strickler a few minutes later noticed that a large pile of greenbacks, done up in packages of $500 and upwards, was missing from the table. Thinking they had been placed in one of the cash drawers, he asked his assistant, Mr. Rockwell, who replied that he had not seen the money, and just about that time it began to dawn upon the officers that their short absence from the counter had cost the institution nearly $4,000, about that amount of money having been piled upon the table awaiting deposit.

About $95,200 in 2015—Ed. 2016

Gen. Cook was immediately sent for. He found the officers of the bank in a state of considerable excitement, and all of them thoroughly at sea. The robbery was to them a terrible mystery. None of them had been out of the bank at all and Mr. Strickler, the efficient cashier, had remained continuously in his office. They could not have believed that the bank had been robbed if they had not had the evidence which their eyes furnished that the money, which a few minutes before had been there, was missing. That someone should have come into the building and taken out $4,000 in money, even at a time when there was a circus around, seemed to them well-nigh incredible. But the fact stared them in the face that the money had disappeared, and they came to Cook to find it. No one could suggest a point that would be of assistance, and he began to put questions, with the hope of getting some clue which would aid him in his apparently almost hopeless search. The clue was at last obtained. Mr. Strickler remembered that while the other officials and the employees of the bank had been out looking at the circus, he had been engaged in conversation with an individual who had brought in a $100 note to get it changed, and the note being of doubtful appearance, he had seemed bent, upon drawing the cashier into an animated discussion, which was carried on on the part of the stranger in an unnecessarily loud and vehement tone of voice.

"That is the man we want to get," said Cook. "He was the steerer for the thieves."

The detective at once jumped at the conclusion that ordinarily a man would not go into a bank to get change while a circus was passing. The man's manner, when further described, confirmed the opinion previously formed, and he obtained a description of the fellow as speedily as possible, upon which thread he went to work to run the case down and restore the bank its stolen funds.

Before starting out, however, he made a survey of the building, for the purpose of completing his theory of the *modus operandi* of the robbery and how many had been engaged in it.

The portion of the building occupied as a bank was composed of two rooms—a large one, in which the active employees were engaged, and a smaller one, used as his private office by Mr. Williams. The two communicated through a partition door, and both had doors opening upon Fifteenth street.

The rear door on Blake street, leading into the private office, was usually locked with a spring lock, working from the inside. It could not be opened without a key, except from the inside. From the private office there was a door leading into the inner portion of the bank, enclosed with counters and railings, and another door leading straight to the front entrance. Gen. Cook concluded that the plan must have been arranged beforehand, and the theft committed without any delay. The rear door being open, a person could gain access to the vaults and cash drawers, and by stooping low would not be visible to anyone on the outside of the counter. It was therefore presumed that while one of the thieves guarded the rear door for his pal and another talked with the cashier, the third craw led deftly on his hands and knees and reached up for the money, sweeping the counter pretty clear, and taking all the currency that was in sight. The time consumed by the procession in passing was sufficiently long to enable the thieves to do this without showing their hurry or doing the work bunglingly.

This work being accomplished, the thief who had taken the money wrapped it in a red handkerchief and crept to the back door. Seeing his friend clear, the man with the $100 bill took his departure and all three joined on the outside, passing hurriedly down Fifteenth street and past the Elephant corral, as had been noticed by spectators, who did not, of course, know what had transpired in the bank. At that corral, as was afterwards learned, a portion of the money was left.

Having a description of one of the men who had been in the robbery, and being in possession of the course that the robbers had taken. Cook went to work himself and sent others of his officers out in the search. They had some hope of finding the thieves through other operations, and some of the detectives attended the circus for the purpose of getting a clue of this kind. The fact that a number of smaller robberies were committed during the forenoon, and, in every instance, in the crow ds where the procession passed, strengthened the theory that there was a well-organized gang at work, and that they were doing their work under cover of Cole's circus procession But a more hopeless task could hardly be imagined. Here was a bank robbed in broad daylight, with the officers and clerks moving about the room and keeping a watchful eye on the money deposits. No one who could recognize them had seen the thieves enter or depart, and no one connected with the bank could give the officers any but the slightest clue as to the character or appearance of the bold outlaws. But Cook is not a man prone to give up the track of a thief because the trail happens to be cold. According to methods and intuitions of his own he went to work, ne relied mainly upon his great knowledge of the thieves of the country, believing that if the robbers had been well-known and experienced crooks, as their work showed they were, he would know them or some of them when he should come upon them.

He accordingly set out to look for his men. Two hours afterwards brought the welcome information to the bank that two out of the three robbers had been captured and part of the money recovered. In his search Gen. Cook visited the American house, and while sauntering about there. Cook's eyes fell upon a form that was not unknown to the eyes of the detective. A brief retrospection caused him to remember the man as one Joe Parrish, a noted thief, whom he had seen ten years before in Chicago. He was observed to be accompanied by another man, whose face could not be seen at first. The two moved about suspiciously, and Cook decided upon a closer investigation of the pair. At last he obtained a full view of Parrish's partner, and found him to be not only a first-water Italian crook from St. Louis, but also that his description answered that given by Mr. Strickler of the man who had called to get a bill changed. These were the men wanted. Of this fact Gen. Cook was quite certain. He consequently left them and went in search of his deputy, Mr. Smith. That gentleman joining his chief, they returned to the American house "for business."

Spotting their men, who did not seem to be laboring under any uneasiness of apprehension, They decided upon immediate arrest, and came down upon them like a thousand of brick. Cook walked deliberately up to Parrish, a genteely dressed young man, with a Jewish cast of countenance, and announced that he was under the pleasant necessity of placing him under arrest. Parrish—who subsequently gave his name as F. Wiggins—made no resistance; did not even raise the slightest objection or remonstrance. Meanwhile, Smith had approached the other party and placed him under arrest. This man—who gave his name as I. H. Russell, though it was an alias—was also neatly dressed and of gentlemanly appearance. He exclaimed, as Smith laid his hands upon him: "Well, well!" Only this and nothing more.

As the officers were conveying their prisoners to a coach, however, preparatory to taking them to jail, Russell turned to Gen. Cook and said: "'Will you be kind enough to tell me what this is all about?'"

He also informed Cook that he was a lawyer in good standing, afterwards stating that he had come to Denver as a commercial traveler, and was selling jewelry. When Cook asked him where his samples were, he replied that he was dealing in cheap jewelry and did not carry any samples.

Wiggins never spoke a word from the time of his arrest till he was behind the bars.

While Smith was looking after the prisoners in the office of the American house, Cook went up to the room—No. 73—occupied by Wiggins and Russell and instituted a vigorous search. The prisoners were also carefully searched, and $800 in all was found upon the two, the bulk of which was identified as money stolen from the bank.

A portion of the money found upon the prisoners was $100 in five and ten-dollar bills, which was hidden in the front part of one of Mr. Wiggins' shoes.

Both the prisoners stoutly protested their innocence of the crime charged against them, but the proof of their guilt was as straight as could possibly have been desired, and no one entertained any doubt that the right men had been taken. The job was one of the neatest ever performed by a detective in any place, and Gen. Cook and his coworker were praised on every hand. Starting out at 2 o'clock without a single clue, they had in two hours found and jailed the robbers and secured a fine roll of money, if not all or the bulk of it. "With such detectives as these in Denver," said one, "thieves will certainly conclude that this is not the place for them." "They are better than all the iron safes in the country," said another. Indeed, the detectives were congratulated upon every hand.

But one of the thieves was still missing, with something like $3,000 in his possession. He proved to be more evasive than the other two had been, and succeeded in getting out of town. The officers were at first nonplussed and unable to obtain the slightest clue as to his identity. They could not turn a wheel. At last they succeeded in getting the man's name, which was Sam Straddler, otherwise known as "Dayton Sammy," from his pals, and learned that he was in Cincinnati. Thitherward Cook dispatched Smith, who arrived just in time to learn that his bird had flown. He had contrived to get away from the police authorities there and could not be found.

Parrish and Russell remained in jail for several months, and at last compromised the matter, so that the bank was out nothing in the end.

It is a fact worth noting that neither Mr. Russell, Mr. Parrish or Mr. Straddler has been seen in the city since they were turned out of jail. They don't get along well with Dave Cook, and prefer to be widely separated from him.

THE HAYWARD MURDER

IN all the criminal history of Colorado—in all the register of the achievements of the Rocky Mountain Detective Association—the ensanguined pages show no more causeless, unprovoked murder than that of R. B. Hayward, in September, 1879. The difficulties met and overcome by the detectives, and the prompt and tragic end of the criminals, lend an additional interest to the case and make it one of the most famous in the far West, as it is most assuredly one of the most noted in Colorado in some of its features. The absence of any material temptation; the temporary escape of the murderers; the accidental finding of the body of the victim; the patient search of the officers; the final arrest of the men hundreds of miles away; the identification and confession; and then the lynching, so rich in dramatic detail, form a narrative reading more like a sensational romance than the cold facts of an actual reality.

On the 10th of August, 1879, Gen. D. J. Cook, superintendent of the Rocky Mountain Detective Association, received a dispatch from Sheriff Besey, of Grand county, Colo., telling him to keep a sharp lookout for a man looking very much like a Chinaman, and evidently with some Indian blood in his veins, who was wanted for the robbery of the house of Mr. Frank Byers, in Middle park. The robber bad secured a watch and a few trinkets of more or less value, and then, helping himself to a mule, had departed for other fields. This robbery had occurred on the 8th, and the intricate machinery of the detectives was put in motion as soon as notified, for Mr. Byers was a well-known citizen, and presently information began to take shape and flow through the properly appointed channels to headquarters.

It was found that on the 12th, four days after the Byers robbery, and two after the detectives had been notified, the robber had appeared in Georgetown and called upon Dr. William A. Burr, giving his name as Joseph F. Seminole, and stating that he came from Emerson Kinney, of Hot Sulphur Springs, who desired the medical gentleman's immediate presence, as Mrs. Kinney was dangerously ill.

"When you get about six miles out of town on the road to Empire," said the cool and crafty scoundrel, "stop at the ranch of Mr. Lindstrom and get my mule, which I left there. It will be much better for you to use my animal than to ride your own on such a long and hard trip. When you reach the Summit house, in Berthoud pass, just present this order and the proprietor will furnish you with a horse and buggy."

The order that was given read as follows:

"Please give to Dr. W. A. Burr, horse and buggy, and charge same to Emerson Kinney, of Hot Sulphur Springs, on same order as before. J. F. SEMINOLE."

When the doctor reached Lindstrom's place he exchanged his horse for the mule left by Seminole, and continued on his way. At the Summit house the foregoing order was presented, but the proprietor declined to furnish a conveyance on the strength of it, saying that he did not know Seminole at all, but offering a horse and buggy if the doctor would be personally responsible for it, a proposition which the latter accepted. At last Mr. Kinney's ranch was reached, and to his utter stupefaction the doctor found that his expected patient was not only never in better health, but had not the slightest idea of being sick. Breathing vengeance deep and dire, the good-hearted but exasperated doctor started on his return, and when Lindstrom's was again reached, he was greeted with the intelligence that Seminole had been there and secured his horse, and to this day that animal has never been seen, or even heard of.

Thus far the detectives got, and then were balked. To them it was but a case of robbery—they never dreamed how soon it was to develop into a ghastly murder. Somewhat piqued at their non-success, although the crime was comparatively but a paltry one, they continued their efforts, and after a while traced Seminole to Leadville, where, on the 7th of September, he, in company with a man known as Tom Johnson, whose correct name proved to be Samuel Woodruff, hired two horses for the avowed v purpose of merely taking a little ride. While skirmishing around, they noticed a Mr. Aldrich draw two hundred dollars from a bank, and learned that he was going immediately to Georgetown. They followed behind him, and when six miles from his destination rode up to him, drew their pistols and called upon him to halt and deliver. Aldrich, however, was not of that kind, and jerked his own weapon and turned loose, though, unfortunately, not hitting either of the two scoundrels, who turned and fled precipitately. When he arrived in Georgetown, he promptly notified the sheriff of Clear Creek county, and that official immediately struck the trail and followed it up without the loss of a moment. So rapidly did he gain on the fleeing desperadoes that they dismounted from their horses, turned the animals loose and made their escape in the brush. The animals were returned to their owners and the sheriff abandoned the pursuit of the men.

The rascals continued on foot until September 10. They reached the place of Mr. Anderson, and hired him to drive them to Denver. They stated that they had no money, but an uncle of theirs kept a livery stable in Denver, and he would pay for all the trouble. While on the trip Anderson noticed that his passengers did have money, and remarked that they had better pay the toll charges at least, as he was not willing to spend cash right out of his pocket and trust them besides. But they refused, and then Anderson said he would go no further; but upon being confronted by two cocked pistols, he changed his mind and drove on. About a mile further two wagons were seen coming from the direction of Denver and going in that of Georgetown, and when almost within hailing distance Messrs. Seminole and Johnson jumped out and look to the brush, evidently fearing that Anderson would call for assistance. Relieved of his undesirable passengers, Anderson joined the other wagons, and in their company returned to Georgetown.

That same afternoon, about half-past four, this pair of precious scoundrels came to the house of R. it. Hayward, near Big Hill, Jefferson county, and engaged him to gear up and take them to a cattle camp they said they were hunting, supposed to be near A. Rooney's place, near Green mountain, just outside of Hogback. They passed the Mt. Vernon toll-gate at about half past six that evening, and from here the fate of Mr. Hayward was an unfathomed mystery until his body was found.

Of course Mr. Hayward's people became uneasy on account of his failure to return the evening after he left, and when he did not come the next day Mrs. Hayward took steps to inform the Jefferson county authorities of the circumstances under which her husband had gone away from home, and of his prolonged absence. They made thorough search, but failed to discover anything, either concerning Mr. Hayward's whereabouts, as to what disposition had been made of his team, or where the men were who had gone away with him.

On the 16th of September, C. P. Hoyt, of the Rocky Mountain Detective Association, reported the facts of the mysterious absence of Mr. Hayward to Superintendent Cook, and gave the description of the two men last seen with the missing man

In the meantime, on September 11, the same two men (though the fact of the murder was not then known) went to Brown & Marr, of the bus barn, on Arapahoe street, Denver, and hired two bay mares and a top-rig buggy, paying four dollars in advance. This was about 2 o'clock in the afternoon, and they said they merely wanted to take a little spin around town and would return at a certain specified hour. As this time had long been passed, Brown & Marr placed the matter in the hands of the detective association late in the evening of the 11th, and they telegraphed all over a description of the missing rig. About 11 o'clock on the morning of the 12th, Superintendent Cook received a message from the town of Loveland, in Larimer county, stating that two men had abandoned a buggy answering the description of Lite missing one, and had mounted the mares and ridden off. An officer was immediately dispatched to the scene, and sure enough it was the identical vehicle taken from the Denver stable.

As it was now ascertained that the thieves had gone north, Superintendent Cook notified Assistant Superintendent Carr, at Cheyenne, to be on the lookout, and on the 11th of the month Gen. Cook received information from him that two men answering the description of the two who had hired the horses and buggy, had remained all night in the vicinity of a ranch near La Porte, Larimer county. The men represented to the owner of the ranch that they belonged to a cattle outfit, and that the cattle were down in the bottoms near at hand, while the wagon containing the camping outfit was far to the rear. They were obliged to be with their cattle, they said, and would like to borrow a couple of buffalo robes until morning. The kind-hearted ranchman acceded to their request, and never again beheld his robes, nor in the morning could he find any signs or traces of cattle.

On the 22d of the same month, a gentleman named Leech, while riding from Laramie City to Cheyenne, on horseback, met two men mounted on bay mares, with folded buffalo robes as saddles, at the crossing of the Union Pacific railroad, four miles east of Sherman station. They stopped him, asked him what time it was, and where he lived, and as they had a hard look about them, he assured them he lived about two hundred yards from there, on the other side of a little butte, though the truth of the matter was there wasn't a house within four miles of the spot. When Mr. Leech reached Cheyenne he met Detective Carr, and mentioned this meeting near Sherman, and when the officer gave a description of the missing horses and thieves, Mr. Leech recognized it immediately.

Carr then went diligently to work, and after a while ascertained that on the 23d two men, riding bay mares, with no saddles, but buffalo robes in lieu thereof, had come to the ranch of Kick Janise, near Sidney bridge, on the North Platte. This Information was forwarded to Gen. Cook, and Mr. Leech, having come down to Denver on business, was interviewed at his hotel by Detective Joe Arnold, as a representative of Chief Cook, who bad, as did also Gen. Cook, shrewd suspicions that the murderers of Hayward and the horse thieves were the same parties. He showed Mr. Leech a description of the men who had engaged Mr. Hayward to drive them to the cattle ranch, and that gentleman immediately recognized them, being especially sure because of the white bone-handled knife and the revolvers carried by the suspicious-looking strangers.

The result of this interview was that Detective W.W. Ayres, of the Rocky Mountain Association, was sent in pursuit of the men, starting from Denver on the 4th of October. By this time the Hayward murder had become state talk, as the mystery was still unsolved and as the cold-blooded nature of the affair had also become generally known. Currency was also given to the fact that he had left an intelligent wife and two bright daughters just budding into womanhood, to watch and wait for the return of the husband and father who would never return.

There remained hardly any trace of doubt that Mr. Hayward had been murdered by the two men with whom he had started out. This suspicion was greatly strengthened by learning the late history of the two men who had gone with him, which history has been given in the beginning of this story.

Mrs. Hayward was for a while almost frantic with grief at the loss of her husband, but she soon rallied with the genuine pluck which is the characteristic of most western women, and determined to do what she might to avenge his death. She offered a reward of $200 for the capture of the murderers. This offer was followed by one from Jefferson county, agreeing to pay $500 for their capture, and soon Gov. Pitkin proclaimed a reward on the part of the state of $1,000 for their apprehension, making $1,700 the aggregate sum offered for the fugitives.

Over $40,000 in 2015—Ed. 2016

As related above, Gen. Cook had already formed the theory, though he kept it to himself, that the two men who had stolen the horses were the Hayward murderers, and he decided to have them followed to 'The jumping-off place" if necessary, or get them. He had already formed a pretty definite theory as to the destination of the two men. He had learned, among numerous other facts which he had gathered together, that Seminole was a half-breed Sioux Indian, and that he belonged at Pine Ridge agency, Dakota, where he had a family going there by the name of J. S. Leuischammesse. As has already been seen, the men who stole the horses had turned their attention, in that direction, and thitherward Cook directed Mr. Ayres, never informing him, however, that he had any suspicion that they were guilty of any crime greater than that of horse stealing, wisely concluding that if Seminole's fellow Indians knew that he was charged with murder and likely to be hanged, they would not permit the detective to bring him away, and believing that the best way of keeping this fact from them was to impart it to no one. On the other hand, they would perhaps even assist the detective in getting him for horse stealing.

Mr. Ayres had a long and arduous journey before him, as he could look forward to at least a thousand miles of stage-coaching and horseback riding in the north, with winter coming on, and with many hardships to endure in a land of savages. But he started out undaunted by the prospect, and the result shows how faithfully he worked and how successfully' he wrought.

While he is making his way across the almost pathless plains of Wyoming and Dakota, it is necessary to stop for a moment to relate to the reader the fact of the discovery of the body of Mr. Hayward. It was found on the 7th of October, three days after Ayres had left the city, and almost a month after Mr. Hayward had left home, in an old culvert on the Golden road, five miles from Denver. The body bore no testimony as to the manner or cause of death. It was greatly decayed, but still was not beyond identification, and the coroner's jury brought in the verdict that death was caused in all probability by dislocation of the neck at the hand of a party or parties unknown. No wound or mark of violence could be found anywhere on the body, and the theories were that either the murderers had broken his neck with some dull instrument or else had poisoned hum

A BRIEF BUT FIERCE STRUGGLE

In the meantime Detective Ayres had gone to Cheyenne, taken horse there and ridden to Horse creek; from there to Big Horse creek, thence to Hawk Springs and into old Red Cloud agency, on the Platte. Here he got information of the men he was after, and without loss of time pushed on to Running Water; from there to Camp Robinson, thence to Camp Sheridan, and then into Pine Ridge agency. The Indian agent, Mr. V. T. McGillycuddy proffered all assistance, and Joseph Seminole was soon under arrest. Not without considerable trouble, however, as shall appear.

Mr. Ayres had taken letters to the agent and the military, and had been assured that he should have every assistance, as the Rocky Mountain Detective Agency was well-known and highly respected in that far-away section.

Not only the officers and the soldiers, but the Indian police as well, were anxious and willing to assist in running Seminole down. They recognized the description as soon as it was given them, and told the officer from the far-away region that they would find him forthwith, and volunteered to lead him to his place of abode. Ayres told them all he knew of the crimes charged against Seminole, the worst being that of horse-thieving, and assured them that he was wanted on no more serious charge than that of showing his undue love for horseflesh. They professed great indignation that their nation should have been disgraced by the stealing of a single horse, and avowed that he should be sent back forthwith to answer for the offense. They seemed to dislike the fellow any way; possibly because he was a half-breed, but most likely for the reason that he was better educated than the rest of them, and held himself in a manner aloof from them. At any rate, they were quite willing to take the officer to him, saying that Seminole should not only be arrested, but that they would see that the officer should get away with him in good shape.

This was as good a thing as Mr. Ayres wanted, and when he was well rested, the Indians, true to their promise, led him to the wigwam of the culprit.

It may not have been a picture of peace and plenty which Seminole presented, but he certainly seemed to be quite contented, surrounded as he was by his squaw and papooses, who prattled about in the dirt, while he sat enjoying the bliss of a long-stemmed pipe. The surroundings were rude and coarse, but the half Indian appeared to be perfectly at home and at ease.

But the officer of the law cannot stand back on account of any qualms of conscience or foolish sentiment when there are arrests to be made. His is not the part of preserving domestic felicity.

When broken in upon, the murderer did not show any signs of fear, and when introduced to Mr. Ayres as an officer from Colorado in search of him, he manifested no disposition to make resistance. It may be that he asked rather impetuously to know the charge against him, but Ayres' answer that it was that of horse stealing reassured him, and he submitted quietly, and walked out of his wigwam stolidly, though with apparent willingness.

The officer was led to believe that he had accomplished a big job with but little effort and was mentally congratulating himself accordingly. But all was not accomplished. There was much yet to be done, ne felt that he had a wide and wild stretch of country to cover in getting home, and the idea of going through an Indian region alone, in charge of a half Indian, was not a cheerful one. Not by any means.

When Seminole was once out of his house the detective undertook to handcuff him. But the fellow had had time for a little self-introspection and meditation. The Hayward murder undoubtedly came into his mind, and he began to feel that, whatever the charge upon which he was to be brought back to Denver, he would be in danger of being discovered as the murderer, and he began to show tight at the sight of the handcuffs. He would not agree to have them put on, and when the officer attempted to force them on, struck at him. He was a strong man and able to get the best of the officer had he been unaided, but the Indian police came nobly to Ayres' rescue, and they laid Mr. Seminole low in very short order, and while he was prone upon the ground and kicking and scratching, the irons were adjusted. The scene was as wild a one in the interest of justice as ever fell to the lot of man to witness.

The capture was now completed, and one of the murderers of "old man" Hayward was in the hands of an officer of the law, though on a different charge and far away from the scene of the tragedy or the bounds of civilization.

The officer found that on September 29, Seminole had sold his stolen bay mare to an Indian chief named Woman's Dress, giving a bill of sale, and signing thereto the name of Joseph Leuischammesse, which, upon being compared upon arrival at Denver with the writing of the order to the proprietor of the Summit house, proved that it was written by the same hand, the letters being formed identically alike. The other man, Tom Johnson, as he is still called, was not there.

With an armed escort of Sioux Indians, Ayres started back with his prisoner. He parted with his escort at Camp Robinson, and at Pine Bluffs boarded a freight train, and took up quarters in the caboose.

About 3 o'clock of the next morning after taking passage on the freight, Mr. Ayres found himself minus the prisoner to capture whom he had risked so much and undergone so many hardships. He had allowed the man to be out of his sight for a moment, and that moment had been embraced by the fellow to regain his liberty. The train was rattling along at more than ordinary freight train speed, so that Mr. Ayres did not dream of the handcuffed man's jumping from the train. But Seminole was a man who dared anything, and he boldly plunged out of the caboose into the darkness, and was once more free. Mr. Ayres' efforts to refind his man proved utterly futile, and nothing was left to him but to notify his chief.

A great deal had been gained, but now everything seemed lost. By this time Cook had become entirely convinced that Seminole, or Leuischammesse, was one of the murderers of Hayward, and for that reason he determined to leave no stone unturned to recover his man. Consequently the matter was again placed in the hands of Assistant Superintendent Carr, and through the aid of the telegraph but a very few hours had elapsed when there were no less than fifteen cowboys scouring the plains under the leadership of Cattle Detective Cowles in the neighborhood of the point at which the escape was made, and in nine hours from the time of the escape the recapture had been effected.

What could better serve to show the complete system upon which the Rocky Mountain Detective Association is organized?

Without further incident of note, the wily rascal was brought to Denver and taken to the county jail. He had become moody and cross, and was generally pronounced a rough customer by those with whom he came in contact. He would not talk at first at all. It was evident to Gen. Cook—who had kept his suspicion concerning the connection of Seminole with the Hayward murder to himself, even up to that time—that the fellow was living in dread of having his identity discovered. But Cook preserved a discreet silence. Mr. Ayres did not yet know the importance of the arrest which he had made.

As soon as the fellow was securely locked in, Gen. Cook sent for Mrs. Hayward, the widow of the murdered man, who was brought to Denver by Detective Hoyt of Golden. Taking her to the jail building, he had seven or eight prisoners, including Seminole, and all of them corresponding in some respects in appearance with him placed in a row in a room.

Into this room Mrs. Hayward was guided, having been told what was expected of her, namely, that she should have an opportunity to identify the probable murderer of her husband. She was told to walk along the line in which Seminole stood as stolid as a block of stone, and find among the array, if she could, the guilty party. She passed rapidly down the line, looking at one man at a time, without stopping to hesitate, until she came to Seminole, when, getting a full view of him, she threw up her hands and exclaimed:

"My God! that's the man. Take him away from me!"

The identification was positive, and was a death blow to the half breed's hopes. Besides this, he was identified by Brown & Marr, by Dr. Burr, and others, so that no doubt as to his identity could by any possibility be entertained. Seeing that he was in for if, Seminole made a full confession.

SEMINOLE'S CONFESSION

While Seminole was in jail here, Detective Cook determined to obtain from him some information which would lead to the apprehension of Woodruff, of whom all trace had now been lost. He accordingly sent a detective to the jail in response to Seminole's request, for a lawyer, and who, while professing to be a legal adviser, obtained from Seminole all he knew of his companion in crime and the particulars of the murder. He stated that while riding with Mr. Hayward they rode behind, the old man in front, driving; that Johnson suddenly clutched Hayward about the throat and choked him to death, while he, Seminole, took the lines and handled the horses; that the breakage of the neck was occasioned when they heaved the body out of the wagon when about to shove him under the little bridge where it was found; that at half-past ten the same night, they drove the wagon and mules into Denver and put up at the Western barn; that in the morning they took the outfit around to Paul & Strickler's, on Fifteenth street, and tried to have it sold at auction, but learning that the sale would not take place until afternoon, they went back to the barn, and finally sold it to a Leadville teamster for $190, Woodruff giving the bill of sale and signing the name Thomas Logan to it; that they then went to Brown & Man's and hired the buggy and mares, and followed exactly the route as traced, and that at Sidney bridge they separated, Woodruff going to the right, in the direction of the Niobrara river, while he kept straight on to the Pine Ridge agency, where he was captured

As to his companion, Seminole said his right name was Woodruff, though he had been known only as Tom Johnson in Colorado. He knew that Woodruff was a stonecutter by trade, and that he had been pardoned out of the Wyoming penitentiary after serving three years for killing a man named John Friehl, with whose wife Woodruff had been too intimate. The fellow gave a complete description of Woodruff, and seemed decidedly reckless as to whether his companion in crime should be caught or not. He made his confession in a cold-blooded manner, and gave no reason for the murder of Hayward, except that they wanted his team, and thought it would be best to have the owner conveniently hidden away while they were carrying forward their operations in Denver and getting out of the country.

Gen. Cook concluded that the best place to look for Woodruff was the place at which he had last been seen by Seminole, and consequently sent detectives to the Niobrara region. This time Mr. Ayres, who had captured Seminole, was sent out, and was accompanied by Mr. C. A. Hawley, who, being one of the most courageous as well as one of the shrewdest members of the association, was selected for this task, because ii was believed that there would be some lively work in arresting Woodruff, who was known to be desperate as well as cunning.

"But you must get him, Hawley," said Cook to his deputy when he left. "I trust the work to you, and expect you to do it up in good shape."

"If he is to be had, you can depend on me," said Hawley. "I am ready for him and go to find him."

'The two detectives made the trip to Niobrara with all possible haste. When they arrived there they began to look around for their man. One day when they came close upon an individual who answered the general description of Woodruff, that individual, finding that he was closely watched by the officers, and suspecting them to be officers, jumped on his horse and rode off at a lively gait. Inquiry revealed the fact that this man was known as Tom Johnson. They felt convinced that he was the man that they wanted, and they went after him with all possible haste. A wild chase he led them, too, over the uninhabited country of western Nebraska. Knowing the lay of the land better than the officers did, he was able to evade them for a long time, and at the end of a week of as hard work as often falls to the lot of detectives, they overtook and captured him.

After taking the fellow, they had doubts as to whether he was the man they were seeking; but concluded that a man who would act as suspiciously as he had been acting must be guilty of some crime, and whether it was that of the murder of the Colorado ranchman, or some other, mattered little to them. Hence they determined to bag him and to bring him to Denver, which determination they put into execution, landing here with him near the middle of November. The fellow proved not to be Woodruff, but it was soon ascertained that he was a fugitive from justice from Omaha, where he had been guilty of horse stealing; and it may be remarked in passing, that he was sent to that city and tried, and that he had to serve out a seven-years' sentence in the penitentiary of Nebraska. Thus the officers only brought down the wrong game when they fired, though they did not waste their ammunition, Shakespeare tells us that conscience makes cowards of us all. Johnson's conscience certainly put him behind the bars at Lincoln City.

This episode did not delay matters a great deal. Gen. Cook had been on the *qui vive* while his officers were out, and had learned that Woodruff had relatives living either in Iowa or eastern Nebraska, and he had come to the conclusion that the fugitive murderer would most likely fly to them for protection and to escape detection. The sequel will prove that in this case, as in most others where he forms a theory as to the conduct of fugitive criminals, he was right. Hence he decided to send Hawley to look up Woodruff's relatives, with the hope of also finding Woodruff. He had heard that they resided in the country before Hawley started, and suggested to him that it would be a good idea for him to play the role of a granger, in case it would serve his purpose. It was also decided to make the most of the capture of Johnson, the story of which was published in the newspapers in such a way as to lead to the inference that Johnson was the man wanted, the belief being that Woodruff would see the papers, and seeing this article, would conclude that the officers had been outwitted and taken the wrung man, he would become careless, and hence be all the more easily come up with.

While the people were reading the story of Johnson's capture, the next morning after his arrival from Niobrara, believing that the murderer had really been overtaken, Hanley was preparing to start upon a second excursion in search of that individual. He again started out to find his man. This time he did find him, "and no foolin'," either.

There was one important point to be gained in making the search. No one knew definitely where Woodruff's relatives lived, though they were known to be residents of the vicinity of Council Bluffs or Omaha.

Going first to Omaha, and then crossing the Missouri to Council Bluffs, the detective took a train on the Chicago, Burlington and Quincy railroad and went down the road about fifty miles, keeping his eyes and ears widely open in the hope of getting the slightest trace of the party he was after; and then, disgusted, returned to Council Bluffs and went to his hotel. From a man whom he met there he learned that James W. Woodruff, known to a brother of Sam, lived at Big Grove, thirty miles distant.

Disguising himself as a granger, he got a pony and a letter from Mr. Phelps, of the Ogden hotel, to his foreman, 'Walter Far-well, on his stock ranch, near the house of the Woodruffs, and started off. The stock ranch was about twenty-eight and a half miles from Council Bluffs, and here Hawley hired out as a corn-husker, and went to work. James Woodruff's place was about a mile and a half further on.

Hawley passed under the name of Charles Albert, and after working one day at corn-husking, prevailed upon the foreman to send him out, the following morning, looking for lost stock. It must be mentioned that while husking corn, the detective was incidentally told by Mr. Harwell of the late arrival of a brother of James Woodruff, said to be direct from the Black Hills, and with a $9,000 bank account in Deadwood. He had been home but ten days, and Hawley shrewdly suspected that this brother was the Samuel he was after. So in the course of his rambles about after lost stock, he stopped at the Woodruff farm, and learned that they had moved into the town of Big Grove. The officer thereupon circled and rode into the little village from the east, and spotted the Woodruff house, returning immediately thereafter to Phelps' stock place.

After unsaddling his pony and getting something to eat, he started for Council Bluffs, halving at about 11 in the morning end arriving at about 4 in the afternoon. Here, on the 25th of November, he swore out a warrant for the arrest of Samuel Woodruff, before Justice

Baird, and securing the services of Constable Theodore Guittar, they took a two-seated buggy, and at 10 that night started for the stock farm again, getting there about 3 o'clock in the morning, and seeking the barn for rest. But two hours later they were rudely awakened by an attendant, who didn't "sabe" the presence of two rough-looking tramps.

After feeding their horses and obtaining breakfast, they drove down to Big Grove, and leaving their team concealed in the bushes on the outskirts, walked into the town. They noticed their man at work near the Woodruff house, but as soon as he saw the two strangers he stopped his labors and went within. The officers then walked on down to the store of a Mr. Freeman, and while Hawley talked about the chances of getting work on the railroad, his companion went out and borrowed a double-barreled shot gun.

The detective discharged both barrels out of the back door, and then carefully loaded the weapon with a handful of buckshot in each barrel, stating to Guittar that it meant "death to either himself or Woodruff," in case of an escape or failure to capture. A little later James Woodruff, the brother, came driving down the street, and hitched his team a short distance from Freeman's store; and, coming up to the latter place, began a series of questioning and re-questioning, evidently endeavoring to pump the disguised detective; however, with little success.

Perhaps an hour was consumed in this manner, and then he left, and a few minutes later Hawley saw the two Woodruffs coming down the street together. James carried an axe and Sam a Revolver.

The detective pulled back the hammers of his shot gun, and watched the men through the windows.

As they neared the store, Hawley stepped out, apparently closely examining something about the locks of his weapon, and when the brothers reached the store, the officer brought the gun to his shoulder and said:

"Sam Woodruff, throw up your hands; I want you."

Quick as a flash the desperado's fist sought his revolver. But the cool, quiet tones of the officer, "Pull that pistol one inch, and I'll blow daylight through you," caused him to let go his grip and throw up his hands above his head.

Constable Guittar then applied the handcuffs and shackles, and disarmed the man, and he was immediately marched down the street a little way, while a boy was sent after the officers' team. The brother, James, attempted a few demonstrations, but Hawley's revolver, cocked and held in position, quieted his ardor.

Five minutes later, and the officers and their prisoner were driving towards Council Bluffs at full speed, and as soon as identified by Justice Baird and turned over to Hawley, he was taken to Omaha and there lodged in jail.

Hawley, being out of funds, now telegraphed Sheriff Cook for money, and though instantly forwarded, through some red-tapeism of the telegraph company he was delayed until too late to catch the train of that day. On the next, however, the detective and his prisoner left, reaching Cheyenne on the 29th at I o'clock in the afternoon. Before starting, the officer telegraphed Sheriff Gregg at Fremont, and Sheriff Con Groner of North Platte, to meet him for the purpose of identification of his prisoner. This these officers did, and fully identified the man as Samuel Woodruff. At North Platte, in addition to the sheriff, Martin Oberst, night clerk of the Railroad hotel, recognized him as having stopped at the house two or three weeks before, when he signed his correct name. At Cheyenne he was further identified by the sheriff, and T. Jeff Carr of the detective association, and upon arrival in Denver, the next day, Mr. Hunter, who was in the city on business, recognized him as having stopped at his ranch on the Niobrara river, on or about the 18th of September.

When brought to the sheriff's office, Woodruff refused to say anything, though on the journey he had denied all knowledge of the murder. He was driven over to the jail, and his co-partner in crime, Joseph Seminole, brought into his presence.

"Hello, Clarke." was Woodruff's exclamation, "what are you doing here?"

To this Seminole merely shrugged his shoulders.

"I used to know that man as Clarke when we were together in the penitentiary at Laramie City," Woodruff added, explanatorily, to the officers.

And with this these two scoundrels were locked up in separate cells. One thing worthy of note was that Seminole's description of the revolver carried by Woodruff tallied exactly with the weapon which Woodruff wore when arrested.

Much of the above is taken from the Denver *Tribune*, as told its reporter by the detectives. At this stage of the proceedings the *Tribune* was led to remark: "To the Rocky Mountain Detective Agency a great deal of credit is deservedly due for the able and persistent manner in which this matter has been worked up and this final capture had added increased lustre to the reputation already borne by this excellent organization. To D. J. Cook. C. A. Hawley, W. W. Ayres, Joe Arnold, T. J. Carr and C. P. Hoyt, the officers who have worked up the affair, special honor is due. They have been untiring in their efforts, and unsparing in their expenditures, and now have the pleasure of seeing total success crown their labors. Officers Cook and Arnold have secured the wagon that belonged to the murdered man from a Mr. Todd, in Douglas country, and will soon have the mules."

On the 3d of December, three days after Woodruff's arrival in the city, Mrs. Hayward and her two daughters, Minnie and Cora, aged then thirteen and fifteen, respectively, arrived in the city, accompanied by Detective Hoyt, of Golden, and proceeded to the jail to identify the prisoner. When all was ready, Woodruff was brought from his cell into the parlor of the jail. Mrs. Hayward sat upon the sofa facing the door, Cora on her left and Minnie on the right. Sheriff Cook stood at the head of the sofa, and the other officials near the windows and the door. As Woodruff entered the room, he shot one glance out of his dark eyes at the visitor on the sofa, and then dropped them, never again raising them during the remainder of the interview except once, and then to reply to a question. His nervousness was quite apparent, the trembling and twitching of his hands being very perceptible.

A moment's silence, after he had taken his seat, and then Mrs. Hayward said:

"Minnie, is that the man?"

"Yes," was the positive and quick reply of the little girl never raising her eyes from the close scrutiny with which she had regarded the prisoner from his entrance.

"You are sure he is the man," continued Mrs. Hayward, and the answer was as quick and as positive as before.

The other daughter, Cora, now spoke. "I know that is the man," she said, and the mother, turning to Sheriff Cook, said slowly: "Yes, that is the man—there is no mistake."

At this moment Joseph Seminole was brought into the room. "And there is the other," said Mrs. Hayward—the two daughters agreeing in like words. Then Gen. Cook asked Woodruff if he desired to ask any questions to test the visitors' belief, and received the reply, "My lawyer will do my talking." There was no longer any room for doubt. The two scoundrels who had killed an innocent man and who had led the officers such a chase as few criminals before or since their time ever did, had been overtaken by the Rocky Mountain Detective Association. It had been a long but a successful chase. They had been taken and securely locked in the Arapahoe county jail, where they had been fully identified and where they awaited orders from the Jefferson county authorities.

CLOSE OF THE HAYWARD STORY

The last chapter of this somewhat remarkable story at last opens. It is, if anything, the most thrilling of the series, as it relates the tragic end of the two men who have figured in these pages to considerable length, and with whom we began when we left Middle park in August of 1879. It is now December 28 of the same year, and the story is drawing to its close. Over three months have elapsed since Mr. Hayward, the quiet citizen and loving father and husband, was killed by these villains, but his neighbors, who knew him and appreciated his worth, had not forgotten the horror of the crime, nor allowed the passing days to carry with them their desire to avenge the great wrong that had been committed.

The scene is now laid at Golden. Gen. Cook, for the Rocky Mountain Detective Association, had taken the murderers to Golden that being the county seat of Jefferson county on the 9th of December, and hearing that there was a likelihood of an effort being made to lynch the scamps, took precautions to prevent such a result. It had long been his boast that no prisoner had ever been taken from his hands and lynched, and he did not propose to have his creditable reputation blackened now. He was fully prepared to meet any attempt upon the lives of the men that might be made, and appreciating the sort of man they were dealing with, the Jefferson vigilantes wisely decided to await a more convenient season" for the putting into execution of any designs they might have. The prisoners feared lynching, and trembled when Cook and his party left them after they' had been identified and placed in jail. Woodruff said: "I fear those old farmers who were Hayward's neighbors. They are a great deal more determined and bitter than milkers."

His fears were well founded. The dreadful hour came shortly after midnight on the cool, crisp Sunday morning of Christmas week of '79.

A few minutes before 12 o'clock Saturday night the late habitués of saloons and billiard halls, as well as others who happened to be awake at that hour, noticed the riding along the principal street of numerous horsemen, who came from apparently all directions and in little squads of two, three, half a dozen or so. They noticed that these silent horsemen all rode toward the jail, and all seemed to be intent on some urgent business. Then, remembering the oft-repeated murmurs of lynching made against the imprisoned murderers of poor old Hayward, a number of citizens followed in the wake of the strangers, who made at the jail a cavalcade of at least a hundred men, armed to the teeth and grimly seated upon their horses, not even talking or whispering among themselves.

A consultation between the chief and his lieutenants took place upon the steps leading to the first floor above the basement of the court house, and a few minutes later, without noise or confusion, a large circle of guards was spread around the jail and some two or three hundred yards distant from it. These grim sentinels were but a few paces apart, and some were mounted and some on foot. Every member of this avenging band wore a mask, or a handkerchief across the face, or had his features blackened with burnt cork, so that recognition was absolutely impossible. No one was permitted to pass this cordon of guards, no matter what the excuse. One man climbed a telegraph pole and the telephone wire from the jail was cut and thus all communication to and from the building was ended. Then the horses were ridden to a vacant lot opposite and tied, while the riders dismounted and closed in upon the jail. There was no noise or confusion. Everything had been carefully planned, and every man had a certain position and a certain duty assigned, and he silently took the one and performed the other,

There were in the building, aside from the prisoners in the cells, Under Sheriff Joseph Boyd, who was asleep with his family in a rear room, and an extra watchman, Edgar Cox, who was lying upon a bench in the sheriff's office. Hearing the sound of feet on the frozen earth outside, Cox rose to a sitting position and looked up at the windows, the curtains of which were raised. At each window he saw, to his stupefaction, two or three men, who had rifles in their hands. Their gleaming barrels pointed directly at him, and a stern voice simply said: "Don't move, or you'll get hurt."

Under the circumstances Cox did not move, but sat gazing at the deadly weapons which so steadily and unrelentingly covered him, while he could hear the heavy tramp of men marching in at the front door and thing down the inside stairs to the basement.

This same tramp, tramp of many feet, foretelling something unusual, reached the ears of Under Sheriff Boyd, who was in bed, and he suddenly awoke with the feeling that there was trouble ahead. Hastily pulling on his clothes he rushed out of his room, and saw the two rooms from which the two doors open into the jail part, teeming with masked and armed men, who apparently paid no attention to him whatever. As he passed the "feeding" door—so termed because through this the prisoners' meals are taken in to them—he noticed that the outer wooden door was splintered and the lock broken off. Pushing his way through to the front room, he mounted to the third step of the stairs leading to the first floor, and raising his voice, said:

"Gentlemen, listen to me one moment. You are, or I take you to be, law-abiding and law-loving citizens, and yet you are now engaged in unlawful proceedings. I beg of you to cease, and not in your indignation or passionate feelings take the law into your own hands. Rest assured justice will be obtained, even though it take a little longer."

At this juncture three men at the foot of the stairs pulled their revolvers and covered the speaker, while one said:

"Hands up sir—we know our business."

To which Boyd replied:

"I'll not hold up my hands. I know you have not come here to harm me," and recommenced his expostulation and entreaty to the men in front of him.

In the meantime, a number of the vigilantes had attacked the iron-grated door with sledge hammers and crowbars. Every blow told, and sinewy and muscular arms sent the heavy instruments to the points where they would do the most good.

The undersheriff still continued his address to the men, and finally the leader, a tall, well-built man, ordered three of his fellows to take Boyd into custody and remove him. They instantly complied and the officer was taken into the inner room, where he still continued his protestations. The blows fell thick and fast upon the great strong lock and at last with a crash it gave way and the door swung open, and those terrible, determined men swarmed within.

Previous to all this the prisoners were sound asleep in their cells, save one, Joseph Murphy, in for petty larceny and who was out of his cell, being on duty in keeping up the fire and such other little chores as might be necessary.

As the assault began upon the bolts of the iron door, Woodruff awoke with a start, and sprang to the grating of his cell, where he glared in tremulous anxiety upon the bars that were trembling beneath the rain of blows. Seminole, too, awoke about the same time, and began a low moaning in his terrible fear, though he did not arise from his bed, but as the door at last gave way, and the crowd rushed in, he gave vent to a cry which is described as being more like the shriek of some wild animal than any other noise.

Without loss of time the vigilantes attacked the padlocks on cells fourteen and twelve, the former being Woodruff's and the latter Seminole's. Noticing the liberty of Murphy, and supposing that he might attempt to escape in the confusion, the leader of these midnight dispensers of justice went to Boyd, who was still under guard, and told him he had better lock up such prisoners as might be loose.

"Will you pledge your word of honor for yourself and men that you will not touch the keys if I get them?" asked the faithful official.

"Yes," was the brief but evidently earnest reply.

Calling the watchman, Cox, and accompanied still by his masked guard, Boyd went to the vault and began to work the combination that opened it. Before giving the last twist, however, he turned to his silent captors, and said:

"'You have heard the pledge given by your captain, or chief, or whatever you call him, in relation to the keys; have I your words of honor also?"

They bowed a grim assent, and a moment later the bolt shot back and the iron door turned on its hinges. Taking the keys the official entered the jail and locked Murphy up. As he passed the cells containing two burglars, they begged to be released, fearing lest the vigilantes would also make an example of them. Boyd assured them that they would not be harmed, or at least he would do all in his power to protect them.

In the meantime cold chisels had cut into the cell padlocks, and sledge hammers completed the job. Woodruff was on his feet and showed fight, but his visitors were determined men, and the cold-blooded murderer was soon rendered docile, a few raps with the butt of a revolver being administered on the top of his head. He was carried out and laid upon his stomach on the floor, his face resting upon his left side, while skillful and willing hands bound his wrists together behind his back. As he was being taken from his cell he made but one remark:

"Gentlemen, you are mistaken. I am innocent of this crime."

When the tying was completed he was lifted up to a sitting posture and asked for the captain, referring to Boyd, and that officer immediately came forward.

Laying hand upon the shoulder of the prisoner, Boyd said:

"Well, Woodruff, what can I do for you?"

Woodruff raised his dark eyes to the kindly face above him, and with a low voice, inexpressibly sad and full of feeling said:

"Captain, write to my wife—and to my brother, and tell them all about this, will you? Don't forget it. Write to (and a name was given which the officer forgets) and tell him to avenge my death—he'll do it."

"Gentlemen," he said, turning to his captors, "this is not the last of this."

Then Boyd said: "Is that all I can do for you. Sam?"

"Yes," said the prisoner, "all—all."

During all this time the men had been hammering away at Seminole's cell, and as Woodruff finished speaking, the door was opened and a number of men sprang within. Seminole was lying upon his face moaning fearfully in his terror. He was quickly picked up and carried out, and his hands bound behind him in like manner to Woodruff's.

Without further hesitation or delay and in perfect silence the prisoners, the manacles on their ankles clanking a dismal dead march, were taken out through the front door of the basement and taken in the direction of the Golden and South Platte railroad, three or four hundred yards distant. Woodruff refused to walk, and was half carried and half pushed, but Seminole did what he could in the way of locomotion, and in a few minutes the men were on the railroad bridge that crosses Kinney creek.

The bridge is a timber one, having three spans, supported on spiles resting on wooden foundations. A rope three-eighths of an inch in diameter was produced, which was supposed to be long enough to hang both men, but being found too short, a delay occurred while a new one, an inch in diameter, was obtained. Woodruff was stationed on the end nearest Denver, and Seminole just five sleepers further away. With nooses about their necks, the other ends of the ropes being fastened to the projecting ends of the timbers (notches being cut to prevent any slipping), the men stood.

"Sam Woodruff, do you wish to say anything?" was the grim question of the masked leader.

The man addressed looked around upon the crowd silence a few moments, and then, without further preface, said:

"Gentleman, you are hanging an innocent man, but I trust God will forgive you, as I do. May I say my prayers?"

Assent being given, the doomed man knelt and silently prayed to the Almighty. When he had finished he arose to his feet and, looking once more upon his captors, said: I have one last request to make. Permit me to jump off the bridge; don't push me to my death."

But his request was not granted, and a few moments later a dozen hands pushed him off the edge—oft the edge into eternity.

When Seminole was asked if he had anything to say, he choked a moment and then, in a clear, distinct voice, said:

"Gentlemen, I have but little to say, and I address myself to those among you who may be erring ones. Beware of the first bad step. The after ones are not to be feared; it is the beginnings. But for my first evil break I would not be standing here tonight with this rope about my neck and death staring me in the face. In relation to this murder, gentlemen, we two are the guilty ones. We committed the crime. I have no excuse to offer, nothing to say."

And then, raising his head toward heaven, his lips moving tremulously, he broke out with, "O, God Almighty, have mercy on my sinful soul; and as Thou hast shown Thy love and tenderness in times past to weak and guilty ones, show such to me now. Guard, oh, I pray Thee, my mother and brothers, and let not them follow in my footsteps or take my sinful path. Forgive me my transgressions, O God, and"—his voice broke slightly—"take me to Thee, sinful though I am." And then, in simple but beautiful and eloquent terms, he prayed for the well-being and salvation of his captors and executioners.

During this prayer the vigilantes stood around, with hats removed and heads bowed, in reverential listening. It was a sombre, impressive picture. The moonlight shining cold and clear upon the scene; the fated man, with eyes turned towards the zenith, one foot upon the iron rail of the track, the other upon the tie to which was attached the rope that drooped from his neck; the swinging, twitching body of his companion in crime dangling in awful solitude below; the congregated men with un covered and bent heads, and their faces hid beneath grim masks; the polished barrels of rifles and guns gleaming in the moon beams, and the grave like silence alone broken by the earnest, feeling words of the speaker—a picture never to be forgotten. And when at last the lips were closed and the fatal push was given even the stern executioners of inexorable law felt a tremor run through their stalwart, muscular limbs.

Seminole died instantly, his neck being broken in the fall, but swinging past the spiles the skin on the knuckles of his right hand was rubbed off Woodruff died hard, his struggles for breath being, distinctly heard, and his limbs twitching convulsively.

The work was done, and the vigilantes slowly retraced their steps to their horses, and without a word mounted to their saddles, while the two bodies hanging beneath the bridge twisted and twirled, and finally rested motionless, stirred only now and then by a passing breeze that played fitfully with their fast stiffening forms.

During the confusion in securing the prisoners in the jail, Mr. Boyd managed to get to the telephone and attempted to communicate with the town. But in vain. Then he sent Cox, the watchman, off to alarm Sheriff Belcher, but ere the messenger had proceeded a dozen yards he was stopped and returned to the building. The sheriff was asleep at his home when, about 1 who told him that something was going on at the jail, and a few moments later a black watchman named Baker, who had been especially instructed in view of such an emergency, came in with the alarm also. A few minutes later and the sheriff was hastening at the top of his speed towards the jail on the hill. But he was too late. The murderers of R. B. Hayward had gone to their final account, and the vigilantes, with the exception of a guard on the ridge near the bodies, had disappeared as quietly and mysteriously as they had come. Then the sheriff went for the coroner, Dr. Joseph W. Anderson, and without loss of time that officer arrived upon the ground. While he was examining the bodies the coroner was hailed by the vigilantes with:

"What are you doing?"

"Examining into your devilish work."

"Are they dead?"

"Yes; deader than hell."

"All right. Hayward is avenged. Good night." And the sentinel horsemen rode off with a parting wave of their hands.

As the main body of men left the scene of the lynching, they tired a farewell shot from their pistols, and as their number was variously estimated at from one hundred to a hundred and fifty, it made quite a volley.

After viewing the hanged men, the coroner ordered the sheriff to cut them down, which was done, and D. P. Maynard having been sent for and arriving with his express wagon, the corpses were taken up and conveyed to an unoccupied storeroom on Ford street. Here they were placed under the care of two watchers, and about 9 o'clock in the morning were conveyed to the court house, where, an hour later, the jury impaneled by the coroner held the inquest, and brought in a verdict to the effect that Seminole and Woodruff "came to their death upon the 28th day of December, 1879, being taken from the jail and custody of the said jailer of said county by force and violence, between the hours of 12 and 1 o'clock a m., and hanged by the neck by parties unknown to this jury, and with felonious intent."

After the tragedy the undertaker laid the bodies out in plain pine boxes, painted black on the outside, and, untying their hands, crossed them in front. Woodruff was dressed in a dark check shirt, duck overall and cotton stockings, without shoes. His eyes were half open, and his mouth, with its lips slightly apart, disclosed his regular teeth beneath. During his confinement in Golden he had not shaved, and a rough growth of beard covered his cheeks and chin. His forehead was covered with blood that dripped from the wounds on the top of his head, caused by the necessary rapping given with the pistol butt when faking him out of his cell.

Seminole wore a checkered vest and a dark sack coat over his undershirt. Dark pantaloons, brown mixed stockings and Indian moccasins completed the balance of his attire. His mouth and eyes were firmly closed, and from either corner of the shut lips a streak of blood ran down upon his neck, while watery matter oozed slightly from his left eye. His face was considerably swollen, and decomposition soon set in. The knots on both nooses had slipped around to the front, immediately beneath the chin, and had cut somewhat into the flesh of both men. The back of Woodruff's neck was badly cut and much swollen, and blood marked the courses on both necks followed by the rope. In order to accommodate Woodruff's body, a box six feet seven inches long was necessary, and six feet one inch for Seminole.

Monday afternoon, succeeding the day of the lynching, no answer having been received from relatives, both Seminole and Woodruff were buried in the Golden cemetery.

And thus Samuel Woodruff and Joseph Seminole pass out of the world's daily history, and another terrible example is recorded to give terror to all evil-doers.

Recording the tragedy as above related, the *Tribune* of December 30 said:

> "In wandering through the town of Golden yesterday, and conversing with business men of all grades of social and intellectual standing, the reporter failed to find one solitary person who condemned this recent lynching. On every side the popular verdict seemed to be that the hanging was not only well merited, but a positive gain to the county, saving it at least five or six thousand dollars. In plumply asking the question from thirteen representative men, the *Tribune* commissioner met with the unvarying response: 'It was the best thing possible, and we are all glad of it.'"

ONE HOPE STILL LEFT

Mr. Joseph Arnold, known to his friends and the community at large as "Joe," has for many years past been one of the most trusted of Gen. Cook's assistant detectives. To him have been entrusted many of the cases which required the closest attention to detail, and a capacity to pick up clues which others less shrewd and less familiar with the small traits of human nature would have allowed to go unnoticed. He is a typical detective. He is one of the best men on a cold trail in the whole country, and is as plausible as a courtier when it is necessary to be plausible. At other times he is quite disposed to be taciturn, and he never gives anything away.

One of Joe's best pieces of detective work was done in the year 1878, and it illustrates his shrewdness about as well as any story which can be told of him. This consisted in the working up of the case of Christian J. Schuttler, as big a pious fraud as ever dawned upon Denver. Schuttler had for many years lived in Johnson county, Iowa, twelve miles from Iowa City. He was a man of over fifty years of age, the head of a family consisting of a wife and twelve children. He was a member of the Amish Society, a branch of the Dunkard faith, and was a leader among them. Indeed, he was at the head of the society in Johnson county if not in the entire state of Iowa. He was the financial agent and manager of his society, attending to all the business of his people with the outside world for the entire community. The society in Iowa was prosperous, because industrious and frugal, and Schuttler, as their agent, had almost unlimited credit. He was trusted everywhere as a man of extreme probity and honor: probably because he wore a long beard, as the Amish people never shave; had a meek look in his eyes, spoke in a low tone, wore hooks and eyes instead of buttons, and carried other external signs which made him appear a man whom the world should trust; but most probably because he had the confidence of his own people, and because they backed him as a body in his financial and other operations. At any rate, he was trusted implicitly, and this fact led to his falling into Joe Arnold's hands.

As general business agent for his organization, Schuttler often made business visits to Chicago. What his general conduct there was on these occasions is not known in detail, but it is supposed to have generally been very loose, though he was not suspected by those who trusted him until after the occurrences which are about to be related.

Schuttler made one of these visits to Chicago in the early part of 1878, and during that visit disappeared mysteriously from the sight of his friends and acquaintances. He had gone to Chicago for the purpose of selling for his society thirteen carloads of fine beef cattle, which had been prepared for the market by his Dunkard friends. Before leaving, as was afterwards ascertained, he had borrowed $4,000 in currency from the Johnson County Bank, of which Mr. John Conden was cashier, and also various small sums from other persons. He had been gone several days before any uneasiness began to be felt; but when at last, after some two or three weeks of waiting, nothing was heard of him his friends began to grow uneasy, and took the initiatory steps towards making a search for him, if alive, and for his body if dead. Letters were written to Chicago, but only elicited the fact that he had arrived there with his cattle, and had sold them and gotten the money for them. The cashier of a bank remembered seeing Schuttler in his bank, where he had gone out with a draft for $10,000. This was the last trace which had been found. Search was made everywhere in Chicago, but no one could be found who could throw any light upon the mystery, which deepened every day. Advertisements were put in the papers. Friends became uneasy for the man's personal safety; creditors grew anxious for oilier reasons; his family was terribly distressed for their own welfare, as well as for that of the father and husband. But no good tidings were received with which to appease the general uneasiness.

Hardly anyone believed that Schuttler had disappeared of his own accord. As has been said, he was trusted by all and suspected by none. It was believed that he had been robbed for his money, and the suspicion that he had also been murdered gradually took possession of the public mind.

At last a heavy reward was offered for the finding of the man, dead or alive, and for any clue which would aid in clearing up the terrible mystery and bringing to justice those who were believed to have been responsible for his disappearance.

At the special request of those interested, Pinkerton's Detective Agency was employed on the case by those interested, and instructed to spare neither money nor pains in their work. They published descriptions in the papers, searched Chicago from one end to the other, and even went so far as to have the Chicago river dragged for the body. They set their men in every direction to work, but failed utterly to find any trace of the missing man, or to offer any theory which would explain his disappearance. Schuttler's friends were quite despairing.

But there was still reason for hope, if they had only known, which will appear in the next chapter.

CONFIDENCE, THEFT AND BIGAMY

One day several weeks after the man's disappearance, and when the Pinkertons had almost ceased their search the Johnson county people received a telegram from the Rocky Mountain Detective Association, asking them for a complete description of Schuttler, and asking what should be done in case there was reasonable hope of finding Schuttler. A reply was sent, requesting that every effort be made, and saying that a reward of $500 would be paid for the discovery of the man and his return to Iowa.

Joe Arnold had read the description of Schuttler in the Chicago papers. Mr. O. A. Whittemore was then a justice of the peace in Denver. One day Mr. Arnold was in Justice Whittemore's office attending to some business when he noticed a rather peculiar looking couple come in and ask to be married. The man gave the name of Christian Schottler and the woman that of Mary Spohr. The detective scanned the pair carefully, and at last came to the conclusion that he had somewhere read a description of the man and that he was "wanted." After thinking over the matter in his own mind he concluded that Christian Schottler, who was getting married to Mary Spohr, was no other than Christian J. Schuttler, late of Johnson county, Iowa, who was supposed to have been murdered for his money and who was being mourned by his wife and twelve children as dead. That he had made many changes in his appearance was quite evident. His long hair and beard had been cut, and the Quaker-like garb had given place to a far more fly costume. Rut the features of the man were those which had been described in the Chicago paper, and the name given here was very similar to that which Iowa man had borne. Mr. Arnold was quite convinced that Schuttler, instead of being the truly good creature which had been described, was a wolf in sheep's clothing, who had stolen the $10,000 in money and deserted his family and foresworn his creed for the purpose of living with the woman whom he had seen become his wife.

Mr. Arnold was careful, of course, to avoid divulging his suspicions to these people or to create any uneasiness in their minds.

He went to Gen. Cook and told him what he had witnessed and imparted his surmise to the chief. Cook then went with him to see the man and to pass his opinion upon him. He coincided with Arnold in his view of the case, and it was after this conference that the telegram referred to above was sent to Iowa.

In accordance with the instructions from Iowa, the detectives decided to keep a close watch upon the movements of the pair. This work was entrusted almost entirely to Mr. Arnold. He seldom allowed the man and woman to get out of his sight, though he was careful to remain unknown to them. He discovered that they spent the greater portion of their time in the retired portions of the city, and found that they had entered into negotiations some few days after their arrival here for a saloon on Wazee street, where it was supposed they believed they could go into business and earn a livelihood, as well as enjoy their illicit love, without being detected. They resided during the time in a little grout cottage on Fifteenth street, near Welton, considered then a long way out of town.

One day, much to his satisfaction, Mr. Arnold traced Schottler to a photograph gallery, and found that he had had some pictures of himself made. What motive he could have had for this step is not known, but it is presumed that he desired to preserve a record of his early appearance in his new garb, which, though that of ordinary life with other men, was strange to him. Whatever the freak that led him to seek the photographer, it proved quite a serious matter for him, and helped, if it did no more, to hasten the arrest. Of course Arnold procured one of these pictures. He sent it post haste to the home of Schuttler, where, although the clerical look was removed, it was recognized as being the photograph of Schuttler. The detectives were then requested to see that Schuttler did not make his escape and to arrest him in case he should attempt to leave town. The telegram was from Mr. Conden, the cashier of the bank which had lent Schuttler $4,000, and he announced his determination to come out and see the man.

In the meantime Arnold had found that the man and woman told different stories about themselves, as to where they were from, one of them stating that they had just arrived from Illinois and the other that they came from Wisconsin. They appeared to be nervous and watchful, and every movement strengthened the suspicion entertained of them by the detectives. The woman at last disappeared, and it was learned that she had gone to Chicago, taking a considerable sum of money with her.

When Conden arrived the man was alone. He was taken to a place where he could obtain a good look at him without being himself seen by Schuttler. He at once pronounced Schottler to be no other than Schuttler, and requested that he be arrested forthwith.

The arrest followed soon afterwards, and was made by Gen. Cook. When Schuttler was apprehended he denied that he had been guilty of any crime, and told the officer that he must be mistaken. He made no objection other than to declare his innocence and to swear that his name was Scholtz instead of Schuttler. In reply to these remarks Cook only told him that if he would go with him to his office the matter could very soon be settled; that there was a man there who would probably recognize him, and that if he did not there would be no harm done, and he could go. To this proposition Schuttler assented, and went with Cook. Conden was awaiting the arrival of the two men at the officer's rooms, and when Schuttler arrived there was a mutual recognition.

"My God!" exclaimed Schuttler.

With this he thrust his hand into his pocket and brought out an ordinary pocket knife with which he made an effort to cut his throat, and an this he doubtless would have succeeded had he not been interfered with by Cook and Arnold. He then acknowledged everything, and said it was useless to make an attempt to conceal his crime. He would, he said, willingly go back home and make any reparation for his offense that was in his power. He now talked profusely, and claimed that then for the first time, though he had been missing for nearly two months, he had realized the wrong which he had done, he protested that he had been drugged and stupefied in Chicago and led astray by the woman to whom he had been married here.

It may be remarked in passing that it was afterwards learned that the woman had been a member of the *demi monde* and that Schuttler had been acquainted with her for several years before his little escapade. It seems, further, that he had deliberately planned an elopement with her before leaving home, and that he had as deliberately borrowed money and procured the sale of the cattle with the intention of defrauding the community which had trusted him with such implicity. The woman had played her part merely for the purpose of getting money from the fellow, and had succeeded to such an extent that when he was captured only $1,000 of the original $10,000 was found upon his person. She had gone away, doubtless, to never return. Be that as it may she has never since been heard from in Colorado. She had undoubtedly played Schuttler for an old fool; and going on the principle that an old fool is the worst fool of all, had undertaken to beat him badly, and had succeeded admirably—tearing the man, as such women are most capable of doing, from his exalted position in his community and from his family, and causing him ever afterwards to be looked upon as a thief, a bigamist, and, worse than all, a silly dupe.

To return to the story. Arnold assisted in taking Schuttler back to Iowa, where he was taken in hand by the authorities. The people of Schuttler's faith, who are generally very honest, were greatly chagrined at his disgrace, and through their intercession he was saved from a term in the penitentiary. They agreed to settle all his debts, and a compromise was effected upon this basis. The man's wife was the only person who professed to believe his story of the manner in which he had been led astray. There was a reconciliation in the family, with whom Schuttler soon afterwards removed to Nebraska, where he is probably still living.

The reward offered was paid promptly to Arnold, and he received much praise for the splendid manner in which he had conducted the case, and especially for the shrewdness he had displayed in the beginning. It is safe to say that among the people of Johnson county, Iowa, the Rocky Mountain Detective Association will forever be considered as superior to Mr. Pinkerton's agency. There are many other localities which feel the same way on the subject.

THE WALL MURDER MYSTERY

Dry creek is the name of a small and unimportant tributary of Cherry creek, which, like a great many other streams in this vicinity, contains but little water, except during the spring and summer months. It is, however, skirted in places by growths of underbrush and cottonwoods and willows. It heads in Douglas county, near the Divide, and runs for twenty miles in a northeasterly direction, until it joins Cherry creek some fifteen miles above Denver. The region is one for the possession of which ten years ago no one but a few sheep-herders disputed with the prairie dog and plains rattlesnake. Lonely and barren as was the country, it has had its tragedies, and Dry creek tells one of the most thrilling tales of cold-blooded murder which is recorded in this calendar.

Some few years previous to 1871, a quiet and reticent man came to the place and bought a small herd of sheep. He gave the name of S. K. Wall. Occasionally, when business called, he rode into Denver; but he never remained for any length of time. Unlike many men of his calling, and those of the kindred vocation of cattle-grazing, he never staid over to have "hi good time with the boys." He did not buy whiskey with his money, but after paying for his necessities, he would visit the book stores and lay in a supply of reading matter. This he would carry with him to his home up the creek. There he lived, in an unpretentious dug-out tent, the life of a hermit, doing his own cooking and tending his own sheep. He had built his hut in a willow copse, near the bed of the creek; and, owing perhaps as much to his retiring manners as to his frugal mode of life, the supposition prevailed in the neighborhood that he had a great deal of money stored away in the place of his abode. His herd had also increased rapidly in numbers and now counted four hundred head of as well-kept sheep as were to be found in the neighborhood. The prize was one likely to excite the envy of those disposed to avariciousness.

Among Mr. Wall's neighbors in those days were Mr. J. S. McCool, who now resides on the Platte a few miles below Denver, and Mr. LeFevre. Employed by Mr. LeFevre was a young man named George

H. Wetherill, while Mr. McCool gave work to one E. E. Wight, commonly then known in the neighborhood as Jack Wight. These two employees became the murderers of Wall, whose sheep and supposed hidden treasure of gold they longed to possess.

Witherill was the younger of the two men, being at that time twenty-three years of age, while Wight was about twenty-seven. Both were doubtless bad enough, but to Wight seems to belong the credit of planning the deviltry. He also appears to have found in Witherill not only a willing accomplice but a pliant tool. Wight had come into Colorado the year before from Iowa, and Witherill had recently arrived from the north west. He was a native of New York, and had gradually drifted westward until he reached Utah and Dakota. For a while he was engaged as a stage driver from Corrinne, Utah, on the Fort Benton route. Afterwards he drifted back to Laramie City, Wyo., and from Laramie came to Denver. The education which he had received as a stage driver in the then almost savage region in which he operated was not calculated to make a refined creature of him.

Witherill and Wight soon became acquainted and were not long in deciding to appropriate Wall's property which had aroused their cupidity. From the time they first discovered themselves to be of common mind upon this point, they talked over the project continually when they met. Both of them were herders, but for different men, and they frequently contrived to bring their herds together for the purpose of discussing this subject between themselves. They also managed to get days off, when they would stroll about and discuss the matter. They also met at night and debated the fine points, going so far at times as to walk over to Wall's place and survey the premises. The horrible nature of the crime of murder seems to have never entered their minds. The only point which presented itself was the feasibility of their scheme. They were not anxious to kill, but they wanted Wall's property, and after discussing various other plans for getting Wall out of the way, decided, as dead men tell no tales, to murder him in cold blood and take the sheep and whatever valuables might be found.

These plans had begun to take root as early as the middle of the summer, but they did not mature until September. The 17th day of that month in the year 1871 fell on Sunday—as bright and quiet a day as Colorado was ever blessed with. The two men had taken the day off for the purpose of putting their long-cherished project into execution, agreeing upon a place of meeting and a plan of proceeding. They came together about 2 o'clock in the afternoon, and about 3 came upon Wall lying quietly upon a peaceful hillside in the shade of a bluff, matching the lazy sheep as they gnawed their Sunday meals out of the tufted grass on the sloping plains below—certainly a picture of peace and quiet. There was nothing there to suggest murder, but on the contrary all was suggestive of brotherly love. The scene was one to call out the warmth and fellow feeling in human nature.

But the two scoundrels had gone to the place on murder bent, and they did not propose to be deterred from their purpose by a Sunday scene or a sparkle, of bright sunshine. They went up to Wall, who did not suspect but that they meant to pay him a friendly call, with smiles on their faces, and began a friendly conversation. Even while they talked they were preparing for the murder which they had come to commit, and when the doomed man turned his head, one of the ruffians—which one will probably never be definitely known—pulled his gun and leveling at the poor man's back, fired, the ball striking him in the neck.

Comprehending for the first time the real intention of the men, Wall instinctively took to his heels to save his life, and started towards his dugout tent. He flew down the hill as if carried on the air, the two men pursuing almost as fast. It was a race for life—a curious interruption of the mild Sunday scene which spread out before them under the bright light of the autumn skies. Even as Wall ran, the blood spurted in torrents from the ugly wound in his neck, marking the path he trod so plainly that he might have been tracked by means of it, had not the pursuers been so close as to need no guide to the course the man had taken. One of them had come on horseback to the place, and he left his animal standing while he should pursue his murderous task. They followed closely in the footsteps of Wall, whose path led over a rugged hillside, down a steep bluff, and into the bed of Dry creek below. He ran so rapidly at first that the shots which his bloody handed pursuers sent after him were of no avail in bringing him to a halt. It is not believed that either one of the bloody bullets except the first hit the mark and it began to look as if the poor man would make good his escape. He was evidently bent upon getting to his cabin, where once arrived he had firearms stored with which he would be amply able to protect himself even against double odds. The murderers apprehended his intentions, and bent every energy to cut off the retreat. Finding that the leaden missiles failed to accomplish their purpose, they quit shooting and doubled their pace.

As they increased their speed, Wall evidently slackened his. The run was a long one, and he was losing a great deal of blood. He had, however, reached the bed of the gulch, and was nearing his home, when his foot struck a boulder, and he fell prone on the creek bottom, the murderers sweeping up behind him like bloodhounds in pursuit of a fugitive slave.

"Good!" exclaimed one of them, as they saw their prey fall so nearly within their grasp.

"I guess the damned scoundrel's done for," replied the other as they slackened their pace to draw a long breath and be prepared for a final struggle.

But a moment more served to change this last expressed opinion. Wall was greatly weakened by the loss of blood and the fatigue of the race, but he managed to scramble to his feet once more, and to stagger onward in a zigzag run up the creek bottom. The assassins had come up to within twenty steps of him and could easily be heard.

"Stop there, damn you or we will fill you full of lead," one of them shouted to him. "No more of this foolishness; you may as well surrender on the spot."

Realizing that further flight was hopeless; that his strength was gone and that he was unarmed, and feeling perhaps that he might save his life, Wall halted, and Witherill and Wight came up.

As they approached Wall he turned towards them and demanded an explanation of their strange conduct.

"What does it mean?" he demanded to know.

"Mean? It means that you are having too good a time of it—that you are making too much money for a damned old snoozer who knows no better how to use it and enjoy it than you do. We want it. We want your sheep, your money, everything you've got, damn you!"

The poor fellow was rapidly sinking under the loss of blood. He replied faintly: "Take everything, but spare my life. I don't want to die. I have done nothing to deserve death. I will give you everything freely. All I ask is that I be permitted to live."

Witherill and Wight were now standing very close to him, and one of them had raised the breech of a heavy rifle over Wall's head. "Spare your life! What sort of a game are you giving us? Spare nothing! A fine idea to let you live and as soon as your damned old head is cured up to go blabbing it to Dave Cook and every other officer and detective in the state. What d'you take us for? A charitable society? Guess, old man, you're a little off, ain't you? It's dead men that tell no tales to detectives, old fellow; we puts our trust in no others."

In vain did the poor quivering man plead for his life. In vain were his promises of secrecy. Even while bending upon his knees and while he lifted his quivering hand to swear that he would deliver every article of his possession to his murderers if they would only permit him to live, even while imploring, the heavy rifle held above his head came crashing down, another shot being fired at the same time. A thundering, deafening noise, a lightning pain followed by the darkness of death, and all was over. Wall fell to the ground with his skull broken in and expired a moment afterwards.

The body was buried beneath a pile of rocks where it had fallen and the murderers prepared to take possession of the property which they had secured by their Sunday's work.

They, had hoped to procure money through the murder of Wall, as well as to get possession of his sheep. They shared the popular opinion that he had many dollars in gold and silver and greenbacks laid away in his hut. Hence they first searched the dead man's person, taking his watch and pocket book, the latter containing some small change and a certificate of deposit in the bank then kept in Denver by Mr. Warren Hussey and after securing these articles of value, though of treacherous and tell-tale character, they hid the still warm body of this victim away and proceeded to search Wall's dugout. Here, contrary to expectations, they found nothing of value to them and went out in some disgust to take possession of the sheep, which had been so suddenly left by their master, and which were still grazing on the quiet hillside almost in sight of the spot which had seen the culmination of the tragedy which had begun in their midst.

A day or two afterwards people living in the neighborhood discovered Witherill in charge of Wall's sheep and also that Wall himself had disappeared. In reply to inquiries Witherill stated that he had bought the sheep from Wall, and exhibited a bill of sale for them, saying at the same time that Wall had left Colorado. There was some little suspicion aroused at first, because Witherill had never been known to have any sufficient amount of money to procure so large a herd as Wall's. It soon, also, became known that Witherill was wearing a watch which Wall had owned and which he had told someone that he would not part with for three times its value.

After this Witherill was regarded with suspicion by his neighbors, and some of them came to Denver and laid the matter before Gen. Cook, who was at that time sheriff of Arapahoe county as well as chief of the Rocky Mountain Detective Association. As the crime, if one had been committed, was outside of his jurisdiction as sheriff, having been committed in another county, Gen. Cook referred the complaints to the sheriff of Douglas county. He, however, determined to keep his eyes open for developments and to lend whatever aid he could to the apprehension of the criminal or criminals, if indeed the foul play suspected had been committed.

THE MYSTERY UNRAVELING

Gen. Cook did not have to wait long. It is a true saying that murder will out. It cannot bide its bloody footprints, especially when there are shrewd detectives on the track. Reports of Witherill's suspicious movements came in frequently. An important item to the detective was the fact which be learned that Witherill had come to the city' soon after he took possession of the sheep with the certificate of deposit at Hussey's bank and presented it to be cashed. This was an important link, and it was greatly strengthened by the fact that the clerk at the bank had declared that the indorsement of Wall's name on the certificate was not in Wall's handwriting, and had returned the paper to Witherill, who had said that Wall bad gone to Laramie City, Wyo., and that he would send him the certificate and get a reindorsement. Cook was now well on till *qui vive*. In about two weeks, the time necessary to send the paper to Laramie and get it returned, Witherill bad returned to the bank with the certificate, the first indorsement erased and the name written in a different hand. But the clerk failed to recognize the signature as Wall's, and acting under Cook's instructions, retained the certificate.

Up to this time Witherill does not seem to have dreamed that anyone suspected him of any crime, and as for Wight, no one did suspect him. They had been disappointed in getting so little money from Wall, and determined, while they had their hands in, to add to their wealth by getting more sheep together.

Hence they made another raid, and this affair seems to have been the hair that broke the camel's back; which at last so thoroughly continued former suspicions that a thorough search was decided upon. Mr. J. K. Doolittle, who is well-known in Denver, and who is now a prosperous merchant in Pueblo, had a large herd of sheep, which he kept up the creek some miles from Witherill's herd. One day it was discovered that about six hundred of his herd had disappeared, and investigation developed the fact that they had been merged into Witherill's flock. George Hopkins, Esq., at that time city marshal of Denver, went out to attend to the restoration of the sheep to their owner, and to arrest Witherill on the charge of stealing the sheep. He had no difficulty in identifying the sheep, but he found Witherill prepared with the papers to demonstrate his own "innocence." He showed a bill of sale from Wall for them, as well as the other sheep. But he was brought into Denver to straighten matters up. He agreed to restore all of Doolittle's stock, and to pay whatever expenses Mr. Doolittle had incurred in procuring his property.

While Witherill was in Denver, however, he was seen by John L. Hayman, whose name appeared on the bill of sale transferring the sheep from Wall to Witherill, who recognized him as the man who had signed Walks name, and who had claimed to be Wall. Here was a clear case of forgery.

Witherill on this occasion got out of the Town before Chief Cook had learned of these developments; but when he obtained the information he decided that Witherill should again be arrested and a thorough investigation made to ascertain whether Wall had not been murdered. Witherill had certainly proved himself a thief and a forger, and there were many circumstances which went to show that he had also been guilty of taking the life of a fellow being.

While Cook was making his preparations for the capture of Witherill, Wight first began to figure before the public as an accomplice of Witherill's in his crime. Knowing that he had so far not been suspected, as he had constantly pushed Witherill forward and himself remained in the background, he came to Denver the next day after Witherill had left, on Tuesday, a little more than three weeks after the murder, and had the temerity to go to the officers and advise them to arrest Witherill, saying that he believed him to be guilty of Wall's murder. He thus partially gained the confidence of the detectives, and learned enough to convince him that the apprehension of Witherill was decided upon. Knowing that when Witherill was once taken he would reveal the part that Wight had taken in the tragedy, he returned to Dry creek that afternoon and warned Witherill of their danger, and they prepared for flight that night.

Detectives Smith and Benton had been selected by Chief Cook to go out and arrest Witherill. They left Denver on Wednesday morning, October 12, in search of their man. When they reached the point at which they supposed they would find Witherill, they found only a report that he was not to be found. The officers were not long in discovering that not only Witherill, but that Wight also had fled, and that they had carried off several valuable horses belonging to persons residing in the vicinity.

Finding both Witherill and Wight gone, the officers determined to devote a little time to ascertaining, if possible, the extent of the crime committed by the fugitives, and, acting under their chief's instructions to search for confirmation of his suspicion of the murder of Wall, they began their investigations. Going up Dry creek towards the missing man's cabin, they were not long in making the dread discovery which proved a complete confirmation of the worst theories. As they walked along the dry bed of the creek, their attention was attracted to a bunch of wolves standing around a pile of stones on the hillside, not far from the gulch. They seemed to be pawing at the stubborn rocks and sniffing the air as if in search of something to eat, evidently satisfied that the object of their search was not far away.

The men determined to investigate that spot. The animals were frightened away by a pistol shot fired into their midst, and the officers walked up to the place which they had just quitted.

Lying on the bare stones and protruding from an opening was the fleshless arm of a human being, showing traces of the teeth of the wolves, shreds of clothing being scattered about the place. The stones being speedily removed, the rapidly decaying body of the murdered man was brought to light. It was covered with bruises and blood, but was still recognizable. Here was the horrible suspicion confirmed. There was no longer any doubt that Wall had been murdered by Witherill, and the flight of Wight made his complicity more than probable.

The body being properly disposed of, the officers set themselves to work to find whatever clue they could to the course the murderers had taken in their flight. It was ascertained that Witherill had some friends at Colorado City, in El Paso county, the old state caput ah and it was believed that the two men would go in that direction. The

140

officers sent information to this effect to Chief Cook, and started in that direction in search of the men.

But Chief Cook had learned more of the movements of the fugitives, even while remaining at home, than his officers who were on the ground knew. He had ascertained, in that mysterious way which has ever made his name a terror to evil-doers, that the men had turned their faces towards the rising sun and were making their way across the plains towards "the states." Even while his officers were still out, he had laid plans to entrap the murderers and to secure their arrest by sending dispatches to all points on the plains where there was any chance of their stopping. Among other places to which he sent these descriptions was Sidney, Neb., and he had the satisfaction a very few days afterwards of receiving from Deputy Sheriff H. H. Tigart, of that place, a telegram, saying. "We've got your man Witherill. What shall we do with him? Wight gone on to North Platte." In reply, Cook instructed the officer to hold Witherill, and he and Smith, who had returned by this time, were off on the next morning's train for Sidney. This was on the Friday succeeding the flight of the two. Saturday night carried them to Sidney, where they learned the facts of the capture.

If all the facts in the flight of these two hardened men from the pursuit of justice could be known they would make as thrilling a story as ever had its foundation on our barren prairies. Compelled to steal horses, guns and provisions, with three hundred miles of what was then a desert lying before them, no friendly shelter offering, with the probability of encountering savage tribes of Indians at any time; with the knowledge that when they should seek shelter in the habitable part of the world towards which they were making their way, they would do so at the risk of their lives—with these thoughts confronting them as to the hardships before them and the officers following their trail from behind, they were certainly between two fires. Let us hope, too, for the sake of humanity that there still lingered in their minds some degree of remorse for the foul deed they had committed—that occasionally, when left to themselves on the boundless plains, with naught between them and the heavens, there occasionally flitted through their minds some degree of bitterness of feeling, some questioning of conscience as to the bloody and unprovoked deed they had committed.

Their flight seems to have been an alternation of mad rides and of skulking hides. We find, them, according to their own accounts, putting in the day lying quiet or seeking their way over the roadless plains where they were certain to encounter no one and during the night riding madly forward towards the eastern horizon, where was the only ray of hope, small as it was, that shone for them.

The fifth day out they ran into a large herd of buffalo, while riding over the prairie. They decided to relieve the tedium that surrounded their almost blank existence by having a little sport with the bison and at the same time capture some fresh meat. They shot into the herd, taking aim at a particularly large old bull, and wounding him so badly that when the others of his herd ran off he was unable to keep pace with them and was left behind. Wight and Witherill put spurs to their horses, rushing across the open plain with the speed of the wind and firing at the wounded and faltering animal as they went, very much, indeed, as they had pursued poor Wall when they sought to take his life as they now sought to take that of the crippled bison who ran before them. He at first seemed destined to evade them as their human victim had done, but, like Wall, had at last faltered and so slowed up as to permit himself to be overtaken,

On their impetuosity, they had rushed upon the animal until they could almost touch him with the muzzles of their fire arms. Wight had reigned his horse up by the side of the animal, which had come to bay, and was preparing to shoot, when Witherill came up behind and landed a bullet from his weapon in the back of the bull. The animal roared with pain, and snorting and shooting fire out of his eyes, made a desperate plunge at the horse and rider by his side. Wight pulled up his horse hastily, but not soon enough to avoid the blow. The bison's horn struck him on the shin and short and dull-pointed as it was, cut its way to the bone, ripping open the flesh of the calf of the leg all the way to the knee, and tearing the sinews out, making a very ugly and painful wound. The blood spurted out so as to almost blind the brute, which did not, however, cease its attack. Wight managed to spur up his horse, the animal having been protected from the bull's horn by its rider's leg, and he and his "brave" partner, although they had had courage enough to shoot down a defenseless man, found themselves unable to stand before this specimen of brutal anger and rode off as rapidly as they could, leaving the field to the wounded buffalo.

The entire herd had stopped on a distant hill, and many of them stood looking back as if they enjoyed the spectacle of the fight, which must have been at least equal to the scene of a Spanish bull fight. But the men were too much put out to further enjoy the sport, and, binding up Wight's leg as best they could, they found their way as speedily as possible to a ranchman's home on the Platte. They represented themselves as hunters, and asked to be allowed to remain until Wight should recover from his wound. Here they remained for two days, but gangrene setting in in the wound, they decided to take the chances and seek a point at which medicines and medical aid could be pro cured. Hence they set off for the settlements along the Union Pacific railroad, coming first to Julesburg, where Witherill stopped with the horses, and where he put Wight on a train and sent him to North Platte, still further down the road, it being Witherill's intention the next morning to follow with the property.

But Chief Cook's messages had gotten in ahead of the men, and Deputy Tigart, of Sidney, Neb., having received a description of Witherill, proceeded on the very evening after his arrival to Julesburg, a few miles distant from his home in Sidney, to arrest the fugitive. The officers waited for night to come on and went after him when he was supposed to be asleep. They found him in a barn, with his arms lying about him. He was at first disposed to resist capture, but discovering that he was well surrounded, he surrendered. The prisoner at first denied that his name was Witherill, and said that he was one William Jackson, but ultimately confessed, and then told of the whereabouts of Wight, who, he declared, was as much to blame as was he (Witherill).

Gen. Cook and Mr. Smith, when they arrived at Sidney, found Witherill safe in hand, and as he had been captured in Colorado territory there was no trouble about him. Wight was known to be in

North Platte, Neb., and it was feared that he could not be gotten away without a requisition; hence Gen. Cook placed a hundred dollar bill in Tigart's hands and told him to go after Wight. That officer boarded the next west-bound train, and the following morning brought him into Sidney with the wounded man, who had been taken without much trouble.

RECITAL OF COLD-BLOODED

Up to this time Wight's connection with the affair had been only a matter of surmise, but Witherill talked freely. According to Witherill's story told at this time, Wight had been the guilty party, and Witherill himself had been as pure and guiltless as if he had never seen Wall. He said on the day of the murder he left Melvin's, where he had been at work, saddled his horse, and went over to Wall's camp. Wall had a small tent or cabin built down in the gulch and concealed from view by willows grown thick on each side of it. When he got up to the tent door he found Wall and Wight quarreling. Wall accused Wight of having taken his pocketbook that day, while he was away from home. After further hot words, Wight came out, and taking hold of Witherill's Henry rifle, asked him if it was loaded. Witherill told him it had a shell in the barrel, at the same time getting off his horse and hitching. Wight sprung the lever, threw the shell out, and loaded the gun. Wall came out and sat down on a rock close to the tent door. Wight set down Witherill's gun and picked up Wall's, and quickly raising it fired at Wall, the ball taking effect in the neck. The wounded man dropped, and presently raising again, said: "Wight, you've shot me." Wight then dropped the gun, and taking up Witherill's rifle, shot Wall again and again in the head and body until he was dead. All this while Witherill stood dumbfounded. He didn't know what to do. He went to untie his horse to leave, when Wight presented the gun at him and told him not to leave or he would put a hole through him. Wight then went into Wall's pockets, took out his watch and handed it to Witherill, also a draft. The latter he isn't certain whether he took from Wall's or his own pocket. Witherill did not see Wall's pocketbook at all. After this the two men arranged to sell the sheep and divide the spoils. Wight also proceeded to write out a bill of sale of the sheep, from Wall to Witherill. Before they left, Witherill gave Wight $25 in money, and the latter said he would dispose of the body and clean up the traces around. All this time Wight was as cool and possessed as if it was an every-day job with him. Witherill then rode away and never saw the body again.

Wight refused to talk, simply saying that if there had been any murder committed, Witherill was the guilty man.

The two men were securely ironed and brought to Denver, where they were placed in jail. Two months afterwards they were tried at Evans before Judge E. T. Wells, having obtained a change of venue from Frankstown, then the county seat of Douglas county. Owing to technical defects in the law, both escaped the death at the gallows which they so much deserved. Indeed, as Wight's complicity was not established by any evidence except the testimony of Witherill, he was allowed to go on a bond of $2,000, on the charge of horse stealing, notwithstanding all were satisfied that he had been as guilty of murder as Witherill, if indeed he had not been the instigator of the whole plot, but he had been shrewd enough to make a tool of his chum and to remain in the background himself. Witherill was sentenced to a life term in the penitentiary. After the trial he made a full confession to Gen. Cook, which, while it is at fault in some details, is doubtless correct in the main, and so interesting throughout that it is here given in detail, as follows:

"Sometime during the week previous to the murder, 17th of September last, E. E. Wight came over to where I was, and intimated this murder, and it was arranged between us that I should come over to his house on Sunday, the 17th of September. I went. He was to watch for me and meet me somewhere on the road—if he could see me—near the sheep herder's grounds. I met him near the sheep herder's tent. The sheep herder wasn't at his tent; he was with his sheep back on the bluffs. We went out there and found him. Wight was on foot and I was on horseback. We found him soon after we got on the bluff or table land. I then gave my gun to Wight to shoot him. When we came up we passed the time of day and held a short conversation about various things—nothing pertaining to this. As the sheep herder turned to go away, Wight spoke to him, and Wall turned his head toward us and then Wight fired at him. The man Wall fell instantly; then he got up and ran down into the gulch; Wight followed him and fired at him several times; I judge that he hit him though I couldn't say. He stumbled and fell several times while going down the hill. He had on his hat as he was running

146

downhill towards the gulch; the next time I saw him he didn't have on his hat. I didn't see the hat anymore until I saw it in court at Evans. I followed after Wight—or near to him—down the hill. Wight and I followed along on the bank of the gulch; Wight fired at him whenever opportunity offered. We couldn't see him all the time, as Wall was running in the bed of the gulch. Wall soon got faint and sat down, from loss of blood; when I saw him sit down I got off my horse and hitched him; Wight and I then went down info the bed of the gulch where Wall was sitting. Wall said as we approached, 'What have I done?' We made no reply. Wight then struck him with the barrel of the gun on the left side of the head, I should judge, perhaps, above the ear. One side of his face and his bosom were covered with blood. He fell, and I think the blow from the gun killed him; he died within two or three minutes after being struck. We examined his pockets and took out his pocketbook and watch. The pocketbook contained about twelve dollars in money and a certificate of deposit for three hundred dollars at Warren Hussey's bank, in Denver.

"Then we left the body lay where it had fallen and covered it up with rocks first and dirt afterward. We then returned to the sheep herder's tent, and as we went we arranged between us that I should take his sheep and herd them; I was to sell them as soon as possible, and divide the money between us. In order to get a bill of sale for them, he agreed to meet me in Denver the next day and have the bill of sale made out for me. While at the tent we hid his diary, with such papers as it contained, and also his gun, near the tent We separated there, then, and I returned to Melvin's and he started towards McCool's ranch. I think we reached the tent, previous to the murder, about 3 o'clock p in., and we finally separated a little after 4 o'clock, I should say, though we had no time, as the watch taken from Wall's pocket had run down. The next morning I came to Denver; I looked around for Wight, but couldn't find him. Then I went to an office in Feuerstein's building, adjoining the Land office, and asked the lawyer to make me out a bill of sale he made it out according to my directions. I signed Walks name to it. I took the bill of sale and went directly home to Melvin's. I went the next day over to Wall's camp, and got the sheep together, and assumed responsibility of their charge. A few days afterwards I came to Denver and advertised the sheep for sale in the Rocky Mountain News. I started back home again that night. I stayed at LeFevre's ranch that night. I met Wight there; that was the first time I had seen him since we separated on the day of the murder. Wight and I had some conversations about my having advertised the sheep. A week or more elapsed, during which time I was herding the sheep and Wight was building a house for LeFevre. The next time we met was on Sunday, at the camp where I was stopping.

"During this time Doolittle's sheep were roaming on Big Dry. On the Sunday when we met Wight spoke to me about Doolittle's sheep. I went early next morning and drove them to where our own were. I stayed with the sheep that day and kept them together. The next day I made an excuse to go down to LeFevre's camp. I told Wight that I had them together, and about how many I judged there were. I told him I thought there were about six hundred of Doolittle's. Wight wanted that I should go and get another bill of sale made out; I did not do it, He then took from me the other bill of sale, and between that and our next meeting he changed and altered it so as to cover six hundred and forty head, instead of three hundred and forty, as It was originally made out I didn't like it; it was made out badly; it would be easily detected, and I spoke 10 him about it. We then arranged it between us that I should come to town and get two made out separate, one for three hundred and forty head, and another for four hundred. I went to Mr. Witter's office in Denver and had both bills made out. Before I started home again I heard that six hundred and fifty head of sheep were missing on Cherry creek. I left word with Loustellot, in Denver, that if any sheep were missing there were some stray ones at the head of Big Dry. I also told Mr. Bowers that there were some stray sheep up where I was stopping. I went back home then to McCool's ranch. Two days afterwards Doolittle, having heard that there were stray sheep there, came out there from Denver. I claimed to him to have seven hundred and forty head of sheep. We corralled them and counted them. They numbered nine hundred and eighty-eight head, and he claimed all over the seven hundred and forty head. Because I told of there being stray sheep up there, Wight got mad. He sometime afterward told me that he came to Denver and told Doolittle that all of his sheep were there.

"The next day after Doolittle had been so informed. Hopkins came out and arrested me, charged with stealing sheep. Hopkins brought me into town, and on the next day Hopkins, Doolittle and I went out to the Twelve-mile house, to where the sheep had been driven, and I delivered to him the sheep he claimed. I settled with Doolittle and was discharged. I explained to Doolittle that the sheep claimed by him I had bought from Wall, and that I had a bill of sale, and the officer discharged me because he thought I had not stolen the stock. I was discharged in Denver, and went right back to McCool's ranch. When I got there Wight was there, and he told me of having had some conversation with Sheriff Cook, and that Cook suspected that I had murdered Wall, and he was about to arrest me. Wight thought we had better leave the country. It was arranged that we were to leave as soon as possible. We went the next day to Mr. Melvin's, where I was to receive some cows I had traded sheep for. We didn't get the cows that day, and stayed there that night. Next morning we went back to McCool's ranch. The day after, Wight came to town with LeFevre's hired man, and brought his box of clothing with him. I came to Denver via Twelve-mile house, having sent my trunk to town. Wight and I took our box and trunk to the Denver Pacific depot and shipped them to Nebraska City. I shipped my trunk in the name of William Jackson, he shipped in the name of E. E. Fox. After shipping our goods Wight traded a shotgun which he had stolen from Bates, on the rancho, for a Winchester rifle, and we bought some ammunition-arid a field-glass. I saw Marshal Hopkins coming down the street towards me, and I started down the street away from him, taking a roundabout route to Bailey's corral, where my horse was.

I then rode over to Rood's gun-shop and got my gun, which had been left for repairs. I then went back to McCool's rancho. I had been there about an hour when Wight came. He brought a saddle with him, which he said he had stolen from William Wulff. We had intended to have left the country that night, but could not find the horses we intended to steal, and also expected Webster over to buy some cows which I had bargained to him. Next morning Mr. Webster came. I let him have eight cows to sell on commission. They were branded W back of the left shoulder. He advanced me $21 on the cows. The remainder he was to send me when I should furnish him my address and the cows had been sold to the best advantage, less his commission. He also cashed an order of his given me by Freeman. I also gave Webster an order for $72 and some cents, which he was to send when collected, with the money received for the cows. Webster informed me that I was accused of murder, and that I had better look out for myself, as Sheriff Cook had written to the sheriff of Douglas county that he had better arrest me. He described the sheriff of Douglas county to me before we parted. "Wight and I then left and went down on Plum creek. We got back to McCool's rancho about dark. We got what things we wanted to take with us, and McCool's mare. Wight took a horse from William Underwood, and I told him he ought to be ashamed to steal from a one-armed man. He then turned the horse loose, and we started for Denver, passing through about midnight, on our way to Johnson's island [Henderson's island], were we expected to get two more horses from McCook We stopped about six miles from town and rested our horses. At about daylight we again started, arriving at Johnson's island about 9 o'clock a m., where we took breakfast. We stayed there in the brush until about the middle of the afternoon, then left our horses and started back on foot towards McCool's rancho. When we got there we could not find the horses we were in search of. Wight thought we were seen, and about dark we started back, and I stole the black mare. We then started down the Platte and arrived at Evans soon after daylight. We left there, traveling down the Platte, and traded off McCool's mare at a ranch six miles below old Fort Morgan. A few days after, Wight got hurt while chasing a buffalo. We then had to lay over three days at Moore's ranch. We left there and went to Julesburg. I bought Wight a ticket and gave him 5, and sent him to North Platte City, and I stayed in Julesburg that night, and was arrested and brought to Sidney the next day, where I was kept until Sheriffs Cook and Smith came for me."

Wight remained in jail in Denver several months after his partner in crime had been sent to Cañon City, awaiting his trial. While in the Arapahoe jail he made a desperate effort to escape, taking a prominent part in the Griswold emeute, the story of which affair will be found succeeding this chapter. His trial took place at Golden, the prisoner having obtained a change of venue, and resulted in a sentence of seven years at hard labor in the penitentiary. He is still at Cañon City. He might now be a free man, had not his propensity to escape from prison prolonged his term of incarceration. After remaining for two years in the state penitentiary he contrived to get away, and, evading all pursuit, was not overtaken for four years, when he was spotted and captured away down in Maine. He was returned to Colorado and, as stated above, is now serving out the sentence which might have been completed ere this but for his desire to escape.

Even to the present time his old tendency to intrigue has not failed to assert itself. Since his imprisonment began he-has made numerous efforts to secure his release and that of Witherill as well. It has been but a short while since Gen. Cook received the following letter, which he is convinced was written by Wight:

Penitentiary, Cañon City,

December 21, 1881

Hon, David Cook, Denver, Colorado:

Dear General—My attention was lately attracted to an article in a Denver paper, wherein you expressed a knowledge of the fact that George Witherill, who is here serving a life sentence, used to drive a stage in Utah. Three years ago the writer became somewhat acquainted with a man in Kansas City, who related to him the following story, in which the said George Witherill plays a most prominent part, and every word of which I have good and sufficient reasons for believing as true. In the winter of the year 1870 this man, by name Edward Neal, was stock tender for the stage company at Corrinne, Utah. One day a man came to the stable and took an extra team and a Concord wagon for the purpose of going up to meet the coach, which he did some miles above Brigham City. At that moment he was joined by another man, a passenger on the coach, and they two immediately arrested three other men, who were also passengers, taking them from the coach and

151

calling for their baggage. The prisoners did not claim it, and the coach drove on around by Brigham City for the purpose of leaving the mail there, allowing the two detectives (for such the two parties first referred to claimed to be) with their prisoners to reach Corrinne before the coach. The captives were then taken to a lonely cabin and tortured, with the result that they confessed to being road agents on their way to the states, with the proceeds of more than a dozen stage robberies; further, that all the money was on the coach. Meantime the coach, arriving at Corrinne, drove to the express office and unloaded everything except a rough box, an old trunk and a gunny sack, all of which the driver of the coach knew belonged to the three men who had been taken from the coach beyond Brigham City. He then drove to the stable, and while Neal was unhitching the coach team he hitched up the team that the detectives had used, loaded the above articles into the Concord wagon, took a shovel and left the stable, driving out over the old pontoon bridge. This occurred at about 6 p m. The driver did not return to the stable until about 9 o'clock, having been absent about three hours. Just as he was leaving the stable, however, to go home, one of the detectives came and wanted the baggage belonging to the three men who had been taken from the coach that day, saying that there was more than one hundred thousand in money in the outfit, besides considerable jewelry, and that he would "whack up" with the driver if he would get it. This the driver refused to do, having safely secured and hid the plunder. Snow falling that night obliterated all traces of the wagon track, and the detectives never found the stuff. Being afraid of these men the driver left Corrinne immediately, believing that the so-called detectives were only sharpers, and would do him bodily harm if he did not divulge the hiding place of the treasure. His opinion of the detectives was probably correct, as they also left Corrinne a day or two afterwards, having made no report at all to the stage company. The driver came to Colorado, and the next Neal heard of him was that he was arrested for murder, tried, found guilty and sentenced to the Cañon City penitentiary for life. The driver's name was Witherill, and he is the only man living who knows where that money is. Witherill probably went on the ranch in Colorado for the purpose of keeping out of sight. I feel quite confident that this George Witherill here is the man. He, of course, keeps all this a profound secret; but you, general, can surely persuade him to tell you where the stuff is. It cannot be buried more than five miles from Corrinne, as Neal said that the horses were cool when he brought them back to the barn. Now, can't you promise to help him to get out of here, or something of the sort, and persuade him to tell us where to find the treasure? After he has given the necessary information, let him go to the devil, for all I care. Please let none of the officers here know anything about all this, as they would only make a botch of it, I am sure. Whatever you may want to say to me in regard to the matter, publish it as a "personal" in the Denver *Tribune*, addressed to "No. 5720, C. C." That paper is accessible to me here, and I shall be sure to see what you say. This goes from here on the quiet, so no one will see it but yourself. I have the honor to be, yours most respectfully, NO. 5720, C. C.

It is almost unnecessary to state that Gen. Cook paid no attention whatever to this curious epistle. He did not believe the story told, and even if he had it would not have influenced him to exert himself in behalf of the two scoundrels who murdered as peaceful a citizen as was Mr. Wall, ne believed that both Wight and Witherill were where they belonged, and considered that he did his duty in assisting in putting them there. Subsequent events show that they should have been left there for life, as the next chapter wall show.

WITHERILL RECOMMENCES HIS CAREER OF CRIME

Among the collection of laws, good, bad and indifferent, passed by the Colorado legislature of 1887, was one which was the indirect cause of the death of at least two innocent men. It was a law that provided that a life sentence in the penitentiary should be construed to mean only sixteen years, i e., that a criminal who had been sentenced for life should be released after having served sixteen years. There were many ugly rumors out in regard to the intents and objects of the bill, but it finally passed by a small majority. It released from Cañon George R. Witherill, who was set free April 8, 1887, and the crimes he had committed before the next legislature assembled caused that body to repeal the law with great celerity.

When the murderer of the inoffensive sheep herder was released from the prison, he at once came to Denver. While in the penitentiary he had made threats that he would kill Gen. Cook if he ever got out, because, as he said, Cook had on two or three occasions prevented him from securing a pardon. When Gen. Cook heard that Witherill had come back to Denver, he thought chat he had come back to carry out his threat, and at once went in search of him. When Witherill heard that Cook was after him, he at once secured the services of a friend who had been a guard at the penitentiary, and started out to find Gen. Cook to square the matter and assure him that he had no intention of carrying out his threats. He learned that Cook was in the Brunswick hotel, and, following his friend in there, threw up his hands the instant he entered the door, begging the general not to shoot him. Cook told him that, knowing his sneaking and desperate character, and the threats he had made, he would be fully justifiable in shooting him down like a dog, but that it he was sincere in his protestations that he wanted to live an honest life, he would let him go, but added that he had better leave Denver to make his attempt.

Acting upon this advice, Witherill left Denver for the mountains, and was not heard of for about a year and a half, and then as the perpetrator of another cold-blooded and atrocious murder, or rather two murders. As previously related, Witherill had gone into the mines, first working at Durango and afterward at Ironton. While at Ironton he formed the acquaintance of a Swede by the name of Marinus Jansen, who owned a splendid four-horse team and a big ore wagon and outfit for hauling ore from the mines. Witherill decided that Jansen would make an easy victim, and so commenced negotiations with him to go to Silverton to haul ore from a mine in which Witherill claimed to have an interest. That was the last ever seen or heard of poor Jansen, and his body lies rotting in some abandoned prospect hole in a lonely mountain side. They had started out early in September, and toward the latter part of the month Witherill drove the outfit into Pueblo, where he disposed of it for $400.

Having now plenty of money to loaf around and live well for a time without work, one would naturally suppose that Witherill would refrain from crime for a time at least, but he appears to have been a maniac on the subject of murder, who could not resist the temptation to kill no more than a hungry man can resist the temptation to eat when tempting viands are set before him. It would have been a good thing for the community had Gen. Cook shot him in Denver before he had time to make his lying explanations. He lost no time in seeking another victim; as before, hunting up a laboring man with some good teams. He hired Chas. R. McCain, and with him left Pueblo at 9 o'clock on the morning of October 25, to go to a point eleven miles west of Cañon City to haul ore. They had two teams, both of which belonged to McCain, who resided in Pueblo. Witherill had represented to McCain that he was the foreman of a heavy shipping mine, and would give the Pueblo man lucrative employment for himself and teams to haul the ore from the mine to the railroad track.

The men proceeded with the teams until night caught them, at Beaver creek crossing, eighteen miles east of Cañon City, and they camped. The point where they camped was not over a quarter of a mile from the house of Mr. Palmer, one of the commissioners of Fremont county. Both evidently lay down in the wagons, McCain never to awaken in this world, and Witherill to keep diabolic watch until his victim was fast asleep. Then he crept, panther-like, to where the unconscious man lay, and sent a rifle bullet crashing through his brain. Fearing, perhaps, that the wound was not of a deadly nature, or because, possibly, the victim in his dying struggles would alarm someone, the fiend grasped an axe and pounded McCain's head into a mass of broken bone and oozing brain. The closeness of the gun when the shot was fired was such that the bullet passed entirely through McCain's head and the bottom of the wagon, to still retain enough momentum to flatten itself on a stone. When found, it had bits of bone and the blanket, which McCain had evidently had his head partially covered with, still attached to it.

The fiend then proceeded with devilish cunning to conceal the body of his victim and indications of his crime. The body he carried or dragged into a neighboring ravine and deposited in a ditch he then covered it with rocks and dirt and effectually, as he thought, hid from the eyes of men the lifeless remains. To destroy the blood spots and other indications of the deed, he covered them with hay and burned it. The bottom of the wagon he rubbed with stones and with hay to efface the dreadful evidences of his crime.

As coolly as if he were upon an ordinary business mission, Witherill took McCain's money and drove both teams on Saturday morning into Cañon City. He camped just east of the city and then, going boldly into the business part of the town, he wrote a letter addressed to McCain's wife, in which he [im]personated her husband. He informed her that he had purchased a ranch at Grand Junction, Colo., and had sold his teams. He asked her to sell all her household effects and join him as soon as possible at the location of their new home.

Familiar with her husband's writing, Mrs. McCain, upon the receipt of the letter, at once knew that it was not indicted by him. But that might not have so much alarmed her as the quick intuition of her heart which told her something was dreadfully wrong and strange in this sudden change of plans and unexpected determination to move to the western part of the state-and make a new home. She placed the matter before an officer, and at once the conclusion was reached that the life-sentenced murderer of

Sheepman Wall had added another to his series of blood-stained deeds.

The alarm was at once sent out and inquiries made. It was; learned that Witherill had been at Cañon City on Saturday morning. Shortly after the search began a man was found who knew him and had seen him on the road to Denver with two teams. On Wednesday afternoon, October 31, Deputy Sheriff Force, of Denver, received a telegram, informing him of the mysterious, disappearance of McCain and of the anxiety to apprehend Witherill. Late the same night the deputy found Witherill at Goulding's stables. He was surly in response to questions and said that his name was Simon Cotter. To this Mr. Force responded: "That may be your name now, but it wasn't Simon Cotter or Simon Says-Thumbs-Up when I saw you in the pen at Cañon." This knocked the bluff out of the ex-convict and he submitted to arrest in silence. He refused to say anything about the whereabouts of his associate and went to jail. Upon being searched, the sum of $250 was found upon him.

Despite his effort to erase the evidences of the ghastly deed; there were found blood stains in the bottom of the wagon. An axe was also found, which had blood stains on the handle. The presence of two pocketbooks, a double set of blankets and other belongings of two men among his effects were also peculiarly suspicious circumstances. Yet with stolid effrontery he maintained that he knew nothing about Chas. McCain, and that he had left him in Cañon alive and well. In interviews with representatives of the press he claimed, in substance, that McCain had business in Cañon and had announced to him his determination to come to Denver and hence to go East. On that account he had obeyed McCain's request and had driven both the teams to this city, and expected him along The following morning, however, when informed that the body of McCain had been found, he refused to say anything more.

Sheriff Griffith arrived in Denver on the morning of November 2, and in the afternoon started with his prisoner toward Cañon City. The reports of the determination to lynch the prisoner when he arrived in Cañon City were, however, the cause of deterring the sheriff from going farther than Pueblo. Witherill was incarcerated there a few days, and then again quietly returned to the Arapahoe county jail. It was only when there was no help for it, and when it became impracticable to longer keep him there, that Witherill was at length taken to cañon. The greatest precautions were taken to convey him there quietly. He was placed in a Rio Grande baggage car, securely manacled, and taken from the train live miles from Cañon City. From that point he was taken to the city in a close carriage and locked in a steel cell. It was believed that so secretly had the transfer been made that no information would leak out. In this the officers were mistaken, for it soon became apparent that everyone in Cañon knew that at last the fiend whom they had determined to rid the world of was within their reach

It was the 3d of December when Witherill was taken to Cañon and the next morning news was received in Denver that he had been lynched to a telephone pole on Main street, within a stone's throw of the penitentiary where he had spent fifteen years of his life.

The night of the tragedy was cold, dark and still. It was not until 6 o'clock that the information of Witherill's arrival was obtained, and the fact was not assured until about midnight. All night the streets were alive with men, and the prospect of a lynching was the only subject of discussion. The terrible details of the McCain murder were discussed, and the spectacle of the grief-stricken wife weeping over her husband's mangled remains was called to mind as demanding sure and speedy vengeance. Little knots of men assembled on street corners and in doorways recounting the infallible evidences of Witherill's guilt, each man sitting in judgment upon the ex-convict. All this time the real organized lynchers were secretly and silently at work. Masks were provided for the entire party and every preparation made for the attack. Two of their party knocked at the back door of the jail, and when Sheriff Griffith opened the door sprang upon him and throttled him without making a sound.

After the sheriff had been put out of the way, the crowd of masked lynchers filed into the jail and secured the keys to the cells from the sheriff's son.

The dim light burning in the jail revealed Witherill in his cell, standing upon the defensive. He was ordered to come out, and cried out:

"Come in and take me out."

He had broken his wooden bedstead to pieces to secure a weapon, and when some of the party stepped forward to take him at his word he used the club with the desperate energy of a doomed man. There is no telling how long Witherill might have held his own against superior numbers had not one of the attacking party drawn a revolver and shot the murderer in the shoulder, knocking him down. He was then quickly overpowered and led out of the cage, with a noose around his neck and his hands secured behind his back.

Surrounded by a solemn but earnest crowd, Witherill was marched down to Main street to a telephone pole, about one hundred yards from the jail. The condemned man was led to this pole and the rope throw n over the cross-bar by a practiced hand, and the end of the rope was grasped by fifty strong and willing hands. The triple murderer was given a minute to confess. This he refused to do, and he was drawn up five or six feet from the ground. After some seconds he was lowered until his feet touched the ground, and he was asked to confess the murders of Wall, Jansen and McCain, and upon his stubborn refusal to comply he was drawn up until his feet cleared the ground by some ten or twelve feet and the rope tied.

Witherill's helpless body, dangling against the pole in the agony of death by suffocation, was watched by the assembled crowd without a single sign of pity or remorse. When satisfied that life was extinct the crowd quietly dispersed to conceal every evidence of the judgment of Judge Lynch, except the ghastly figure at the end of the rope.

As soon as daylight came, the fact that the anticipated lynching had been successfully accomplished was noised through the town, and hundreds of men, women and children went to the scene to view the terrible but significant sight. Old women and young girls stood in the bright sunlight, and gazed at the murderer's body swaying slightly in the morning breeze, without a shudder, and if their looks could be relied upon they, too, had given Witherill a mental trial and found him guilty. In all the crowd that viewed the remains of the dead murderer, there were none who could forget the murders of Wall, and of Jansen, and of McCain, long enough to pity the wretch who had in a measure paid the penalty of his many crimes.

A SLICK SCOUNDREL

One morning in May, 1885, the people of Colorado generally, and of Denver in particular, were very greatly surprised to read the announcement in the papers among the Washington dispatches, that "Hon." C. P. Judd had been appointed by President Cleveland agent and statistician for the government labor bureau for Colorado and the adjacent territories.

The name of "Hon." C. P. Judd in connection with democracy in Colorado was totally unknown, and the fact that it was the first appointment made in the state by the new administration, gave it an added importance. Prominent democratic politicians were besieged with inquiries as to the identity of this new democratic star that had so lately burst into such meteoric brilliance; their only reply was: "Don't know; never heard of him before." While the politicians were still speculating, a reporter for the Denver Times happened to remember that Gen. D. J. Cook, of the Rocky Mountain Detective Association knew almost everybody of any importance who had ever lived in Colorado for any length of time, and to the general he went with his inquiry. He was rewarded with what is termed in newspaper parlance, "a bully good story."

Gen. Cook had known Judd for years. In fact, his acquaintance with the newly made labor agent was so familiar that he had at one time taken a trip to Cañon City with the gentleman, at which time Mr. Judd had taken up his residence there for a period of one year for having appropriated a valuable horse and buggy belonging to a man named Veasey, living in Denver.

This was only one of a long list of crimes of which he was guilty. He was a born thief, with a predisposition to horse-flesh, and had done time in more than one penal institution for his thieving proclivities. His first exploit in this line, so far as known, consisted in stealing a wagon load of groceries-and provisions from a freighter, who was hauling supplies from Topeka, Kan., to Fort Riley, at an early day before railroads were built through that section. The freighter's horses, which had been turned loose to graze at night, had strayed away, and while he was away hunting them, along came Judd, who lived near. There was no one about and he deemed it too good a chance to lose. Securing a team of his own he hitched to the wagon and drove off. The owner soon returned with his horses, and finding the wagon gone, set out to tracking the thief, whom he overtook after following him fourteen miles. Judd was convicted and sentenced to the state penitentiary at Leavenworth for three years.

After serving his term out, he decided that the boundless West afforded better opportunities for the exercise of his peculiar talents, and accordingly he came to Colorado early in the 70's.

When he came to Denver he showed the same fondness for other people's property. In 1871 he stole a horse and buckboard belonging to A. H. Jones, the liquor man, and in 1872 he stole a bicycle or velocipede from a man whose place of business was on Fifteenth street, next door to where Celia's restaurant was located. On both of these charges he was cleared by Gen. Sam Browne, who proved to the court that Judd was a kleptomaniac.

In 1872 he was arrested and sent to the county jail for one year (there being no state penitentiary at that time) for stealing a gold watch from a lady in West Denver, at what is known as the Williams house. He served this sentence and was discharged on February 28, 1871. In 1875 he was arrested, tried, convicted and sentenced to the state penitentiary for one year for stealing a horse and buggy and several hundred laths from a man named Veasey, as related above. The last crime he committed before breaking into politics so suddenly and so successfully, was the theft of a horse and buggy, the property of William Dingle, a Denver druggist, on the 14th of October, 1883, while the rig was standing in front of the store of the owner, in the Tabor block. He was seen by several parties to cross Cherry Creek bridge at Larimer street and drive out in the country. The matter was reported to the police, and Detective Mart Watrous was put to work on the case. He went to Judd's house and charged him with the crime. After denying it for a time, Judd finally confessed and went with Watrous, gathered up the property and turned it over to the detective.

The horse had been turned loose and wandered home. The buggy was found in a piece of woods down the Platte. A valuable lap robe belonging to Mrs. Dingle was found buried with the harness and the whip was found in another place. Judd was taken before Justice Sopris.

While that official was busily engaged in making out the warrant, Judd slipped out of the court room and made his escape. After getting away from Denver, Judd went to Leadville, where he succeeded in identifying himself with some labor organization, soon after starting out on the road as an organizer. He traveled over the state considerably, and through his connection with this organization he was enabled to make the acquaintance of several prominent men, whose endorsements later secured for him the government position.

At the time he was appointed to his position, Gen. D. J. Cook stated, in a published interview, as related above, that he was the same man that had served several terms in prison for larceny.

At the time the interview was published, Hon. C. S. Thomas cut it out and sent it to the commissioner of the labor bureau at Washington. He shortly after received a letter from the commissioner, stating that there was evidently some mistake, that he had consulted with Mr. Judd regarding the matter, and that the latter had stated to him that there was another C. P. Judd—a criminal—in Colorado, and that this fact had frequently caused him much annoyance. Mr. Thomas showed this letter to Gen. Cook, and the latter told him to write again to the commissioner, asking for the appointee's photograph. This was done, and on the 22d of June the commissioner wrote in reply that Judd had started by a circuitous route for Colorado, and that he would, at some time during his trip, be at Leadville. It was, therefore, impossible for him to secure his photograph. The commissioner further expressed the hope that the Colorado officials would look him up, and see if he really was the criminal and fugitive from justice, or whether his story was true.

Gen. Cook immediately went to work on the case, and in a short time was on the track of his man. Soon after this Judd's wife came to Denver and stopped at the house of a relative in West Denver. The detectives began to watch her and her correspondence. In a few days she received a postal from Judd, dated Leadville, telling her to come to Alamosa and meet him there. On learning of the receipt of this postal by Mrs. Judd, Gen. Cook went before Judge Sopris and swore out a warrant for his arrest for stealing Dingle's horse and buggy. This he placed in the hands of Joe Smith, who happened to be in the city at the time, and the latter took the same train with Mrs. Judd for Alamosa.

When Judd came forward to meet his wife, Sheriff Smith stepped up and arrested him. He was not very much disconcerted, and immediately sent his wife to Silverton, where she had a sister living, and without any further proceedings announced his willingness to come to Denver. Upon his arrival in this city he was taken to Gen. Cook's office, where he made the following statement in writing:

"Denver, Colo., August 12, 1885.

"This is to bear witness that, whereas, the undersigned was appointed by Secretary L. Q. C. Lamar, a special agent of the bureau of labor on the 10th day of May, A. D. 1885, and was thereafter represented by certain members of the democratic party in the state of Colorado as the identical C. P. Judd who had served a term in the penitentiary at Leavenworth, Kan., in the county jail of Arapahoe county in the state of Colorado, and in the penitentiary at Cañon City in said state; and, whereas, in an interview with a reporter of the Denver Times with D. J. Cook, superintendent of the Rocky Mountain Detective Agency, Gen. Cook made the above charges and statements concerning the undersigned, which interview was published shortly after said appointment, and a copy thereof forwarded by C. S. Thomas to the interior department, at Washington; therefore, I hereby declare that the above statements and charges are correct, and that I am the identical C. P. Judd referred to in said interview and in said charges. "C. P. JUDD."

Of course after this Judd lost no time in resigning the position, and Mr. Dingle agreed to drop the prosecution if Judd would leave the state never to return. This he readily agreed to, and he seems to have faithfully kept his word.

Judd originally came from Illinois, where his family was well-known and respected. He was a large, good looking man, a fluent and persuasive talker, and a man whose opinions changed as rapidly as a kaleidoscope. Early in the campaign he published a card claiming to be the first man in the United States to suggest the name of Grover Cleveland for president. Subsequently he made several speeches for Blaine, presumably for a cash consideration. After he found that Cleveland had been successful, he at once became a good democrat once more, and at once set out to secure endorsements for the position which he was afterward lucky enough to secure. As a matter of course, he gave Denver a wide berth, but he was fortunate enough to secure the influence of several prominent democrats in other parts of the state, among whom were Dr. J. J. Crooke and Hon. George Goldthwaite, of Leadville, who had both written letters to the interior department endorsing Judd in the strongest terms, besides this, the Hon. Harley B. Morse, of Central City, had gone to the department in person to recommend the rascal, whose suave manners and glib tongue had deceived him thoroughly. After Judd's exposure and consequent downfall, he decided that the West was too swift for him, and he was last heard from in Iowa, where he was supposed to belong to a gang of counterfeiters.

At all events, Colorado was well rid of a scoundrel who would have brought disgrace upon her fair name, had it not been for Gen. Cook's wide acquaintance and perfect recollection of men and events, and his untiring efforts to bring criminals of whatever age or station to Justice.

A BOGUS DETECTIVE'S FATE

There are snide detectives just as there are shyster lawyers, quack doctors and dead-beat newspaper men. We have our share of the pretenders and dead beats, and they do us more harm than good. The worst case which has ever disgraced our annals here in Denver was that of one L. P. Griswold—a hard nut, too, he was. His machinations here resulted in his own tragic death, and in that of one other man, certainly, if not of a third; also developing several plots of intricate and diabolical design, and bringing many people into the affair before it was ended.

The series of occurrences with which Griswold was connected had their beginning in the summer of 1870, and did not terminate until in the winter of 1872, covering a period of eighteen months, owing to the delay of the law. Griswold had been a great deal about Cheyenne [Wyoming]. Cheyenne was a bad place in those days. It was enjoying its railroad boom. Times were lively, and murders, holdups and burglaries were frequent. There was a vigilance committee which did some good work. It was frequently considered necessary by this committee to pronounce sentence of death upon offenders in the community, and Griswold was for a long time employed to, execute the decrees of the court of Judge Lynch This was not wrong, but the committee made a mistake in the employment of Griswold as the executioner he was a bad man—such a man as would kill a fellow being for a few dollars. Whenever sentence of death was pronounced upon a victim he was turned over 10 Griswold, who would secure a gang and hang and rob him.

But to come to the story. Cheyenne finally quieted down and Griswold was without a calling. He came to Denver and to Gen. Cook, of the Rocky Mountain Detective Association, one day, wanting employment, professing to be a detective. Cook told him he could do nothing for him, but would give him a "pointer" on a case which he could have if he desired, not knowing his real character then.

Some weeks before, the Myers Fisher ranch on Clear creek had been burned—houses, stables, etc.—and Fisher had come to the conclusion that the fire had been caused by an incendiary, and he offered a reward of $400 for the capture and punishment of the perpetrator of the crime. Cook looked into the case, and he became convinced that the fire had been caused by accident, and would have nothing to do with it. This was the case which he gave Griswold, who was glad enough to get it. In the hope of receiving the reward offered, as it afterwards developed, Griswold then began to lay a plot which was simply hellish in design.

It so happened that Fisher, the owner of the ranch, had had some trouble with one James O'Neal, a man who lived some twelve miles away, near Littleton, and, although O'Neal was a quiet and law-abiding man. Griswold determined to fasten the crime of incendiarism upon him. He also discovered that there had been a fire on another ranch near that of Fisher's, owned by a man named Patrick. To this man and his sons he went with his story. Knowing that he could never convict O'Neal, he asked the Patricks if it could be proven—as he afterwards stated in his confession—that O'Neal had fired both places, they would consent to the capture and lynching of him. They were willing. He brought them what they considered sufficient proof of O'Neal's guilt, which Griswold had procured in his own peculiar way.

Griswold and George Patrick, son of the old man, then came to Denver and swore out a warrant before James S. Taylor, then a justice of the peace in Denver, under false names, for O'Neal's arrest, Griswold getting himself appointed a special officer. He accomplished this by stating to the justice that he had seen Cook, who was then sheriff, which was not true, and that Cook had stated that he was unable to go out to make the arrest. The constable he declared he could not find. He further represented that it was essential that O'Neal should be arrested that night, and at last succeeded in making it appear necessary that he and his friend should be sent upon the mission. Their statements proved to be false in every respect, as will appear, and were the first clue which the detectives had when it came to looking up the case.

Having procured their warrant, the two men drove out to O'Neal's ranch, where they arrived late in the afternoon of the same day.

They introduced themselves to the unsuspecting man as officers and told him their mission, but were, withal, so pleasant as not to create any suspicion that his arrest was merely a trap to secure the poor fellow for execution. He never dreamed what character of man he had to deal with in Griswold, and that hell-hound had coolly made up his mind to take his life, although he believed him not guilty, for a pitiful sum of money.

"All right, gentlemen," O'Neal replied. "I will go with you. I am willing to stand my trial, especially as I feel confident of my own innocence, and know that I can prove it. I have nothing to fear. But it is late; come in and take supper with me before starting."

This invitation, extended in all courtesy and hospitality, was accepted by the two men, who, although they may have been hungry, were more anxious to gain time than to appease their appetites.

Supper being over, dark was coming on, and the three men prepared for their ride, the terminus of which it was supposed would be for all in Denver. Griswold and Patrick had ridden out in a two-seated buggy, but they requested O'Neal to take a seat between them, and all three started off in quite a jovial mood. This joviality was soon increased, for the vehicle was loaded down with whiskey and cigars, and the three men were soon laughing and joking and drinking with each other like old-time friends.

Thus they journeyed on to the crossing of the Platte. The chances are that by this time poor O'Neal was filled with whiskey and capable of making but little resistance, against any attack upon him. Be that as it may, he was taken from the buggy at Browrite bridge, and when he was next seen his soul had deserted its flesh tenement and taken up its abode in another realm.

When found the next day the body was dangling from a girder of the bridge, with a card pinned on the back stating that the man had been lynched because he had burned Fisher's and Patrick's ranches and stolen cattle, and that he had made full confession of the fact. In conclusion, cattle thieves and evildoers generally were warned to beware of their ways, and notified that the vigilantes were ever on their track.

Gen. Cook was among the first to view the body. Griswold and Patrick were the murderers. So much may be stated here. They early sought to cover up their crime and, like many more enlightened criminals, made the newspapers useful in their work. Coming into Denver that night, they went to the offices of the public journals and told how they had been sent out as special officers to arrest O'Neal on the charges above related, giving the same false names which they had given Justice Taylor, and stating that they had proceeded as far as Brown's bridge with their prisoner when they were set upon by a band of disguised men, who compelled them to deliver over the prisoner at the muzzles of a hundred revolvers. They told how they had pleaded in vain for the life of the prisoner, and how that individual, after quivering and quaking and making a faint denial, had at last confessed the crime. Their prisoner being taken, they had, they said, been compelled to drive on, and were then ignorant of his fate, though they supposed he had been lynched.

The newspapers which told this story the next morning bore a revelation to Gen. Cook. He had kept no track of Griswold and the O'Neal case, supposing that when the supposed detective should find that the charges were unfounded he would drop it and cease his efforts. Furthermore, he was sheriff of the county, and thought he would have known, or at least thought he ought to have known, if any arrest of as much importance as that of O'Neal had been made. But he was totally in the dark. The names of the officers given in the papers were not even recognized, Griswold and Patrick having used their false names in the story.

Mr. Cook began to investigate. His work was soon well under way. He obtained his first clue from Justice Taylor, who related the circumstances of the two men swearing out warrants for O'Neal's arrest and stating that Cook had refused to go and make the arrests. From the justice's description of the two "special deputies," Cook inferred that the two men were Griswold and Patrick.

"A clue and a big one," he soon afterwards told one of his men. "Griswold is the murderer of O'Neal. He gave his wrong name to the

169

justice, and he lied about me. Here is where he began to cover up his tracks. Griswold is the man we want. This newspaper story is all bosh."

But the case had still to be worked up. So far he had no basis for his operations but inference. There was a great deal more to know before an arrest could be made. And he must operate rapidly and shrewdly, otherwise his man might escape. He determined to visit Brown's bridge and obtain whatever clue he might there.

Gen. Cook, accompanied by one of his officers, rode rapidly out the road towards Littleton, feeling quite confident that he would find that O'Neal had been murdered, and hopeful of obtaining some clue as to the identity of the murderers, ne was not disappointed, and every step taken confirmed his suspicions previously formed, that Griswold had murdered O'Neal, and that the report of the lynching was a mere pretense. He found the body swinging as it had been left, awaiting the action of the coroner. Some of the country people had begun to gather about the scene of the killing, having heard of the finding of the body. They viewed the ghastly sight with horror and with manifestations so marked as to destroy all idea which the bogus special deputy had sought to convey that the enraged populace had taken the man from them and hanged him.

A few were found by the officers who had seen the two men who had come out to arrest O'Neal, and their descriptions of the men were so accurate as to clear away whatever trace of doubt that might have remained with the detective as to their being Griswold and Patrick.

But still a stronger circumstance remained to aid in completing the theory which Cook was gradually forming. The snide officers had told the newspapers that a large number of mem stopped them and took their prisoner from them. Cook found the place at which the buggy had stopped, and where the prisoner had been removed; but instead of the tracks of a hundred men, or of fifty, or twenty, he discovered the footprints of but three of them. Of these, evidently only one had approached the buggy, while three had left it, dragging the prisoner, as the surface of the soil afforded every evidence. Hence Mr. Cook decided that the two men in the buggy with O'Neal

170

had strangled him there while, perhaps, he was under the influence of liquor, and that they had been assisted in taking him out and stringing him up by a confederate who had joined them at Brown's bridge.

One more clue only is necessary to make a complete chain of very strong circumstantial evidence. The rope with which O'Neal was hanged—where did that come from? Bringing it to Denver with him, Gen. Cook succeeded in ascertaining where it had been bought, and that it was purchased on the afternoon before the night of the murder by Griswold.

If there are any who think Dave Cook not a shrewd detective, they ought to be convinced of their error after reading the story of the working up of this case.

CAUGHT IN A TRAP—A CURIOUS LETTER

There was now left nothing to do but to arrest the two men who had betrayed and murdered O'Neal, and for this denouement preparations were now made. While working up the O'Neal case, Griswold had taken a fancy to a woman living with her husband on Clear creek, a quiet and peaceable man, and the two becoming attached to each other, he had driven the husband away and remained with the wife, filling the role of husband himself. Griswold lived with this woman at her former husband's home, and seemed to feel no delicacy whatever concerning the fine points of the situation.

Two days elapsed before Gen. Cook had succeeded in obtaining the clues set forth in the preceding chapter, and while it was feared that the murderers might make their escape, the fact was not lost sight of that the offense charged was a heinous one, and Cook felt that a great injustice might be done in arresting the men as long as there was any doubt as to their guilt. Hence the delay in taking the culprits into hand.

Detectives Frank Smith and Charley McCune were selected to make the arrest of the precious pair, and were ordered to Clear Creek valley for that purpose. They went first to the residence of Patrick, and found to their regret that they had come too late. That worthy had folded his tent and stolen away, leaving home and friends behind, evidently fearing apprehension.

The officers proceeded with caution to Griswold's home, fearing detection from a distance, and in case of detection a decidedly warm welcome. But they at last succeeded in getting to his house, and upon making inquiry for him, found that he had just gone out—out where no one knew.

The officers began now to feel that they had happened in a day after the feast, and sadly turned their horses' heads towards the city, disappointed and dejected that they had had such bad luck as they felt that they had had. But there was nothing left but a return to the city, with their report; so at least they felt, as they quitted the house where Griswold had so recently been. Yet there was still reason for hope of at least partial success, and they very soon came to realize that all was not lost.

Shortly after leaving Griswold's late place of abode, the officers discovered a mounted man moving in advance of them, and across a held. They spurred up, and were not long in discovering that this man was no other than Griswold. The officers had come prepared to deceive him. They were dressed as cowboys—wore large sombrero hats, tucked their breeches legs into their boot-tops, and carried whips in their hands, which they twirled about and cracked as cowboys do. Taking a different road from that which Griswold was pursuing, the two men contrived to ride around and come up so as to cut him off without creating suspicion. They had no hope of finding him unarmed, and hence were desirous of avoiding a fight if possible. Their disguise was so excellent that it served to save them from this necessity. They rode very close to Griswold before he took any notice of them, and were less than thirty feet distant when Griswold recognized Smith's face, with which he was familiar.

The murderer showed his colors in a moment. Appreciating that the two "cowboys" were officers come to arrest him, he was prepared to defend himself. He sought his gun with great celerity, and was raising it to fire, when he found himself staring along the barrels of as pretty a pair of weapons as were ever presented.

"Put that gun down. Griswold," commanded Frank Smith. "Put it down, or you die."

The gun dropped.

"Now, hands up!"

Reluctantly the fellows hands went up.

He was then disarmed and was soon on his way to Denver.

It was then discovered that the fellow was well provided with provisions and ammunition, and that he was just starting to make his escape from the state when come upon by the officers.

Griswold had a long trial. He took a change of venue from Denver to Evans, Weld county, and there, after the case was thoroughly tried, he was remanded to jail in Denver for a new trial. Eleven of the jurymen favored hanging, and the twelfth was for bringing in a verdict of manslaughter and sending him to the penitentiary for life. No one doubted the man's guilt. The splendid chain of evidence which Gen. Cook had prepared left no room for doubt on that score. But the twelfth man was not a believer in hanging and held out to the last, causing the jury to go before the court with a disagreement report. The murder of O'Neal had been committed on the 10th of July, 1870, but, owing to delays, the month of February, 1872, had now come around, and the law was only preparing to take its course. Griswold, who had been the cause of so much summary punishment, looked forward to his own fate with the greatest dread, and began to make preparations to escape. His plans were well laid, and as he had plenty of outside assistance, it is a great wonder that he did not accomplish his purpose. He was certainly desperate enough, as will soon appear.

It was on Saturday, the 24th of February, that an attempt was made to escape from the county jail in Denver, and which attempt resulted in one of the most exciting scenes ever witnessed in a prison. Two prisoners, Michael Henesee and a negro, named Dan Diamond, were engaged scrubbing the premises and making a general clean-up. While in the companion way leading between the cells from the front office to a room adjoining the day cell in the rear, they had occasion to wash the cells of Griswold and E. E. Wight, the last named being the man who figures in the Wall murder story. The turnkey, Sanford W. Davis, allowed these men to emerge from their cells for the purpose of going to the water closet, a few feet away, and in the enclosure, there being no accommodations for them in the cells, and as both were heavily ironed no fears were entertained of any outbreak. Griswold passed to the front office and called out to L. F. or "Till" Davis, brother to the turnkey, for a chew of tobacco. Davis was in the bedroom adjoining and did not answer, whereupon Griswold turned back, and as he did so he suddenly drew a bludgeon, consisting of a boulder in the toe of a stocking prepared in the water closet, from some place of concealment and dealt the turnkey a blow on the back of the head. This had the effect to fell him to the floor, but he soon regained his feet, and after a scuttle with Wight, Griswold and Diamond, the negro, who had joined the mutineers, he ran towards the large room in the rear, closely followed by Griswold.

During this melee, Henesee, the other prisoner, acting promptly and looking to the welfare of the turnkey, dragged Wight away from Davis and to his cell, and called for help., While the matter stood thus—Griswold and Davis, the turnkey, in the back room, and Griswold in possession of the latter's pistol, Henesee holding the door against Wight and endeavoring to readjust the tumbler lock— the brother of the turnkey grasped a revolver and courageously entered the companion-way and tried to lock Wight's cell door, in the meantime holding his revolver in his right hand. This all transpired in a few seconds.

Griswold, finding that Wight's exit was barred, returned to the rear doorway, stepped down into the companion-way and stood facing young Davis, who was endeavoring to lock the cell, only a few feet distant. The situation, of course, demanded desperate action on the part of one or the other, and as Griswold leveled his revolver at the young man, the latter in turn drew bead upon the prisoner, and both fired simultaneously. The ball from Griswold's pistol probably passed through the front doorway and into the street; the ball from young Davis' revolver entered Griswold's body, inflicting a mortal wound. He however, pressed towards Davis, who retreated and discharged a shot, when Wight emerged from his cell, seized Griswold's pistol, passed to the rear and made a second attack upon the turnkey, who endeavored to make his escape. Wight, however, fired two shots at Davis, one of which grazed the back of his head. The desperado then passed out at the rear, and secreted himself in the jail barn under the hay.

Of course, all the foregoing had happened in less time than it takes to read the account of it. The sheriff's office at that time was where it now is on Fifteenth street, on the alley between Larmier and Lawrence, and the jail was on Larimer between Fourteenth and Fifteenth, running back to the alley, so that they were not far apart. Gen. Cook was sitting in the sheriff's office at the time of the shooting, and, hearing it, hurried over through the alley to the

175

prison, and stationing a man at the back door, told him to let no one in or out. The crowd was already gathering, and Cook was afraid of a general row. Running in he found Till Davis, one of the guards, with a smoking pistol in his hand.

"What's up?" he demanded.

"Oh, the devil's to pay," he replied. "We've had some serious work here."

"Where's Sanford?"—Sanford Davis was a brother of Till's—"Where is Sanford?" he asked.

"Oh, he's dead," replied Till; "shot by Griswold."

"Where's Griswold?"

"He's back there somewhere—I don't know where."

Cook went to work to investigate, and found a confused state of affairs, which has been described as well as can be in the foregoing. The officers of the jail had not yet had an opportunity to ascertain the true state of affairs. In fact, the smoke of the late affray had not yet cleared away. It was generally believed that Sanford Davis had been shot, and no one knew that Griswold had received the liberal dose of lead for which his malady called so loudly. Confusion reigned supreme, and everybody was excited. The jail was a pandemonium. Nothing was known. There was chaos everywhere. A half dozen men might have been killed.

Gen. Cook lost no time in beginning to straighten matters out. Finding that Wight had taken part in the melee, Cook hurried to his cell, but found Griswold in it instead of Wight. Cook demanded his pistol. He said he had given it to Wight.

"I am dying, don't you see?" he muttered, "and couldn't use it if I had it. So I opened the cell and came in and let Wight out and told him to make his escape if he wanted to get away, as I couldn't."

"Shot! Of course you are! Come out of here!" exclaimed Dave, who never dreamed that the old scoundrel had been hurt in the row which he had instigated, and did not dare, hope that he had been mortally wounded. With this exclamation he dragged the fellow out by the coat collar, large as he was, and laid him out in the office, when he discovered that the man was really not feigning. He then found That Till Davis had planted a ball in the old fellows breast, and left him to make his peace with his Maker; and went to look for Wight.

Cook tracked Wight to the stable and began looking for him with a pitchfork in the straw. He had sent the steel prongs of the implement piercing through the hay but once or twice, when out he crawled, leaving the pistol cocked lying on the floor. When Cook took Wight back to jail, old Griswold was dead. He had been shot through and through.

Everybody considered that he deserved his fate, and there were few mourners to follow his body to the old cemetery on the hill the next day. There may have been one or two. It was afterwards discovered that the jail delivery had been planned with the assistance of two citizens of the town, who had horses in waiting for the murderers. One of them has since died.

The woman with whom Griswold had lived was another mourner. She seemed to be sincerely attached to the man, whom she now called her poor, dear husband. It was discovered after Griswold's death that during his imprisonment this woman had done everything in her flower to assist him in his escape, and had been his confidant and adviser throughout.

After Wight, one of the prisoners who attempted to escape from the jail, had been rearrested, it occurred to the officers to-search his person in order to ascertain, if possible, the origin of the difficulty which had resulted in the death of one of the parties thereto. In one of his pockets was found a package of letters, which scrutiny disclosed to have been written by Griswold. These letters were perfectly unintelligible to the ordinary reader, being traced in cipher, probably invented by Griswold himself. To pick them out was, however, a comparatively easy matter to the detectives, as they had already discovered the key to the cipher. One of the letters, developing the plot for escape, ran as follows:

"Dear Jennie—The horses must not be more than two blocks away; we will come out of the front door, and you or Alex — ought to be on the opposite side of the street, so that when we went out you could walk by where the horses were, and then there could be no mistake. We only want the horses now to go to the mountains. I want Alex to come and get them. Then you or him see Henry and have other ones got. I do not know whether we will have Spencers or Winchesters; we will have one or the other, but we may not get cartridges. Have Alex get 5 hundred rounds of each, so we can take which ever we want; also twenty-five rounds of 36, and the same of 44. Those we don't want he can take back. Have plenty of cakes (provisions). Take two sacks, a part full of eatables; they must be more than half full, so that we can lay them across the saddles, one sack on each horse. The principal things are bread; hard tack if you can get it; no more than seven or eight pounds of bacon; lots of salt and pepper, and lots of coffee, ground. Mind you, lots of that is all that has kept me alive. You had better have a quart of whiskey on each saddle, for we are nothing but skin and bones, and very weak. We cannot ride far without stimulants. We will stay near Denver until we get strength; we are getting worse here every day, and I assure you I will not leave here until I square accounts with Smith.

"But we must have plenty of ammunition, for it makes no difference whether we fight in the streets or anywhere else. I will never be taken, and if I should have the good fortune to get killed, you will find the address of those you want, with full directions. It will be in the waist bands of my pants that I have on. If I am not killed I will write and have some money sent to you. The 'old man' can go for wood and bring provisions. I don't expect you to buy anything, but tell Alex to get them. Better get some chewing tobacco. I want one bottle of morphine, for riding will hurt me. I wear napkins. I can almost span my arm above my elbow. I am the poorest I ever was but I must or die. I have some time thought you was afraid of me if I should get away. I have never showed myself a brute yet. I don't think I will begin now. I will send for you as soon as I can. I will send you money very soon, if I go to hell for it. Remember that I think everything will be furnished, if I once get out. They are all scared about it. We will go sometime between 12 and 3—I think about 2 o'clock. Let Alex be on the opposite side and walk near the houses, but not come near us; he must follow so to get the horses. If you are bothered or insulted, we know I will make their blood run a rain [sic] of terror or burn their city until they stop. I tell you, if they cross me I will have their hearts, but to you I will be as I always have been, your husband; will stake my life for you in any way it may be necessary. If I am killed, remember my waist band. Be careful of the key I gave you. I will risk my life for it. They can't read. Good-by.

"L. P. G."

This letter was not fully deciphered until the body had been buried. It was afterwards disinterred by W. F. Smith, the county jailer, in order to ascertain whether it had been buried with any valuable papers, as the above would indicate. He searched the clothing thoroughly, but found only two scraps of paper—one two leaves from Harper's magazine containing the poem "Hannah Jane," and the other a piece of paper with a few words in cipher. On the former was the following significant problem—significant in the light of recent events. Griswold was probably trying to study it out. It was as follows: "A problem: A prisoner anxious to escape, and a dead man awaiting burial; how were these two things to be exchanged so that the living man might pass out without going to the grave?"

So ended, with his own life, the bloody work which "Old Griswold" had begun. His wife, or "woman," is still living in or near Denver. Wight, his accomplice, was the man who had assisted Witherill in the murder of Wall, the herder on Dry creek, an account of winch crime is elsewhere in this volume related.

Dan Diamond, the negro, was one of the worst that ever came to Denver. He, as well as Wight, is probably also at cañon. He never stays out more than a few months, as he is always stealing when out. But he escaped on the day of the fracas. The officers heard of him a few days afterwards at a ranch twenty four miles down the Platte, and followed him down there. They were told that he was in the second story of a house there. Cook went with a posse after him and stationed men outside with guns pointing at every window, and went up to where he was himself, with drawn revolver. They expected him to jump out and be killed. But he didn't. He was a downright disappointment. Cook found him lying flat on his face on a bed, crying: "Oh, Missah Offisah, I dun gib up; don kill me now; I'se yer man. I go right along wid you." And he did go.

As for Hennessee, the gambler, who came to Davis' rescue, he was pardoned out immediately and voted a resolution of thanks.

Till Davis was but slightly hurt, after all. He thought he had been shot, but wasn't. The wound caused by the stone stunned him and the blood flowed freely for a while, but he soon recovered and is supposed to be still living.

Patrick, the man who went with Griswold to arrest O'Neal, and who was supposed to have been equally responsible for his death, has never, since the day after the murder, been seen in Colorado. It was believed that he went to Kansas, but no satisfactory clue being obtained, he was not searched for in that state.

With one other name and one other fatality this record closes. John Tusawn was a brother-in-law of Patrick. He lived near Brown's bridge previous to and after O'Neal's death. Common report made him a party to the murder of the victim; but, although circumstances pointed to his guilt, evidence sufficient to convict him was never found, and he was not molested. It is, however, known that ever after the ghastly tragedy he lived a moody, gloomy life. When the grasshoppers came along in 1875, he lost his crops, and that fall he ended a now thoroughly miserable existence by committing suicide. It was given out that the ravages of the locusts had produced his despondency, and had indirectly caused him to take his own life, but those who knew him best say that he took this step to avoid the further sight of the horrible, spectacle of O'Neal's dead body dangling constantly before his eyes.

Old Griswold was a curse to all who came in contact with him. He did not die any too soon, and the world would have probably been better had he never been born.

THE LEICHSENRING ROBBBRY

One of the boldest robberies on record was committed one cold evening dining the Christmas holidays of 1879, at the saloon of C. E. Leichsenring, then on the corner of Sixteenth and Holladay streets, Denver, supplemented by one of the most adroit captures ever effected in the city. The particulars in the case are about as follows: It was near 8 o'clock when Mr. Leichsenring was induced to open his safe, in the rear of the saloon, by a man named Ayer, who represented himself to be a United States marshal from Leadville, and expressed a desire to examine the complicated workings of the time lock on the inner door of the safe, which was one of the small Hall patterns, and an object of great interest as a mechanical contrivance.

While Mr. Leichsenring was explaining the process of locking and opening the door of the same to Ayer, his attention was for a moment attracted to another part of the house, and it is supposed that the robbery was committed during the brief period that his back was turned. The theory is that during this interim, an accomplice of Ayer, named Rocky McDonald, took out of the safe a canvas bag containing $4,800 in $20 and $10 gold pieces and some government bonds, altogether amounting to $5,090, and walked out of the saloon before the absence of the bag was noticed.

When Mr. Leichsenring turned around he immediately detected that the safe had been robbed, and thinking that Ayer was the guilty party, immediately seized him and turned him over to Officer Newman, who at that juncture happened to enter the saloon. The report of the robbery spread like wildfire, and the amount stolen was quickly exaggerated to $8,000 in gold. McDonald's presence had been noticed by three or four other men, who were seated in the saloon at the time, but no one had seen him take the money.

Mr. Leichsenring notified the sheriff's office and the police as speedily as possible, and officers flocked to the scene of the robbery by the dozen. Gen. Cook was at that time neither sheriff nor chief of police, but his detective association was as active as ever and "just aching" for a neat job in which it might distinguish itself.

Consequently Gen. Cook proceeded to Leichsenring's saloon, and, after elbowing his way through the crowd of policemen and deputy sheriffs who lined the sidewalk on the outside, found Mr. Leichsenring very much excited. He welcomed Cook with open arms and asked him to go to work in the case. He offered first a reward of $500 and then of $1,000 for the recovery of the money, and proclaimed in loud tones, as Dave went out:

"I'll give $1,000 for the capture of the thief and the money, and if Dave Cook finds him, I authorize him to take his pay out of the bag."

The officers scattering in all directions, policemen, deputy sheriffs and private detectives, started out to scour the town. There was incentive to work for now. A big reward was offered. Mr. Cook walked quietly back to his office and put several of his best officers to work, including Joe Arnold and Capt. C. A. Hawley. He then started out himself.

He had been on the street less than an hour when he was approached by a business man and furnished with la clue which very soon led to the arrest of the guilty party. This man told the detective a story which interested him very much. It was to the effect that a man answering the description of McDonald had applied to Lou Rothgerber, the pawnbroker, doing business then, as now, on Larimer street, between Sixteenth and Seventeenth, for a peculiar land of expensive watch, used only by horsemen in timing races, and not having anything in his show cases meeting the demands of his customer, Rothgerber procured one at the jewelry store of Messrs. Hatch, Davidson Co., which he sold to McDonald, together with a heavy chain, for $580, receiving his payment in gold.

Proceeding to Rothgerber's shop Mr. Cook found a policeman standing near the entrance, who being questioned stated that he had seen McDonald enter,

"Did he have any money?"

"Yes, a pile of it."

"Where did he get it?"

"He told me that he had just sold a mine for $10,000."

"Which way did he go?"

"I don't know."

The policeman had heard of the Leichsenring robbery, but he did not suppose that a man who had been shrewd to get away with $5,000, as the Leichsenring robber had been, would be fool enough to carry it around so loosely as McDonald had been doing, hence did not connect him with the theft. Cook knew more than the policeman did, and now felt sure that he was on the right track, and that he would get his man. Proceeding into Rothgerber's place he succeeded in ascertaining that his man had been there, though, for some reason, his actions did not arouse any suspicion. He had not only been in and bought a costly watch, but had left all his money with the exception of a few hundred dollars with Rothgerber for safe keeping. Here was a big point gained already. The money was virtually recovered, leaving nothing to do but to secure the thief. Taking Rothgerber into custody that the money might be held secure, the detective went on his way. It was not difficult to trace McDonald. He had spent his money freely, giving it away wherever fancy dictated, and tossing a $20 gold piece to the policeman at Rothgerber's door.

Leaving Rothgerber's, McDonald had taken a hack a short time previous and driven up Holladay street. Gen. Cook then prosecuted his search, and among some of the houses of ill-repute abounding in that portion of the city, and finding that at one of these places McDonald had spent $10 for two bottles of wine, was soon in a condition to direct Officers Dorsey and Phillips to arrest not only McDonald, but another man whom he suspected of complicity, named Davis, telling the officers that he wanted the two men for larceny, but saying nothing about the suspected connection of them with the Leichsenring case. The two men were picked up with but little difficulty and turned over to Gen. Cook, who, after returning Mr. Leichsenring's money to him, made public the fact of the arrest and the securing of the treasure. As may be readily supposed there was considerable rejoicing on the part of Mr. Leichsenring, and the public was not slow to recognize the service 'which had been rendered. Commenting upon the case the next morning, the Rocky

Mountain News said: "The rapidity with which the capture followed the act—no matter how it may have been accomplished—speaks volumes for the sagacity of the Rocky Mountain Detective Association, and they are honorably entitled to a liberal reward."

Ayer, it should here be stated, was also arrested. The prisoners were taken to the detectives' headquarters, searched, the watch and six $20 gold pieces found on McDonald's person and two more in the possession of his partner. Rothgerber, who had been detained, was released upon producing the total amount deposited by McDonald and proving that he had no knowledge of the robbery at the time he sold the watch. McDonald, together with Ayer and Davis, were locked up to await examination.

All these men remained in jail for several weeks. The trial resulted in the discharge of Davis and Ayer, whose complicity could not be fully established, but McDonald was sent to Cañon City to remain until 1887.

The entire case was concluded, the prisoners jailed and the money returned to its owners in two hours after it was placed in Cook's hands. With the exception of a few assistants of his own association he had no aid, while there was a small army of police and sheriffs on the lookout. Comment is unnecessary.

THE BLACK HILLS ROAD AGENTS

The years 1876,'77,'78 and '79 were characterized by numerous stage-coach robberies in Wyoming, Dakota and Montana, performed by highwaymen, who found refuge in the wild and mountainous region of the north. The roads leading to the Black hills were the scenes of some of the boldest exploits of the kind ever known to criminal history. Many thrilling stories of the dare-devil work of these highwaymen are told, and will long be remembered as a part of the history of the settlement and development of the region round about Deadwood. Large treasures of gold dust taken from the mines were frequently shipped out on the stages, and many men of wealth traveled over the line, going in for the purpose of starting in business or making mining investments. The stages were stopped by these knights of the road, who soon became known as "road agents," at places convenient to the hiding places of the highwaymen, who, safe behind protecting trees or bluffs, commanded a halt and compelled driver and passengers to hold up their hands while they should "go through" the coach and the people on board, one or two of the agents performing the search while others held their cocked guns loaded upon the terrified travelers, who were, as a rule, only too willing to escape with their lives and let their valuables go to enrich the stores of the brigands. Often, however, the travelers "showed fight," and then there was sure to be bloodshed, the highwaymen sometimes getting the worst of it, but most frequently coming out best.

See historian Agnes Wright Spring's excellent The Cheyenne and Black Hills Stage and Express Routes.—Ed. 2016

When the travel to the hills began to slacken and the coaches to be better guarded than they had been in the earlier days of the gold excitement, the "agents," not finding their field as profitable as it had been before, started out to look for new fields in which to show their prowess, and fresh fields to conquer. They turned their attention to the railroads.

And thus it came about that a member of the Rocky Mountain Detective Association came to have much to do with them, in the story which is about to be related as well as in others of a like character. This member of the association is Mr. N. K. Boswell, a resident of Laramie City, Wyo., for several years back, who is now warden of the state penitentiary at Laramie City, and has frequently been sheriff of Albany county, and who has for very many years been considered one of the most efficient of Gen. Cook's assistants.

It was in August, 1878—August 14—that a bold attempt was made by' a party of these road agents to commit one of the most fiendish crimes ever perpetrated by outlaws in any land. The party consisted of Frank James, one of the James brothers, but who went by the name of McKinney; of Dutch Charley, Frank Toll, Sim Wan, Big-Nosed George, Tom Beed, Sandy Campbell and Cully McDonald. They had come in from the northern country to a point on the Union Pacific railroad where it crosses the Medicine Bow river, eighty-two miles west of Laramie City, in Wyoming. The embankments of the road approaching the river are exceedingly steep, about sixty feet high, and are made of large, rough stone taken from the cuts in the road. A more jagged or more broken place than these embankments it would be difficult to imagine.

It was to this place that these road agents had come with the intention of throwing the west-bound passenger train, on the 14th of August, from the track, and of precipitating it down the embankment, hoping to kill or to badly cripple all the train operatives and passengers, and thus make easy work of the robbery, which was the purpose of the undertaking. To accomplish this task they had cut the telegraph wire at the point and had tied one end of a long piece of wire, after loosening the spikes, to a rail; the other end being in the hands of the robbers, who were secreted behind a convenient embankment. The plan was to pall the rail out just as the locomotive should reach it, and to tumble the entire train and its burden of treasure and humanity down this fill. The time as well as the place was well chosen, the train at that season of the year passing the spot about dusk.

But for what really seems a special act of Providence, the entire train would certainly have been hurled over this precipice; and the wires being cut, the highwaymen would have been far away with their booty before the terrible deed could have become known. The instrument whom fate chose to avert this terrible catastrophe was a humble member of the race—the boss of the repair section of the road—who, finding after quitting his day's work that he had left his tools on the Medicine Bow bridge, returned to procure them. Passing along he noticed that the spikes were out, and saw the wire attached to the rail. He comprehended the situation in a moment, and his heart must have leaped into his mouth. But he was a man out of a thousand in coolness and self-possession. Manifesting no sign that he had made a discovery, he walked quietly forward, picked up his tools, came back and passed the dead-fall again on his return, still showing no concern whatever by his manner. Had he made the least sign, there is no doubt that he would have been killed, and that the robbers and murderers would have been enabled to put their hellish plot into execution.

Walking past the trap, he proceeded towards home. He bad scarcely gone around the next curve when he heard the train humming forward at a fearful rate of speed. He quietly flagged it and, of course, when he had told his story, the train was backed. The robbers were foiled in their purpose, and one hundred and fifty lives, to say nothing of property, were saved.

The whole country was aroused to vengeance when the full scope of the terrible plot was developed and comprehended in its hellish entirety. Large rewards were offered for the capture of the outlaws, and numbers of good people turned out to hunt down the men who had demonstrated that they lacked opportunity only to be guilty of a deed which would have caused the entire continent: to shudder in the contemplation of it.

But the robbers were not caught then. Indeed, some of them, including Frank James, are still at large. The pursuit was kept up for several days. Detective Boswell joined the pursuing party, but they succeeded only in driving the rascals out of the section; not, however, until they had shot down in cold blood two deputy sheriffs—Vincent and Widowfield—who were searching for them in the Elk mountains. After this shooting the robbers left for the north, maintaining for a short time a rendezvous on the Dry Cheyenne river, and evaded all pursuit, which was ultimately abandoned. Soon after the band began to operate on the stage lines again, and it gradually changed until there were but two left who had been in any way identified with the railroad raiders, these two being Dutch Charley and Joe Manuse. Frank James had left for Montana, and John Erwin had become leader of the Dry Cheyenne band.

THIRTY DEGREES BELOW ZERO

Early in December, 1878, a portion of this band, consisting of Erwin, Manuse, Dutch Charley, Frank Ruby, A. C. Douglas, Hank Harrington, Frank Howard and Charles Condon (alias "The Kid") decided upon another raid upon the railroad, and this time selected as the point of their attack the bridge across Rock creek, fifty-six miles west of Laramie City. Their programme included the robbery of the train, and also of the hotel kept at the point by ex-Gov. Thayer, of Wyoming.

The plot was quite as devilish as that which had been frustrated at Medicine Bow, but it never came so near bearing fruit as the former one did. It was frustrated through the efforts principally of two men, named Frank Howard, one of the party, and Detective Boswell, who succeeded in taking the entire band by a very bold and shrewdly arranged move upon them.

Frank Howard was a member of the party as it started from the north for the purpose of committing the robberies planned as above stated. The party came south to within a few miles of their destination and, camping in a spot where they supposed themselves safe, decided to send a member of their organization to the station to look over the land and make report upon the prospects there. The performance of this duty fell to Howard, whose conscience appears to have been considerably wrought upon, and whose heart failed him in the work in which he was about to engage. As a consequence of this state of his mind he decided to frustrate the plans of his associates, prevent the raid and assist in securing the capture of the band. He laid the entire story before Gov. Thayer, who was not slow in communicating it to the authorities of Albany county.

Mr. Boswell was not then acting sheriff of the county, although he had but recently been elected to that position. The sheriff was notified, but did not act. Gov. Thayer then informed the officials of the Union Pacific railroad of the intentions of the cut-throats, some of them being at Ogden, Utah. They took the matter in hand and began to communicate by telegraph with the sheriff of Albany county. But he did not heed their dispatches or take any steps to grant their request that the contemplated train wrecking be prevented and an effort made to overtake the criminals while there was a chance of finding them.

Two days were spent in this way, and at last the Union Pacific people telegraphed Mr. Boswell, as a member of the Rocky Mountain Detective Association, and requested him to see if something could not be done, offering a reward of $250 each for the capture of the gang. Mr. Boswell went to see the sheriff, who, upon being approached, declared that he had been unable to get men to go along with him to make the effort to arrest the "agents." Mr. Boswell thereupon undertook the case. In a very few minutes he had found ten determined men who were willing to go with him, and he announced his readiness to proceed with the undertaking. A special train was provided and the men were soon on their way, starting after nightfall of Saturday, December 24.

The hour of midnight had already passed when Bock Creek station was reached, but Boswell decided that if anything was to be done it must be promptly done, and, gathering up horses for his men, they started out at 3 o'clock on Christmas morning in search of their game. It was dark; the ground was covered with snow; there was a stiff wind blowing, and the mercury touched at 30° below zero.

Howard bad been faithful to his trust, and was willing to give all the information which he possessed as to the whereabouts of his gang. But they were discovered to have moved since his most recent visit to them, and their exact whereabouts were unknown to him. The officers chanced to learn that an old ranchman in the neighborhood bad supplied the robbers with food after their change of base. His house was found, and he was dragged out of bed and, by means of threats and tender of reward, he was prevailed upon to accompany the officers to the biding place.

The locality pointed out was a deep ravine which had been cut into a hillside. Indeed, there was a network of gulches and ravines, and the robber gang bad chosen a place near the center, where, under ordinary circumstances, they would never have been discovered, and where their biding place would have proved an excellent fortress for them if their cunning had not been met by equal shrewdness on the part of their pursuers. They were hidden away under a protruding cliff and a little niche in the ravine formed by a tributary stream, now dry.

Daylight was just beginning to dawn when the old farmer pointed out this place, received his reward and took his departure. A moment later a blue streak of smoke shot up through the cold air, and the officers were no longer in doubt that they had treed their game. They were also convinced that, if they would secure the robbers without a fight, they must act with dispatch.

It required but a few moments for Mr. Boswell to dispose of his men, who were stationed with guns cocked at the best places surrounding the hiding place. Having left his assistants with their guns in their hands and ready to fire at a moment's notice, he crawled up behind a large rock standing in front of the robbers' den and looking down upon their sleeping place.

Creeping along with extreme caution he reached the edge of the rock and cautiously looked over. There were six of the scoundrels in camp, namely, Erwin, Ruby, Condon. Harrington, Douglas and Dutch Charley. He saw at a glance that only one of them had arisen from his bed. He had made the fire and was standing in front of it unarmed, with the others still lay wrapped closely in their blanket beds and apparently enjoying their morning naps. Getting his guns ready he shouted to them, clear as a clap of thunder:

"Hold up your hands!"

All was virtually over.

The men awoke with a start, and almost in an instant five pairs of hands shot into the air. There was but one exception in obeying the command, and that exception was noticed in the one from whom it would have naturally been least expected, "the Kid" being the only one to fail. Instead of throwing up his hands, he began to draw his pistol.

"Put that gun down, boy," said one of the older members, "He will kill you in an instant. Don't you see he's got the drop on us? It's Boswell, you d—d fool. You can't get away with old Boswell."

190

The boy dropped the gun. Mr. Boswell's men came up, and the capture of all was effected, with the exception of Manuse, who had gone out to hunt the horses. He was found and taken without any difficulty, and the entire party marched into the station and afterwards taken to Laramie City, where they were safely lodged in jail and afterwards disposed of.

It was believed that several of the captives had participated in the Medicine Bow affair, and that some of them were partially responsible for the murder of Widowfield and Vincent. Such proved to be the ease. Mr. Boswell, as a detective, advised a measure which he thought would assist in the discovery of the truth in the matter. Manuse was believed to have been one of the members of the gang, and the railroad employees were given an opportunity to remain alone with him long enough to find out. Refusing to reveal anything, he was stretched up with an ugly rope around his neck, and held in a choking position until he was almost dead. Being let down, he again declined to talk. He was strung up again, and this time, beginning to fear that his own life would be taken then and there, volunteered to make a confession. From this it appeared that he had started out with the gang to go to Medicine Bow, and was separated from his party and failed to reach the railroad with them. Dutch Charley, one of the captives, was, however, with the gang, and proved to have been the very man who had first fired upon the deputies. As he had told the story to Manuse, these two men had gotten upon the trail of the would-be wreckers and were pushing them hard. They had followed them into a Cañon in the Elk mountains and came near going upon the scoundrels just as they were leaving camp after remaining all night. The robbers left hurriedly, tossing the burning chunks from their fire into a stream of water near the camping place and taking to their horses. Being well mounted, the robbers stopped a few rods away and concluded to watch the movements of the officers, being concealed themselves. The officers coming up to the fire, one of them dismounted and stuck his hand into the ashes, exclaiming to his comrade:

"We are close upon their heels. It's hot as hell."

191

"Yes, you son of a bitch, it's pretty damned hot, and we'll just give you a chance to find out how hot hell is."

Thus responded Dutch Charley for his gang, at the same time drawing a bead on the dismounted officer and notifying him to prepare to die. He attempted to mount, but was shot down by Charley as he got up. The other officer attempted to escape by flight, but a dozen bullets were sent flying after him as his horse ran at full speed down the cañon, and he fell dead with three holes through his body, the gang then disbanding and making their escape.

This story of Manuse's was sufficient to seal the fate of Dutch Charley. It was decided that as the killing of the deputies had taken place in Carbon county and not in Albany, he should be tried there, and he was put on the train and started for Rawlins for trial. He never reached his destination. He was taken off of the train when near the place, by a party of armed and masked vigilantes, and swing up to a telegraph pole to expiate this terrible crime, and his body left hanging for several days as meat for the buzzards.

The other members of the Rock Creek gang were tried. Harrington turned state's evidence, but being sent to Fort McKinney to identify supposed stage robbers, was shot by a man named Smith, who claimed that Harrington had killed his brother. Very little could be proved against Douglas, except as to his evil intentions. He had been superintendent of the Rock Creek stage line, and used his knowledge obtained through his position to aid the stage robbers in their work, notifying them by letter or telegraph, signed "Henry Ward Beecher,"* when there was treasure or "good plucking" on the coaches. He had never been in a robbery, so far as could be proven, and was given only one year in the penitentiary. Manuse and Ruby were sentenced to four years each, and Erwin, the captain, and Condon, "The Kid," were sentenced for life. As for Howard, he was made a detective on the railroad, and rendered the company valuable service. The robbers have sworn to have vengeance upon him for betraying them and being the primary cause of their getting into the hands of the officers instead of procuring big booty and retiring to the safe recesses of the great Northwest.

IN THE EXPRESS BUSINESS

Along in the '60's and early '70's when Colorado was not covered with a network of railroad and telegraph lines as it is today, bankers and others who washed to transmit large sums of money from one point to another were often put to sore straits for some means to accomplish their object. The stage coaches which carried mail, passengers and express to nearly every part of the state, were too risky. Holdups were of frequent occurrence, often it was thought through the connivance and assistance of the drivers themselves. Then, too, they were slow and uncertain; a washout or snowslide might detain them for days at a time.

Accordingly it became necessary to secure the services of men who were not only honest and trustworthy themselves, but who wore known to be "handy with a gun" and who would risk their lives if necessary for the protection of the property entrusted to their care. It was because of this that the Rocky Mountain Detective Association was often called upon when any particularly large sums of money were to be carried from Denver to mountain towns. One or two cases are called to mind, not only by the implicit confidence displayed by the bankers in Gen. Cook and his aides, but also by the faithful manner in which they discharged the responsible duties which they were called upon to perform.

In January, 1870, Kountze Bros., of the Colorado National Bank of Denver, who are still the leading bankers of the whole western country, were running a branch bank at Central City, known as the Rocky Mountain National. A well-known mill man, whose name has been forgotten, carne in one day to secure an additional loan of $2,500 on his mill, which was already mortgaged for $25,000. The local manager, of course, refused to make the loan, and the fellow went out of the bank with the threat that he would "fix 'em." And he came pretty nearly doing so, too he rode around to the various camps, telling the men that if they had any money in the bank at Central they had better get it out in a hurry, as the bank was practically "busted." "Why," he said, "I couldn't get $2,500 on my mill from them." As his property was popularly supposed to be worth $30,000 or more, this of course frightened hundreds of timid depositors, and a run on the bank was begun at once.

The local manager hurriedly dispatched a messenger to Denver for aid. Mr. Charles Kountze, one of the firm, hastily counted out $50,000, and placing it in a grip, sent for Gen. Cook to accompany him to Central. Placing the grip under the buggy seat and a couple of good guns where they could be easily got at, Cook and Kountze drove out of Denver at 11 o'clock at night, and arrived in Central the next morning after a hard drive. A wild mob surged around the bank as soon as the doors were opened, and though the tellers were paying off depositors as rapidly as possible, Kountze feared that there might be trouble, and employed Gen. Cook to remain in the bank as a guard that day. At the close of banking hours they hitched up their rig and drove back to Denver, reaching the city about I o'clock that night. As they crossed the Platte bridge, Kountze said to Cook: "Dave, you'll have to go right back again tonight."

Although fatigued with two long drives over rough mountain roads and nearly sick from cold and loss of sleep, Gen. Cook did not hesitate, but securing a fresh team, started back once more, this time accompanied by an employee of the bank named Potter, who carried the grip containing $75,000. They reached Central in good time, and by 2 o'clock the next afternoon confidence in the bank's stability was again restored, and the run was over. Gen. Cook received not only a substantial pecuniary reward for his three days' and two nights' hard work, but the lasting gratitude of the bank officials as well.

During the exciting times in Georgetown in May, 1875, which grew out of the Dives-Pelican mining suits, and culminated in the murder of Snyder, the superintendent of the Pelican mine, by Jack Bishop, the Dives mine superintendent, the Pelican people employed Gen. Cook, C. B. Hoyt, the present warden of the State Reformatory at Buena Vista; W. F. Smith and other members of the association as a body guard for their legal counsel, Senator Henry M. Teller and ex-Congressman James H. Belford, who flatly refused to go to Georgetown unless accompanied by an armed guard to protect them from the excited mob.

Learning that Gen. Cook was going to Georgetown, President Moffat asked him to carry $75,000 in currency to their branch bank at that place, as he feared that a run might be started on the bank during the excitement. Gen. Cook agreed to this, and he and J. L. McNeal, an employee of the bank, put the money in a buggy and drove up there one night, reaching Georgetown in safety.

During the trial, one of the opposing counsel took occasion to make a sarcastic reference to the "armed both guard of man-killers" that the Denver lawyers had brought with them, and he and the lawless element that then dominated Georgetown got the worst roasting from Congressman Belford that they had ever heard in their lives. The Pelican people won their suit, and the trouble finally quieted down, although the murderer, Bishop, was never apprehended.

In the latter part of June, 1878, a company that was working the Goneabroad and Small Hopes mining claims at Leadville under lease and bond, made an exceedingly rich strike, the first made in the camp. They made the strike only a week before the expiration of their lease, and unless they could raise the $20,000 on the date when their lease and option expired, the valuable property, worth at least $300,000, would pass into the hands of the original owners. The company sent a man to Denver to make arrangements to borrow the needed sum, in which he was successful, returning to Leadville with a certified check on the Colorado National Bank for $20,000. To their surprise, the owners refused to accept the certified check, and announced that nothing but the money would do. By this plan they expected that they would obtain possession of the mine, as the time had so nearly expired that they thought it would be impossible to get the money there in time. Parker, one of the lessees, hastened back to Denver to secure the currency, if possible. President Kountze of the bank did not know Parker, but told him if he could get Dave Cook to carry the money through he would be willing to trust him with it. Otherwise he did not care to take the risk. Parker hunted up Gen. Cook, and arrangements were made to start at once. This was the till of July and the lease expired on the 5th—the distance to be traveled was 145 miles over rough

196

mountain roads—a seemingly impossible feat. Gen. Cook hunted up Frank Smith, and just about noon they, with Parker, in a light rig, started on their long drive. They drove rapidly all afternoon, all that night and until noon the next day, when they reached Fairplay, stopping only long enough to change horses. Almost worn out with the long ride and loss of sleep it appeared that they could not possibly reach Leadville before the bank closed, and if they could not, all was lost. Parker gave up in despair. Gen. Cook, however, resourceful as usual, hunted up Sheriff John Ifinger, and found out from him that it was possible they might get through in time by taking a short cut on horseback across the Mesquite range through Mosquito pass.

Gen. Cook gave him $50 to guide them, and offered to pay for all horses killed in making the attempt. The party secured good saddle horses and left Fairplay at twenty-eight minutes after 1 o'clock. Spurring their horses across the more level parts of the trail, dismounting and leading them up steep, slippery paths, and around walls of rock overhanging cañons hundreds of feet dee]), where the slightest misstep would have proved fatal, they at length crossed the pass, and just three minutes before 3 o'clock, when they supposed the bank would close, rode up to that institution with the money.

The chagrin of the owners who had felt so certain of regaining possession of the property was only equaled by the joy of the lessees. They overwhelmed Cook and Smith with attentions, and during their stay in Leadville nothing in the camp was too good for them, and they were given a handsome reward besides.

These are only a few of the many eases in which the Rocky Mountain Detective Association has been called upon to perform difficult and seemingly impossible tasks, and to its credit be it said, it has never yet been "found wanting," but has ever performed every duty.

A FARM HAND'S AWFUL GRIME

There has been but one execution of a criminal in Denver to the present time since the 24th day of January, 1873. On that day Theodore Meyers gave up his life on the gallows in expiation of the crime he had committed on the night of the 8th of August, 1871, in the murder of George Bonacina, a ranchman living on the Platte [River], twelve miles above Denver, and four miles beyond Littleton.

Meyers was arrested not alone for the murder of Bonacina, but also for an attempt to murder his sister, a Mrs. Belle New ton, who lived with her brother on the ranch. Mrs. Newton was a woman at that time about thirty years of age, and was of prepossessing personal appearance. She was possessed of fascinating manners, and had the reputation in the neighborhood in which she resided of being quite too "exclusive" to please the other residents. She had resided in Omaha previous to 1860, when she came to Cheyenne, whence she removed to Denver in 1870. Soon after coming to Denver, Mrs. Newton established herself in the millinery business, and while so engaged she became engaged to and married a Mr. Benjamin Friedenthal, removing with him soon after their marriage to the ranch already described on the Platte, where they lived for a few months. But their married life was not a happy one, and they separated. Mrs. Newton's brother had joined her on the farm, and they continued to reside there after Friedenthal had taken his departure.

To properly understand the interest which was taken in the tragedy at the ranch it should be known that rumor had wagged a busy tongue in the neighborhood in which Mrs. Newton resided. It was alleged that Bonacina was not the brother of the woman, but a clandestine lover, and some asserted that his intimacy with Mrs. Friedenthal, or Mrs. Newton, had been the cause of the separation between her and her husband. One supposition, when the story of the murder was first told, was that Friedenthal had been in some way responsible for the crime. Another theory was that the murderer had sought to establish intimate relations with the woman himself, and that Bonacina had stepped in the way of his desires.

These were some of the surmises which filled the air, and which rapidly grew into reports which professed to be accurate.

Mrs. Newton brought the first account of the tragedy into Denver herself. She arrived in the city about 11 o'clock on Friday, the 11th of August, 1871, and was conveyed to the Tremont house, standing then as now on Twelfth street, at the intersection of Blake.

A physician was at first sent for he dressed the ugly wounds which the poor woman bore. As many as seven buckshot were ascertained to have been planted squarely in her breast, near the heart, four of them passing entirely through the body and the others lodging under the skin in the back. None of the balls had touched the heart, but it hardly seemed possible that so many pieces of lead should have plowed their way through a human body without producing a fatal result. Her physician told her that she did not have one chance in a hundred But Mrs. Newton was a woman of nerve, and she replied that whether she lived or not she wanted the murderer of her brother brought to justice.

Sending for Gen. Cook, who was then sheriff of Arapahoe county, she told him the story of the shooting so far as she was able. She lay on a bed in her room as she related the circumstances. Her face was as white as death from loss of blood, and her voice sank to a mere whisper as she attempted to make the patient officer understand sufficiently well to pursue the murderer with some certainty of capturing him. Her talk was a series of moans and groans, interspersed with words painfully drawn out.

She had no doubt, she said, that the man whose name is given as Meyers had done the shooting, but she did not know his name, describing him as "a Dutchman, whose first name was Theodore." Delating the circumstances of the affair, and those leading up to it, she said that this man had come to her and her brother some few weeks before the killing to obtain work, and had been employed as a hand on the farm. He had previously been engaged by a man named Lewis, who resided in the neighborhood, but had been discharged. Bonacina had stacked his grain some distance from the house. Meyers represented to him that while working for Lewis he had heard threats made to burn it, and so wrought upon the feelings of his employers that they procured guns and ammunition, and Bonacina and Meyers began sleeping at night at the grain stacks, some fifty yards from the house, for the purpose of protecting the grain from the attacks of incendiaries. They had been thus engaged for about two weeks, when the murder and attempted murder occurred.

The two men went to their out-door beds as usual on the fatal Thursday night, leaving Mrs. Newton alone in the house, where she retired soon after the men had taken their departure. She was sleeping soundly when she was awakened by the sound of a pistol, which was soon followed by a second report. The reports appeared to be in the direction of the grain stacks, and Mrs. Newton rushed to the window, thinking that someone had come to burn the grain, and that her brother and the German had fired upon the intruder. She had been out of bed but a second when she heard someone evidently approaching the house from the direction of the grain, and calling her loudly by her first name, "Belle! Belle! Belle!" three times in succession.

Mrs. Newton was clad in the thinnest kind of night clothes, wearing nothing but a light undergarment. She was so thoroughly excited, however at the noise of the pistol reports, and at the calling out of her own name, that she rushed to the door and opened it. As she swung it back, the German employee stepped up, with a shotgun in his hand, and appeared to be considerably excited, replying to her hurried inquiry: "They're here! They're around!"

"Who's here?"

"The grain burners; don't you know!"

"But where is my brother—where is George?"

"Oh," replied the man, "he is pursuing one of them—he's down there."

The moon was just about its first quarter and was sinking over behind the adjacent mountains, but still gave out sufficient light to afford an indistinct view of surrounding objects. It was a mellow, warm evening, and a thousand flies, bats and whippoorwills buzzed and sang around. Long shadows fell upon the ground and seemed in their great length and intensity to add a hundred fold to the already lonely and weird view surrounding. It was a still, dead scene that presented itself as Mrs. Newton, clad in her ghost-like garb of white, stepped out of her door with her hand raised over her eyes to peer along the lines of the shadows down to where her brother was. She had scarcely turned her back when—bang! crash!—thundering came the report of a gun in her immediate proximity, and she felt the hot leaden messengers tearing through her vitals.

The entire load of buckshot from one barrel of the gun had been emptied into her breast.

"My God what—what is this? I am shot! You have murdered me. You have murdered George and now you have murdered me. You have shot me to the heart. What does it mean?"

The badly wounded woman did not fall, but staggered to the door and continued to support herself and got into the house. Meyers cried out as she disappeared:

"They have shot you, too; I will find them," and started off around the house. Seeing that his second victim still lived, he concluded to make sure of her and before she had entirely disappeared he raised the gun in the attempt to fire another shot. The weapon missed fire, and a second later the door was closed upon him, and the wounded woman was alone with her agony and her blood.

As she staggered into the house she took her right hand from her breast, where it had served to stanch the flow of blood, and caught at the door facing. For long years afterward, and probably such is still the case, the imprints of Mrs. Newton's hands, as she clenched the wood with the grip of death, remained to mark the scene of the tragedy. Wash and scrub as much as one might, the stain refused to come out.

A lone, long night it was that followed—full of intense bodily suffering, of great mental anxiety for her own welfare, full of distress for her brother, and with death staring her, a lone woman, square in the face. Fearful that a vital spot had been touched by the bullets, and considering it probable that her would-be murderer would return at any time, she must have been filled with fear and anxiety. She chanced to pass a large mirror in the room as she went in, and then for the first time fully appreciated the extent of her wound. Her one garment was even then a mass of blood. The life fluid was running out from the bullet holes in spurts. Little wonder that the poor woman at first became frightened and lay down upon her bed undetermined what to do.

"But I will not be a coward," she at last said to herself. "I will save myself if I can. I am dying. I must not die. If I die no one will know who has committed this horrible deed. I will at least live long enough to see that this murderer is brought to justice."

She had strength left to get up and procure towels to wrap herself and stop the blood flow and to get a bottle of liquor which she knew to be in the house, and finding that she did not bleed so freely when standing or sitting as when lying, she mustered all her strength and remained up the greater part of the night, thinking over the thousand horrible things that would naturally troop through the mind of any one situated as she was, even the strongest nerved of the stouter sex.

Added to her other horrors was the knowledge that there was no one nearer than a mile from her, except, perhaps, the man who had shot her, and his proximity was her greatest dread. She had already convinced herself that her brother had been killed; otherwise he would have come to her assistance. "And all was silent then, and I was alone through the whole wretched night," she said to Gen. Cook. But we shall not attempt to picture the agonies of those few lonely, dark hours. The reader may well imagine the experience of the woman, and if he cannot, no description would prove adequate.

At last the glad signs of day began to make their appearance. The gray dawn first peered in through the windows and cracks, and soon afterwards the long, slanting rays of the big summer sun were coursing their way across the floor of the dreary, bloody room, bringing with them messages of faint hope to the sufferer. How she must have prayed for the sight of a friendly face! By and by there came a rumbling sound as of an approaching vehicle. She went to the door. The road was some distance front the house, but there was a wagon passing by. Mrs. Newton cried out to the driver and waved her bloody hands in the air to him. Again and again she shouted at the top of her voice. But to no purpose.

She saw another hope pass away as the driver went on without turning his head, and gradually disappeared around a turn in the road, to be seen no more.

Once out of the house the wounded woman determined to obtain assistance of some sort. Her nearest neighbor was a Mr. Lyman, living down the road almost a mile distant. Thitherward Mrs. Newton bent her footsteps, dragging herself along with an energy and courage that would have done credit to a strong man.

At last this haven was reached, and, after taking a rest, Mrs. Newton's desire to be brought to Denver where she could have medical assistance and see the officers was granted. She was accordingly brought into town, and with her arrival we are brought back to the beginning of the narrative.

This is the story to which Gen. Cook had listened. It had been told with great incoherence, but he had kept the threads of it well together, and was relieved when the tragic tale had been concluded. Although the description of the murderer, who Cook believed to be the German farm hand, was not complete he had hope of finding further evidence at the ranch, and started out with the promise to the woman that he would overtake the murderer of her brother and her own would-be slayer. And he kept the promise to the letter.

ON THE TRACK OF THE ASSASSIN

Chief Cook decided immediately upon the apprehension of the murderer. Accordingly, immediately after heating the wounded woman's story, he started out to the ranch on the Platte, accompanied by Frank Smith. The only clue the officers had as to the identity of the murderer was his first name, which the woman had given them. After a thorough search about the house, the floor of which was covered with blood, the officers found the German's naturalization papers, and then for the first time learned his full name, which was Theodore Meyers. From these papers they learned further that he had been naturalized at Pueblo, Judge Bradford having signed the papers. From' this fact they concluded that he must have resided at Pueblo for some time, and that he must have friends there, and hence-decided that to be the point towards which he most probably would turn his face in his flight.

The officers were astonished to find that of all the nearest neighbors, only Lyman's family had the slightest cognizance of the dreadful tragedy. The people of the vicinity, some of whom were harvesting close by, when informed through the officers of what had happened, evinced their astonishment in utter speechlessness.

The officers instituted a diligent search of the entire premises. The bed in Mrs. Newton's room had absorbed pools of blood, and upon the door panels, staring at them in vivid outlines, were the impressions in blood of the woman's clutching hand. Near the wheat stack, where Bonacina and Meyers had lain, they found a collection of robes, and close by, under some sheaves of oats, and snugly wrapped in robes, was the body of the murdered man. From the position and nature of things, aid from the attending circumstances, it was concluded that Meyers must have sat upright in bed, reached forward and placed the muzzle of his piece against Bonacina's temple, and finished his victim while he lay asleep. The body was elsewhere perforated by two bullets.

It was also discovered that a horse was missing from the pasture, and that a saddle and bridle were gone. Hence it was concluded that

Meyers, who was nowhere to be found, had stolen these articles and disappeared on horseback.

With this theory fixed in his mind, Gen. Cook returned to Denver, and prepared to take the coach out that evening in pursuit of his man—for, be it known, the Rio Grande railroad was in those days a railroad on paper only, and travel to the southward was done either in private conveyances or on the stage coaches.

Gen. Cook went out alone, having confidence in his ability to cope with Meyers, should he overtake him, notwithstanding chat individual was a young man weighing two hundred pounds, and a desperado, as had been shown by his recent acts. He, of course, went well-armed, carrying a pair of revolvers and a derringer with him, for he felt that the chances were that the man would make a desperate fight if he should not succeed in getting the drop on him in making the arrest. He argued that the man who would shoot down a defenseless man and woman, as Meyers had done, must expect to be pursued; that he must expect to be severely dealt with if caught, and that for these reasons he would resist to the last if come up with by an officer.

The trip south was almost devoid of incident. The fugitive had a day's start of the officer, but the latter had not been long on the road before he began to pick up information as to the course the man had taken. Several persons had seen him riding along, and readily recognized him from the description which Cook furnished.

The tragedy had occurred on Thursday night, Meyers leaving on Friday morning and Gen. Cook following Saturday morning. Saturday night about 11 o'clock Cook ended his pursuit, and had the satisfaction of having his theory as to the course the murderer had taken verified by suddenly overtaking him at a place called Woodbury's, twenty-live miles north of Pueblo, where the fellow was waiting to take the same coach that Cook came in on, in pursuance of his journey. The capture was an easy one, although Cook had prepared for a death struggle, which might have ensued if Meyers had not been "caught napping." Previous to leaving he had telegraphed to parties at Colorado City and Pueblo to be on the alert for the escaping murderer. It was known that Meyers had chosen that route. The officer in question felt virtually assured of being able to overtake his man. Meyers had stopped at Woodbury's, and was awaiting the arrival of the coach from Denver. He was discovered to be partially intoxicated. News of the murder had preceded him; he was immediately suspected; and when he retired, to sleep until the arrival of the coach, the caps were removed from his shotgun and he was dispossessed of his pistol. The coach brought the sheriff, and the murderer was awakened by the officer who was standing over him with a revolver, and to find himself a prisoner, instead of a passenger to Pueblo.

The accommodations at Woodbury's were insufficient, and there was also some fear that if the prisoner should be allowed to remain there he might be lynched, as the story of his crime had gotten out. Hence Cook decided to go on to Pueblo and to take his prisoner with him, with the intention of starting on his return the next morning. Putting this plan into execution, Meyers was tied with ropes and lifted into the coach, the officer carrying a lighted candle that he might keep a close watch upon his prisoner. They had as fellow travelers a lady and a gentleman, and it may be easily imagined that the woman did not enjoy the prospect of her ride. Her fears were, however, assuaged by the assurance of Gen Cook that there was no danger, an assurance to which his firm bearing added great weight with her.

Once in the coach, but not before, Meyers demanded to know why he had been arrested. When told of the charge that was made against him he at first denied it but asked where Cook had gotten the information.

"From the woman you tried to kill at the time you killed Bonacina."

"The woman! Ain't she dead?"

"No, sir."

"Well, it's not my fault if she isn't. She would have been, though, if my plans had not miscarried."

"What were your plans?"

"Why, to fire both barrels of the shotgun into her at once. That would have stopped her blabbing tongue. But one of them missed fire."

After this, Meyers, without displaying the least compunction of conscience, told the entire story of The murder, claiming that he And Bonacina had quarreled, and that after killing the man he had been so excited that he did not know what he was doing, and hence had made an effort to finish Mrs. Newton as well.

It was after daylight when Pueblo was reached, and the return stage was soon ready to start for Denver. Cook had already been two nights without rest, devoting the first to searching for clues and the second to the journey and the arrest of Meyers. He was already pretty well worn out, but he did not have time to rest. One more day and night of hard work was before him. There was but one additional passenger on the coach, Capt. H. L. Thayer. During the night, Cook rode with his derringer in his hand and sat on his other pistols that he might have them ready for use at a moment's notice. He had been so long without sleep that he feared that he might drop into a nap at any time, when he could expect nothing from his prisoner less than an effort to get away and a probable attack upon himself. But the journey was devoid of more than ordinary interest, and Meyers was early Monday morning locked up in the Arapahoe county jail to await his trial. The capture was speedily and well executed, for which Gen. Cook was generally complimented.

ALL TO NO AVAIL

Mrs. Newton rapidly recovered from her wounds, much to the astonishment of her physicians and of herself, and by the time that the trial of Meyers for the murder of her brother came on she was entirely well. Meyers was indicted for murder by the grand jury which sat subsequent to his arrest, and on the 5th, 6th and 7th of February. 1872, he stood his first trial. The jury were out about three hours, when they returned a verdict that the prisoner was guilty of murder and that the killing was premeditated. A motion was at once made for a new trial, and it was granted by Judge Wells, before whom he had been tried. The second trial was set for the April term, 1872 but a continuance was granted on account of the absence of important witnesses. The case came up for second trial on Monday, October 21, 1872, and on Wednesday, October 23, a verdict of murder in the first degree was returned. In all respects the trial was a fair one and it was conducted with marked ability on both sides.

On the 30th of December, 1872, Meyers was brought into court, before Judge Wells, for sentence. When asked by the court whether he had anything to say why sentence of death should not be passed upon him, he replied that he had not, and the court then delivered the sentence, which was that Meyers should be hanged on the 24th day of January succeeding. The scene in the court room when the sentence was pronounced was very affecting, the judge and members of the bar who were present betraying visible signs of agitation. But Meyers preserved the same air of indifference which had been so frequently remarked during the progress of his two trials. Although his appearance was haggard, and his pale countenance and emaciated frame showed signs of internal suffering, yet he kept up a brave front and appeared to be undaunted by the terrible doom which stared him in the face.

Every effort was made by the counsel and friends of the man, of whom, considering the heinous nature of his crime, he developed a surprising number, to obtain a writ of error from the supreme court, but all failed; and then the friends turned their attention to the territorial executive. Gov. McCook was at that time governor of

Colorado, but was absent, and Gen. Frank Hall, being territorial secretary, was acting as governor. Upon him, therefore, devolved the responsibility of deciding upon the question of immediate death or prolonged life for Theodore Meyers. The most touching overtures were made to him, but he remained as firm as a granite wall, saying that the courts had passed upon the matter, and that he could not interpose except upon the recommendation of Judge Wells, who refused to take any action in the matter.

Thus the awful day approached, and the murderer's fate drew nearer and nearer to him. At last the day before that set for the execution arrived. Meyers proved equal to every emergency. During his stay in jail he maintained a stolid indifference as to his fate. He chatted pleasantly with all who came to visit him in his unfortunate condition, and rested soundly and ate his meals regularly. Beyond this he amused himself as best he could reading and smoking. Throughout the day preceding the hanging he did not change in his demeanor. No burden appeared to rest upon his soul he passively regretted the deed, when reminded of its great enormity, but it seemed to him that it would be the passport to a better world, which he expected soon to reach. He calmly smoked a cigar and read his German prayer book. Now and then he would speak to a few persons who were allowed to approach his cell. He conversed freely on the circumstances attending the crime, and then referring to the close approach of death, said: "I have made my peace with my Maker, and I die happy in the Catholic faith, feeling that I will soon be in heaven." Being questioned as to whether he did not feel the pangs of remorse, he said: "Oh, yes, a little; but then there is no use crying over spilt milk—the thing is to be, and it can't be helped. I've made up my mind to it, and am satisfied." To a visitor who was moved to tears, he said: "Don't feel bad about it, it cannot be helped; I have no fear of the gallows; there is a better world ahead, and I think I'll reach it." To Sheriff Cook he said: "I will go to the gallows as you want me to; there's no use, though, getting a wagon, for I would just as leave walk as ride."

During the evening previous to the execution, Meyers made a confession to Gen. Cook which supplied many details theretofore lacking to make the story complete. He stated that he had been born in Baden, Germany, in 1815; that he had come to America with his mother and two sisters in 1859; going to the war in 1861, and arriving in Pueblo, Colo., in 1867. As to the events which occurred on the night of the murder and those preceding and following, he said:

"On Sunday, the 6th of August, Bonacina went to Denver after Mrs. Newton, and she came back that evening. As he went to town he asked me to lend him $25, telling me he would return it when he returned. I loaned him the $25. When he asked me for the money he inquired if I had plenty of ammunition for the shotgun, rifle and revolver. I told him I had some ammunition, and to suit himself about getting more. Tie brought back some caps, and, I think, powder. Before he went to town he loaded his rifle with some buckshot I had, and, I think, his revolver, also, with the same. He said he expected the neighbors would come around some night and burn the stacks, and he would shoot the first son of a bitch that came near there after dark. When Mrs. Newton came back from Denver, she told Bonacina that she would give a suit of clothes worth $100 to the one who would kill the first man who came and attempted to burn the grain. She asked Bonacina at the same time if he knew where her derringer was, and he said it was in the trunk. I did not like to stay there any longer, as he was a man who swore, and I did not like his ways. A couple of days before this we had a quarrel over his treatment of horses, while loading grain, but no blows were passed. Between 8 and 9 o'clock on Thursday night, August 10. Bonacina told me to go out to the stacks, or the men might come while we were there in the house. We quit playing cards, and I went out there. In about fifteen minutes he came out to where I was. We made our beds under the stacks then, and I asked him for the $25 I had let him have on the preceding Sunday; also told him I did not want to work for him any longer he asked my reasons for leaving, but I told him I did not want to tell him he then told me he didn't want me to leave until the grain was threshed and other work done. About an hour after we went to the stacks I told him again I wanted the money, as I desired to leave the next day. Bonacina said: "You damned lousy son of a bitch, I won't pay it, but I'll pay you

210

now." At the same time he reached over towards his weapon, the rifle lying by his side and his revolver under his head. I then drew my pistol, which was lying by my side loose, and shot him, or shot at him, and he fell back saying something I could not understand. I then shot at him again with my revolver; did not shoot the shotgun, which was under my head. Bonacina was about six feet from me when I shot. I am not positive where either bullet hit him. I was excited, and shot the second time because I thought he was not dead. I did not know what I was doing.

"I took my shotgun and went to the house, and called Mrs. Newton by the name of Belle. I went there with the determination of killing her, as I was afraid she would give the alarm, and cause my capture before I could get away. She was at the window at first, and upon my calling came outside the door.

I told her, 'they were around,' meaning the men who had attempted to burn the stack. She asked: 'Where are they?' I said: 'They are around, and George (Bonacina) is running after them.' My shotgun was cocked and at a make-ready position.

I was about fifteen feet from her at the time. I pulled the trigger and fired, and she said 'Oh!' and went back into the house. I then went to the barn, back of the house, and remained there about ten minutes, doing nothing, but very much frightened. Afterwards I walked back to the front window of the house, and heard Mrs. Newton walking inside. I could see her moving in there as there was a light in the room. Then I went back to the stack and rolled Bonacina up in the buffalo robes and threw his rifle into the straw. I think the rifle was full cocked, but cannot positively state. I then moved my bed to a diagonal position against his, and took sheaves of oats and covered his body. Then I went to bed and slept only a little that night. After daybreak I heard what I thought was a wagon passing, and at the same time I saw Mrs. Newton come out of the house. She walked to the bridge before she cried to the man to stop. He did not stop. She kept on, and looked towards the stack, and went towards Lyman's. When she got away I went down into the brush and went up to the top of the hill. I did not know what I was doing. I remained there a short time, when I saw Lyman coming towards the place with a span of horses and no wagon. He went first into the barn, and then to the stacks, hitched up Mrs. Newton's wagon and drove back home. I then went back to Mrs. Newton's house, got something to eat, and took a bottle of whisky. Then I went down into a field the other side of Lyman's to get a horse, and got the horse, took him to the house, saddled him and started south. This was about 9 o'clock. I had a shotgun, a revolver, some whisky and a loaf of bread. I struck the road and went over the Divide.

"I was so excited I did not know what I was doing. I thought at first I would go to Cañon City and then into the mountains. On second thought I concluded to go to Pueblo. Had no thought of being captured, but if anybody had attempted to take me prisoner I should have fought. I traveled the day I left the ranch to a point about two miles south of Sloan's mill; the next day I continued the journey and got to Woodbury's, when I was captured that night. While at the foot of the Divide I sold the horse to Mr. Wilson for $75, and continued to Woodbury's afoot, if I had retained my senses and not drunk any liquor, I wouldn't have been captured so easily."

This confession of the condemned man was delivered in a straightforward and plain manner. During its delivery Meyers lighted fresh cigars occasionally and assumed a pleasing expression, now and then interlarding the recital with quiet and dry jokes. Soon afterwards Judge Harrison, of his counsel, was admitted, and the prisoner gave way, the only time at which he manifested any great concern. This interview was truly affecting, and was the occasion of a copious shedding of tears. Meyers spoke feelingly, even pathetically, of his aged mother and his noble sisters, and handed the judge a lock of hair which he desired should be enclosed to them, accompanying a message of love to all.

The next morning, a little before the fatal hour, Sheriff Cook, accompanied by the officers under him, and one or two friends, stepped to the door of the prisoner's cell. He arose from his mattress, extended his hand, and assured him that he felt comfortable and resigned.

Sheriff Cook then spoke as follows:

"Mr. Meyers, by the law, the painful duty of carrying into execution the sentence of the court passed upon you is imposed upon me. That sentence is in the following document, which I will read."

The sheriff then read the death warrant to the doomed man.

The procession started from the jail, then on Larimer street near the Cherry creek bridge, at precisely 2 o'clock. The prisoner, before leaving the inside, bade the remaining inmates an affectionate and touching farewell, and then stepped firmly upon the sidewalk, leaving tearful eyes and aching hearts behind. He was dressed in a suit of black, given him by a philanthropic citizen, and his feet free from the chafing shackles. He entered a carriage—Sheriff Cook and Deputy Smith in advance, then the prisoner, and in the rear the two clergymen, Fathers Robinson and Borg. The carriage moved toward the scaffold, near the mouth of Cherry creek, on the West Side, followed by the Denver Scouts on foot. In the neighborhood there was, of course, considerable excitement. Men and boys, and even women, lined the sidewalks and clambered to observation points. The upper windows and roofs of many of the buildings were crowded with spectators.

The carriage containing the prisoner, together with the officers and ministers, was driven to the foot of the scaffold. The prisoner walked firmly on to the platform, placed himself beneath the rope, and facing to the east, the officers and ministers standing around him. One of the fathers offered up a fervent prayer, though in a voice scarcely audible to the crowd, in which he implored God to give the dying man strength to pass through the trying ordeal, and to receive his soul as it escaped into the shadow of death,

Meyers met his doom with an exhibition of nerve the most extraordinary. Once only, and then for but a moment, did he change countenance. The place had no terrors for him. Upon being asked by the sheriff if he desired to say anything, he replied, seeming to address the crowd:

"Farewell, men! I'm going to another world!"

The noose had been adjusted. The black cap was pulled down over his eyes. Almost before any of the lookers-on were aware of it the fatal spring had been touched, and the body of Meyers was dangling in the air, and human justice, so far as he was concerned, was satisfied. The body had dropped about four feet. There were a few convulsive twitches, the body spun around five or six times, and all was still. The trap was sprung at twenty minutes past 2 o'clock. Four minutes after the pulse stood at lid; five minutes after it had been reduced to 72, and in six minutes life was extinct, as pronounced by Misters Manx and Heimbarger. The body was allowed to hang thirty minutes, and was then taken down and placed in the coffin, and taken to the city cemetery for interment, alongside of Duggan, Franklin and Griswold.

Mrs. Newton soon afterwards left Denver completely restored to health. It was announced at the time of her leaving that she had been discovered to be one of the heirs to the Stewart estate in England, and that she had inherited a fortune of £60,000 sterling. The trial exculpated her husband, Mr. Freidenthal, from all blame, and also went far towards establishing the fact that Bonacina was the woman's brother, as was claimed.

A HALF-MILLION-DOLLAR ROBBER

Although as a rule Gen. Cook's experience with criminals has been with the class who kill, he has also had a great deal to do with burglars and thieves, and others of the less demonstrative classes. One of the most notable cases of this latter class with which he has been identified was that of James Saeger, who was engaged in the robbery of a safe in Pennsylvania in 1868, from which half a million dollars' worth of greenbacks were taken [nearly $8.5 million in 2015]. The loser by the robbery was an old German named Bennehoff, who resided at Petroleum Centre, in Venango county, Pa., and whose wealth had been accumulated with rapidity through the magic instrumentality of petroleum. Be had, previous to the discoveries of oil in the Keystone state, lived there a quiet and frugal life, residing in a plain country house with his family around him. When his good fortune came upon him he did not change his mode of life, but continued in the same house, the only innovation being the addition of a small iron safe, which was deposited in a hallway in the dueling. This piece of furniture was, compared to others of its kind, a fragile thing, but old Bennehoff considered it a secure depository for his fast accumulating wealth he grew rich with wonderful rapidity, as those were the days of the coal ml boom. His wells were numerous and apparently inexhaustible, and the petroleum was worth a great deal more then than it ever has been since. He was in the habit of carrying his money home loose in his pockets every evening and pitching it carelessly into his little iron safe, going about his business feeling assured that his treasure was secure.

Naturally enough the facts of his great wealth and his careless disposition of it began to be noised abroad, and the cupidity of some of his neighbors became sorely tempted. Among these was James Saeger, who lived at Saegerstown, near Meadville, and no great distance from Venango. Up to this time Saeger had borne an enviable reputation. He was a member of an old and well-known family, in whose honor the town at which he resided was named. He was at that time a man of middle life, of splendid personal appearance, had long been engaged in mercantile pursuits and was the head of an interesting family. Yet the temptation of Bennehoff's weak safe was too much for him. It outweighed all considerations of good name and of family ties. He did not, of course, undertake the robbery alone, but was assisted by four other men of his locality, all of whom masked and boldly entered the house of Bennehoff while the family were at supper, and at the muzzle of their pistols compelled Bennehoff to deliver up the key to one of his safes, in which he kept an enormous sum of money. This was done, and the robbers secured their booty, over half a million dollars in United States notes, which they emptied into a pillow case and made good their escape. Two of the robbers were afterwards arrested and convicted, one getting seven and the other fifteen years in the Pennsylvania state prison. Two others have never been heard from, while the fifth, Saeger, has been a fugitive from justice ever since, followed by detectives nearly into every corner of the world, until his arrest in Denver, since which time, for reasons which will appear, he has been let alone. It appears that after the robbery the money was secreted for two days, it being the understanding amongst the robbers that they w*ere to meet at a specified time and "whack up."

Once entered upon his downward course, Saeger moved with great celerity. He even neglected to observe the regulations which have led the world to adopt the general conclusion that there is honor among thieves, but before the time for the meeting of the robbers and their "divvy" had come around, Saeger stole the whole amount from the hiding place and jumped the country, leaving his companions with no money and the guilt of being parties to the burglary, and also deserting his family. It was one of the most remarkable cases on record, and, at the time, created much excitement amongst the people of that section, and was heralded through the press of the land.

Old Bennehoff was almost wild when he came to fully realize his loss. He was still wealthy, notwithstanding $500,000 had been stolen from him, and he announced his determination to capture the thieves at any cost, ne offered first a reward of $5,000 then of $10,000, then $25,000; then capped the climax by offering $100,000 for the taking of Saeger, when it was discovered that he had all the lost money and that he seemed in a way to effectually evade the officers, unless Bennehoff should make it an object to them to search "the world over for him," as he stated it to be his desire that they should do.

As a consequence, detectives flocked to the humble home of this rich man to obtain clues for the purpose of working up the case. They came from all sections of the Union—from New York, Chicago, Philadelphia, Pittsburg and numerous other places. In fact, almost the entire detective skill of the Union was concentrated upon the case. They searched the country for their man in its every nook and cranny. Doubtless as much money was spent in the aggregate in making the search as was offered in the reward.

Among those who demoted several months' time to the case was Capt. Hage, chief of the detective force of Pittsburg, who, after visiting Venango and taking elaborate notes, conceived the theory that Saeger had come to Colorado soon after the robbery, and he came to Denver himself, crossing the plains on a stage coach, making this city his headquarters while he scoured the country round about. But his efforts were of no avail. After spending much time and considerable money he returned to Pittsburg. During his stay here Capt. Hage conferred frequently with Chief Cook, of the Rocky Mountain Association, who cooperated with him. He furnished the Denver detective with complete information as to the robbery, and also left a description of Saeger.

Bennehoff never gave any notice of having withdrawn the reward, and Cook determined to keep a lookout for the bold robber, and did so for years. At last, after six years of waiting, his patience was rewarded by getting a view of the evasive and long-sought for safe blower.

THE STORY OF HIS WANDERINGS

Gen. Cook had learned that Mr. Gus Potter and his wife, who then, as they do now, kept a restaurant on Blake street, had known Saeger personally before coming to Colorado. He naturally concluded that if Saeger should come to Denver he would be found at Potters place. Hence he decided to keep an eye on this establishment. One day, in passing the Potter place, he saw a man walk out—tall, dark-haired, dark-complexioned and fine-looking, answering, in fact, the description of Saeger to the letter. He allowed the stranger to pass on unmolested, but when he had disappeared sought Mr. Potter, and to his great delight learned that his eyes had not deceived him and that his inference had been correct. Cook virtually had his man and was in a fair way to secure a prize for which his entire profession had "been contending.

Gen. Cook first caught sight of his man June 15, 1874, and he soon learned that this was the second visit which Saeger had paid to Potter s place, having come in first on the day preceding. Mr. Potter told the detective all he knew about Saeger, who had adopted the alias of Thomas L. Magee, and related the fellows story as he had received it. Saeger had stated that he had come to Denver with a large herd of cattle and a force of thirty herders. The cattle were halted about eight miles distant from Denver, up Cherry creek, and Magee came to town to transact some business. White here he stepped into Potter's restaurant to get some oysters. He had no idea that-he was anywhere near people who knew Mm, not being acquainted with the locality.

While partaking of his meal, Mrs. Potter, happening to pass through tire dining room, heard Magee speak, and she at once noticed a familiar tone in his voice. Taking a keen look at the man she at once discovered that it was James Saeger whom she had not seem for years, or since she was a little girl, but whose features had made such am impression upon her memory as to remain there indelible. Mrs. Potter accosted him with "How do you do. Mr. Saeger?" whereupon he turned instantly, as though a voice had called him from another land, and answered her. So completely overcome was he—not knowing at first his interrogator—that he confessed his identity and engaged in conversation. Mr. Potter and his wife and Saeger then spent several hours together in conversation. He was also recognized at once by Mr. Potter, when called in for he had many years ago, adopted Potter as his son in Saegerstown. He told Potter that he was now in the Texas cattle trade, and was the owner at between 30,000 and 40,000 head [of cattle] in that state; also, that he had several herds on the road between Texas and Colorado. He returned to his herd near the city that night, and came to town again the next day in the meantime informing Potter that he desired to make him his attorney for the transfer of a large quantity of property. It was on the occasion of this second visit that Detective Cook had discovered his man. Potter knew all he particulars of the Bennehoff robbery, and Saeger's complicity in the affair, but had been ignorant of his whereabouts until the strange incident occurred which brought the fugitive into his restaurant tor a dish of oysters. Knowing that Detective Cock had been advised, several years before, of the occurrence, and had a fall description of the man and as Saeger had played a dirty trick on his (Potter's) uncle in Saegerstown by which that relative had to suffer the penalty of the lawn Potter made no effort to screen the man, and entered into a plan to assist in the capture of him. He induced his brother, Charles Potter, to go out to Saeger's camp, up Cherry creek, and get Saeger to come into town on the Sunday following. This was done because there was danger of Saeger's getting wind of the operations of the detectives, and his giving or attempting to give them the slip. Potter went to the camp, when Jaeger was found in a genial mood. He partook freely of some good spirits Totter had along, and finally, when night was well advanced, and there was supposed to be little danger of detection, he himself suggested coming to Denver, and together the couple came in. They were met promptly upon their arrival by Mr. Cook, who approached the fugitive on the street, and without any ado made him a prisoner. The fellow was given no opportunity to make any defense, and, seeing that he had at last been caught in a trap from which he could not, at any rate not then, extricate himself, he surrendered with good grace and went quietly to jail.

In conversation with Cook, Potter and others, after his arrest, Saeger freely admitted that he was the identical Bennehoff robber, but averred that had he been armed the officer would never have taken him. It was the first time, he said, that he had ever been taken unawares, although he had been followed and watched for six years. He also related somewhat of his life since the time of the robbery. After leaving Saegerstown with the money—which he had in an old clothes bag—he engaged as a coal heaver on a steamer on the Ohio river. The first, stopping place was Pittsburg, after which he went to New Orleans, becoming a gambler further down the Mississippi. From New Orleans he passed over to Cuba. He did not stay there long, but went to Mexico, from which country he went to Texas. In short, he had been a wanderer over the face of the earth, fleeing constantly from the detectives who he knew were hounding him down, and resorting to every possible means of disguising himself. In Texas he found himself comparatively safe, and if he had been content to remain there, buried away off on the Llano Estacado, as he was, he might have remained there in safety. He had lost all his money when he went to Texas, for he had gambled constantly and had led a fast life, and had engaged there as a cowboy, but he was too shrewd to disclose this fact in this interview. He preferred to have it believed that he was still very wealthy, and the sequel shows that he adopted the wise course in this respect. Saeger stated further in the conversation that he had been cornered several times before, but managed to get away through the free use of money. The money, or the bulk of it, which was stolen, he said was placed where it never could he touched. Saeger told Potter that he had always intended to repay Bennehoff in full, trusting to speculations to realize money enough to double his pile, bur that he had had reverses and lost a good deal.

Saeger was also called upon at the jail by a Texas detective, who chanced at the time to be in Denver, and who knew all the particulars in this case, having been retained to capture Saeger immediately after the robbery. He was at the Bennehoff house and took notes of all the circumstances, and searched for Saeger eight months without so much as getting a "pointer" as to his whereabouts, and finally gave up the chase. The gentleman had a talk with the prisoner, who confessed to him that he was the man they had been looking for. The Texas detective, although perhaps a slight bit jealous, was loud in his praise of his Rocky Mountain brother. For that matter, everybody congratulated and praised Gen. Cook for the good work which he had done. The *Rocky Mountain News* said:

> "Our detective force has achieved a signal victory in this capture. We congratulate Mr. Cook on his good luck in capturing the robber. It is a great deal better for people to remain honest, or, if they wall commit crimes, to keep away from the country where Dave Cook officiates. His eagle eye and insinuating manner will spot and fool the keenest of thieves."

But what of the $100,000? the reader will be anxious to know. The result shows how ungrateful some people can be, and how great the risk that defectives take in hunting down and arresting wrong-doers. Bennehoff was notified of the arrest soon after it was made, and he sent his son, in company with an officer, forthwith, to secure the prisoner and whatever of valuables he might have retained. When the son came he offered Gen. Cook the paltry sum of $200 for his services. The offer was spurned, and negotiations as to the reward were then broken off with the young man, though suit was begun to recover the entire sum offered. But before papers could be served, Bennehoff had stolen out of tow n. So that part of the transaction ended. Having been treated so shabbily, Cook left Bennehoff to conduct his business with Saeger as best he could. The young man hurried his work through, fearing the suit and detention and started back to Pennsylvania with notes from Saeger for part of the money which had been stolen, and which were secured by mortgage upon Saeger's herds of cattle—which, by the way, it was discovered he did not own—not a single Texas steer. Indeed, it was ascertained by Gen. Cook soon afterwards, that Saeger had merely attached himself to a Texas drove and had come to Colorado as a herder he had been driven out of Texas for his misdoings there. While in that state, and sailing under an alias, he had been chosen as an inspector of cattle at the Red River crossing, and as such used his official position to aid a few accomplices, with whom he had stolen 1,400 head of cattle. This fact became known before the stock was driven off, and Saeger only escaped lynching by hasty flight. This circumstance brought him to Colorado.

Gen. C. W. Wright was Saeger's lawyer, and he was also busy at this time, and before the town knew it, Saeger had been released on a writ of habeas corpus, and was far away on a horse provided for his escape.

So far as is known, the Pennsylvania safe blower is still at liberty, if he is not dead, simply because a miserly old man was unwilling to pay a detective for his work. But the capture will go down to the future as one of the neatest ever made by an officer in the West.

A UTAH MURDERER'S CAPTURE

Mr. T. Jeff Carr, for a long time city marshal of Cheyenne [Wyoming], and for many years past a resident of that city, has long been one of the most vigilant as well as one of the most successful members of the Rocky Mountain Detective Association, ever working in perfect harmony with Gen. Cook.

On the 24th of July, 1881, Mr. Carr made an arrest in Cheyenne which resulted in the development of the facts in an unprovoked and heartless murder, which had previously occurred in Utah. The man arrested was one Fred Welcome, a young man, but, notwithstanding his age, thoroughly hardened in crime. He had come to Cheyenne about the 15th or 16th of July of the year above mentioned, and had been residing in that city, leading a pretty gay life, for a week, when Mr. Carr received a telegram describing the man and offering a large reward for his capture on the charge of murdering J. F. Turner, near Park City, Utah, early in the same month. On a train which came in from the west on the day of the arrest was J. W. Turner, father of the dead man and sheriff of Utah county, Utah, and William Allison, sheriff of Summit county, Utah, who were tracking the murderer, and from them and others afterwards the details of the crime were learned.

It appears that the elder Turner, who resided with his family at Provo, Utah, had been sheriff of his county for some time past, and that his son had frequently been associated with him in bringing the guilty to justice, and among others who had been brought to punishment through his instrumentality was this Fred Welcome, a young fellow who lived about town and who was never known for any good that he had done to anyone. On the contrary, he was considered as a loafer and beat, and was frequently arrested for crimes of greater or less magnitude, and being arrested, was placed in jail. He seems to have held young Turner to blame especially for one term of his imprisonment, believing that Turner, who was cognizant of his crime, had informed upon him. He laid this up as a grudge against the young man, and threatened vengeance upon him for the act, saying to one of his fellow prisoners while incarcerated in

223

the jail: "By G—d, I'll kill him if it is ten years from now! I'll follow him to his grave."

But nothing was thought of this threat and others like it at the time they were made. They were considered as merely the vaporings of an idle mind. However, they were brought to mind soon afterwards in connection with the horrible suspicion that young Turner had been murdered after leaving home in company with Welcome, who had been released from jail.

As soon as he was out of prison, Welcome set himself to work to prevail upon the son of his jailer to go with him to the mining districts near Park City, saying that he had a claim there which was rich, and agreeing to give half of it to Turner on condition that the latter would go along and take two teams and wagons. The proposition was at first declined, but afterwards, upon the urgent and repeated solicitation of Welcome and the constant reiteration of his assertion as to the value of the mine, Turner consented to go, and all being in readiness they started out about the middle of June. Turner had two good wagons and two pairs of animals quite tempting to the eye of the lover of horseflesh. The wagons were also well laden with food for both man and beast, there being about a thousand pounds of barley in one of the wagons.

The teamsters camped near Park City for several days, but do not appear to have begun work immediately, and while there were joined by another party, a man named Emerson, who seems to have been a pal and an accomplice of Welcome's. Together the three lived for a while, sleeping in a tent and making frequent excursions to the city together. Whether there were any quarrels among them does not appear, except upon the testimony of Welcome himself, who says there was a quarrel on the night of the murder, but his story is probably not good testimony in the connection.

The murder occurred on the evening of the 3d of July, 1880, but was not suspected for some days afterwards, as no one paid close attention to the movements of the teamsters or to their coming or going. There had been no witnesses to the crime to tell the story, and the murderers were allowed to move on unmolested and unsuspected. The first suspicion of the crime was formed by the

family of young Turner, who, not hearing from the son for several days, began to fear that some evil had befallen -him.

Being then told for the first lime of the threats which Welcome had made that he would kill the young man, they became exceedingly anxious for tidings from the son, and began to set inquiries on foot. They heard nothing until one day a telegram came to them from Green River, Wyo. some twelve days after the murder, from a friend, informing them that a team which had once belonged to the Turners had been sold at that place. "My boy has been killed!" exclaimed Mr. Turner with sudden conviction, and the young man's mother fell down in a swoon upon receiving what she too considered positive evidence that her boy had been slain by a murderer.

A day or two afterwards the news of the finding of the body of young Turner was taken to the already heartbroken parents. A mountain man named Leonard Phillips, living in Echo cañon, a stupendous and lonely gorge in the Wasatch range of mountains, familiar to all travelers over the Union Pacific railroad, had gone out one day to look up the outcropping of a quartz vein of whose existence he knew, and noticing a peculiar odor, determined to investigate the cause of it. The stench was so strong that he did not have to look a great while until he came upon a pile of stones thrown in between large rocks.

Looking down upon this mass of rock, Mr. Phillips beheld the limb of a human being protruding from the mass—quite a different outcropping from that which he had gone out to seek. He was naturally horrified at the discovery which he made, but after taking time to collect his thoughts, determined to investigate further. He soon succeeded in bringing the body to daylight, and was astonished at finding that, although there had been considerable decay, he was able to recognize the remains as those of J. F. Turner, whom he had known.

The fact of the ghastly find being made known to Mr. Turner, senior, he ordered the body sent to Provo, and there gave it a decent burial.

The sad rites being performed over the boy's grave, Mr. Turner determined to hunt the murderer down. "I will follow him to the end of the earth but what I will find him," he said. "The slayer of my boy shall not live a free man while I have life and means." He accordingly prevailed upon his brother sheriff, Mr. Allison, to go along with him, and together they started in search of the murderer. There was no doubt in the mind of either that Welcome was the man wanted, but it was not known until afterwards that Emerson had had any connection with the case. Gradually they became possessed of the facts, which they found sufficiently horrible to shock anyone not related to the murdered man, to say nothing of the sensation which must have been produced upon the father.

ARRESTED AND CONFRONTED

At Park City there were found witnesses who had seen the murderers on the evening of the tragedy, before and after its occurrence, and their conduct had been shameful in the extreme. Whether a quarrel was picked with Turner was not known, but the circumstances went to show that there had been no quarrel, but that the murderers had found their victim sitting, and had advanced upon him from his rear, striking him in the head with a heavy axe, the blow being of such force as to cleave the skull and produce instant death. Welcome asserted after his capture that the blow had been struck by Emerson, but all the circumstances went to show that Welcome himself had wielded the death-dealing weapon. The skull wound showed that the blow had been struck by a left-handed person, and Welcome was left-handed.

There were also several persons who had seen blood on his garments after the tragedy had occurred, as it had spurted upon him from his victim. His threats, too, were remembered. About 11 o'clock on the night of the killing, and after it had occurred, there were several who had seen Emerson and Welcome at a dance house where they seemed to be especially hilarious, drinking and dancing with the girls and making themselves especially agreeable to those whom they met. One man who was in the dance house at the time noticed blood on Welcome's shirt front and asked him what it meant. Welcome at first tried to hide the bloody apparently upon second thought, threw his vest open and showed the blood, and also pulled up his coat sleeve and showed blood on that saying as he did so:

"I hit a son of a bitch tonight, and I hit him hard, too. I not only hit him, but I pinched his windpipe for him."

Several others saw the blood and to them he made this same speech, but no one supposed that anything more than an ordinary fight had occurred, and none gave the matter a second thought.

The murderers remained about Park City for two days and three nights after committing the crime, mingling freely with the lower classes of people and having as before a gay time. They had laid the body of their dead companion in the wagon with the barley sacks, and, cold-blooded and merciless as they had been, had been afraid to stay at their camp during the night, and had gone to town each night to carouse and to sleep, when they could sleep. They appeared to be nonchalant, but they found, as all murderers do, of however hardened character, that the crime bore down upon them. It was a heavy weight. They tried to drown it in drink and in the gayeties of dance house merriment. But they failed signally.

The murderers concluded that they must get rid of the body and that then they would find peace of conscience. They determined to move on, taking the body as well as the property of the murdered boy with them, and to find some place to hide it from view thinking that in this case, as in some others, the object being out of sight would be out of mind. They journeyed on, however, selling some of the barley by the way, until they came to a lonely and secluded spot in Echo cañon, where they camped for the night, and where they lifted the body of their former companion from its resting place in the wagon from among the barley sacks, and as the darkness came on in the deep cañon, laid it to rest, leaving the crows and night hawks to sing the funeral dirge, and the moaning pines to offer up prayers for safe passage to the Great Beyond.

So the murderers were freed from their burden and they passed on over the country. But were they happy? And did they find that contentment of mind which they had hoped would come after getting rid of the corpse of their late friend? At Green River, Welcome said to a barkeeper whom he met there: "I cannot sleep well at night; I am afraid."

He then asked the barkeeper:

"Did you ever kill a man?" and added, "I never did." Then he stopped for a moment as if engaged in thought, and said: "Yes, I have; I have killed a young and innocent man in cold blood."

He seemed lost for a moment, and soon took his departure with a troubled countenance.

From the time the body was disposed of in the lonely spot in Echo cañon, the men pushed rapidly eastward, making an effort at every opportunity to dispose of their barley and their teams and wagons. They disposed of the grain at Evanston, and of the first team at Piedmont. Journeying on, they stopped for a few days at Green Diver, where the second team and wagon were sold. The articles were all offered at prices below their real values, and some suspicion was created. The murderers declared that they had owned the animals for four years; but they at last found a man who had known the team as belonging to Turner, and who had telegraphed him of the effort of a stranger to sell them.

This was the first clue which the father had of the son's murder. While he was coming to Green River, accompanied by his friend, Sheriff Allison, the two men, having at last disposed of the property, took their departure quietly, and no one seemed to know which way they had gone. The pursuers only reached the place to find that their game had flown, and to find them-selves arrived at the place with nothing to do, and with the prospect of starting back home without finding the object of their search. The old father's heart was almost broken. As a last resort they telegraphed to Detective Carr, Superintendent Cook's assistant at Cheyenne, on the 2nd of July, and succeeded in getting him interested in the case. He had no idea that the murderer was near him at the time of receiving the telegram, but he immediately set to work with his usual vigor and shrewdness to bring down his game. He did not have to wait long.

Mr. Carr soon learned that there was a young man in the city who answered the description given of the murderer of young Turner. A brief investigation convinced the officer time this was the man that was wanted, but the detective determined to "make haste slowly," and as he knew that the fellow could not dodge him, he decided to watch him awhile before taking him in; merely for the sake of entirely satisfying himself as to the correctness of his conclusions he found that the young man had been a guest at a leading hotel for a week past, and that he had been making himself generally agreeable, spending money freely and seeming to be in very easy circumstances. He was especially fond of buggy riding, and was a liberal patron of the livery stables. On the day that the telegram was received the young man went out for a drive, but, although he did not know that such was the case, he was closely shadowed by Carr.

The dispatch came just in time, for later in the day the murderer undertook to continue his journey eastward, going to the depot to take the train for Omaha he was followed to the platform by Detective Carr, who by this time had learned that the pursuing officers would arrive in Cheyenne on the same train which Welcome had intended to board.

The scene as arranged and enacted proved tragic in the extreme. As the old father and his friend Allison stepped off the train at one end of the smoking car, Welcome undertook to step on at the other end.

Carr had stood around carelessly up to this time, but as the young man started to the train he said, *sotto voce*, "No you don't," and walking up to the young man laid his heavy hand on his shoulder, causing the youth to look with something of an astonished air, and exclaim:

"What is it?"

"I am a detective."

"Oh, you are?"

"Yes, sir; come with me."

"What for?"

"For murder—for the murder of young Turner."

"So you've overtaken me. Well, by G—d, I suppose I'll have to go! I did it, and there is no use to kick. Where are you taking me?"

"To meet the father of the man you murdered."

At this suggestion the fellow trembled visibly, but went along. When he was brought face to face with old man Turner, the latter's face turned ashen pale, his teeth were set in a moment, and his hand was thrust into his hip pocket. A moment later and the sun's rays were gleaming along the barrel of a large revolver which the old man had pulled, and with which, in a second more, he would have laid his son's murderer low.

Mr. Carr, seeing the turn affairs were taking, stepped in to prevent further bloodshed.

Welcome was taciturn and sullen in the presence of the father of his victim, but being again alone with Carr, he said: "By God I done it, and I expect to swing for it. I killed Turner and sold his team, and have spent the money. I am guilty and I expect to swing; of course I do."

Before leaving for home with the prisoner, Mr. Turner said to a Cheyenne reporter, with whom he talked:

"I want you to distinctly understand that Mr. Carr of your place deserves all the credit of catching this rascal, and had it not been for him he would have slipped our fingers."

The reward in this case amounted to a round thousand. Once on board the train bound for Utah, Welcome became quite communicative. He had told Carr before leaving that he himself had killed young Turner, and that he had done so because he had a grudge against him, and because he wanted his property. Now he denied all connection with the murder, and said that the crime had been committed by Emerson, saying that Emerson and Turner had quarreled, and that Emerson killed Turner in the fight.

The trial took place at Salt Lake City, on the 18th day of February, 1881, and resulted in proving a clear ease against Welcome, who did not introduce a particle of rebutting testimony. The jury was out only a few minutes, when it brought in a verdict of guilty in the first degree. The sentence would necessarily have been death, had not Welcome's lawyers succeeded in getting his case before the supreme court, where it was remanded back for a new trial.

Emerson, Welcome's accomplice, was disposed of more summarily. He was captured near Green River, in August, 1880, and tried at the succeeding May term of the Salt Lake district court, and sentenced to the penitentiary for life, and he is now serving out his sentence.

CHOSE TO BE SHOT INSTEAD OF HANGED

The second trial of Welcome, or Hopt, as he declared his name to be, did not bring out any new evidence to materially affect the case, one way or the other, and the verdict was the same as in the former trial.

Again his attorneys carried the case through the territorial supreme court, and then on to the supreme court of the United States, securing another trial with the same result.

Still hoping to wear out the prosecution, and especially the unceasing efforts of Mr. Turner, the father of the murdered man, the attorneys for the fourth time invoked the aid of the supreme court and secured a fourth and last trial. Despite the cunning of his attorneys, and the sympathy of the powerful Mormon church, which he had in some manner secured, there could be but the one verdict, and that of willful and premeditated murder. Hopt heard the verdict with stoical indifference, and as the laws of the territory permitted a man to choose between shooting and hanging as the death penalty, Hopt chose to be shot, and Judge Zane set the time for his execution on Thursday, August 11, 1887, more than seven years after the commission of the awful crime.

Another and final appeal was made by his attorneys to have the United States supreme court set the verdict aside, but that patient tribunal finally refused to longer retard justice, and declined to interfere. Strong pressure was then brought upon Gov. West, but he, too, decided that the murderer had been given too many chances to escape the consequences of his crime already, and declined to interfere.

Finding that there was no alternative but death, Hopt gave up all hope, and as the date of the execution approached. Marshal Dyer began his preparations. A space was cleared within the prison walls, and a doth tent for the executioners, who were live in number, was set up.

Hopt's nerve staid with him to the last. He ate his meals regularly, and his sleep was apparently undisturbed by any apparitions of his victim. At 11 o'clock on the day of his execution he ordered his dinner, which: he ate with a relish, and then called for a cigar. It is doubtful whether any martyr ever met his doom with greater fortitude or more real stoicism than that which Fred Hopt exhibited in accepting the fate which the law dealt out to him. He faced Winchester rifles with a boldness and intrepidity that were remarkable, and while some fifty or sixty men who had been specially permitted to witness the execution stood aghast at the scene, he exhibited not the least evidence of excitement.

He sat on a cane-bottomed chair, posing as though he were looking into a camera instead of gazing down the muzzles of five death-dealing weapons. Four of the 45-70 Winchesters were loaded, the fifth carrying a blank cartridge, so that none of the executioners could lay the flattering unction to his soul that his gun carried the deadly missile. The names of the executioners were kept a profound secret. They were covered with black cambric to their ankles, holes being cut in their hoods to see out of.

They were sent to the firing tent at 12:30 o'clock, to which United States Deputy Marshals Pratt and Cannon had already carried the weapons. This tent, which was thirty-six feet from the victim's chair, was of canvas, all enclosed, with five three-inch square loopholes cut in the north side. The shooting took place in the northeast corner of the penitentiary yard, the other prisoners having all been locked in the dining room fifteen minutes prior to the time when Hopt was brought forth.

It was 12:30 o'clock when Hopt was told that everything was ready, and he marched deliberately from his cell to the spot where, seven minutes later, he paid the penalty of his crime, he was dressed in a suit of black diagonal clothes, his Prince Albert coat, low shoes, white shirt, white tie, and derby hat giving him a ministerial appearance. He walked unfalteringly beside Marshal Dyer, and on reaching the chair, said:

"Now, gentlemen, I have come here to face my fate. Had justice been done me at my first trial, I would not have been here today for this purpose. I have no ill will toward any man living, and now consign my soul to God."

A paper one and one-half inches square was pinned over the condemned man's heart, the good-byes were said, Marshal Dyer gave the order to fire, the guns clicked as though operated by one man, and in the twinkling of an eye Hopt was dead, two balls piercing his heart, and the other two passing through the body half an inch below that organ. There was a slight spasmodic action of the muscles of the throat, but not a muscle of the arms or legs twitched. Death was instantaneous. Father Kelly, the Catholic priest who had been with Hopt in his last hours, administered extreme unction. The body was prepared by the physicians, placed in a coffin, and taken to an undertaker's establishment in the city.

Sheriff Turner was not permitted to witness the execution of his son's murderer, but stood outside the walls and heard the shots fired which put an end to the wretch's existence.

Hopt made no confession. He was very guarded in all his utterances during his last hours, but he made no protestations of innocence, nor did he say aught implicating Jack Emerson, who was at least an accessory after the fact.

The execution of Frederick Hopt for the murder of John F. Turner, seven long years after the crime, rung down the curtain on a drama as replete with startling incidents as any to be found in the realms of fiction. It is certainly one of the *causes celebre* of the West, and its thrilling events find but few parallels in the annals of criminal judicature. The case was made interesting, not only by the fact that the crime was a dastardly one, but also because one of the officers who tracked the murderer was the father of his victim; not only by reason of the fact that that father on three or four occasions saved the villain from mob violence, nor yet, because of the patience with which that parent for seven long years waited to see justice meted out and the law vindicated, but it is interesting because it emphasizes the marvelous safeguards which the law throws around a prisoner in this country, and the maudlin sentimentality which a criminal can arouse, no matter how cold-blooded his crime may have been.

A TALE OF TWO CONTINENTS

During the latter part of October, 1877, Judge Foster, a judge in one of the districts of the United States courts in Kansas, was spending a few days in Colorado, enjoying the delightful autumn weather of this climate, when there came a sudden call upon him to go home to hear proceedings in an important railroad suit, in which the Kansas Pacific company was interested. It was a case demanding almost immediate attention, and distance must be annihilated in some way. The Kansas Pacific railroad was the connecting link between Denver and the point at which the judge's presence was wanted. He had hardly expressed his desire one evening to be in Lawrence, Kan., the next morning in time to open court, when an engine with a sleeping car attached was announced to be at his disposal. A few moments later and Judge Foster had seated himself in the car and the engineer was told to fly.

Just as the car wheels were beginning to revolve, an excited individual rushed unnoticed through the dark and caught the car as the rear end passed by him. Swinging himself from the ground to the seat of the rear platform he became a fellow traveler with Judge Foster on his lightning express, they being the only passengers. There was considerable difference between the two men, in social position, in official rank and all that makes man well-to-do and respected in the work. The man who had joined the judge was a thief, a bigamist, a strolling fiddler and now a fugitive from justice. A queer combination—the same fast train hurrying one individual off that he might mete out justice and another that he might evade justice.

The train rushed out of Denver into the prairie land beyond, and pushed on through the darkness towards the east at the rate of fifty miles an hour. Judge Foster lay back in his cozy apartments and went to sleep. His fellow passenger clung desperately to his hard board seat in the rear and busied himself in holding his place, while the train bounced junkety junk over the rail couplings. The subject of his reverie as he sat thus confined to his seat must have been a medley of women, of dance hall music, of police officers, of a lovely little home with wife and child down in the silvery San Juan, of a voyage and illicit courtship on the ocean, of wandering along the banks of foreign streams talking of home in the Booty mountains, while still he was far away in the Faderland. Whatever the reverie may have been, it was suddenly interrupted after it had had full sway for some five hours, by a heavy hand falling upon the shoulder of the fugitive.

"Who are you?" was demanded.

"My name is Bernheim."

"What are you doing here?"

"I am going east."

"How did you get on?"

"I jumped on."

"With whose permission?"

"With my own."

"Then you will have to get off."

"All right."

This is a portion of a conversation which our fugitive had with the brakeman of the little train. The party was nearing Wallace, Kan., where it was desired to stop, and the brakeman had come out to be at his post of service when the whistle of the locomotive should warn him that it was time to apply the brake. The shrill cry was heard just as the conversation was concluded, and the trainman turned to do his duty. In a few seconds the train had stopped perfectly still and the brakeman turned to the unwelcome passenger to renew his command to move off. Slut the fellow had anticipated him-and had jumped off as the train slackened and had disappeared, he thus hade adieu to Judge Foster and his fast train, the latter having been of all the service to him that it was possible to be, as he had cleared the limits of Colorado and felt that he had given the officers a slip which one scamp in ten thousand does not have the opportunity to give.

236

We, too, dismiss the judge and his whirling car and also for the present the fugitive from justice and take him up at another time of life. We still for the present stick to the Kansas Pacific road, however.

In the fall of 1876, a year previous to the occurrence above described, on an eastern-bound train, two Germans, a man and a woman, became acquainted. At first the acquaintance was commonplace, made up of formal courtesies, but when upon comparing notes the two travelers found that each was bound for the same country, Germany, and that that was the native land of each of them, and when later they became passengers on the same vessel across the ocean, the acquaintance assumed something of a romantic nature. To make it brief, they landed in the old world affianced. The lady's name was Miss Maggie Harencourt, of Denver, a cousin of Mr. Jacob Schuler, of the same place, and she was visiting Germany for her health. The man's name, as given the lady, was Sally Bernheim, a native of Dusseldorff, Germany, and as he represented to Miss Harencourt, a merchant from Lake City, Colo., on his way "to visit the scenes of his boyhood."

In Germany they saw much of each other, Bernheim urging the lady to become his wife, and she repeatedly refusing on account of her health. When he returned to America, which he did in the following spring, he obtained from his sweetheart a promise to marry him on her return to this country. She at the same time informed him of a legacy to which she had recently come into possession, the amount of which she did not disclose, but it was supposed to be something handsome.

A correspondence was opened between the two, which was kept up with regularity and fervor on both sides. The lady had proposed that the marriage take place upon her arrival in New York, Bernheim to go to that point from Colorado to meet her. Pleading the unnecessary expense and the demands of his business, the lover succeeded in gaining the consent of his fiancée to a marriage in Denver, to be consummated whenever Bernheim should learn from her of her arrival in the city. Miss Harencourt arrived October 20, 1877, and registered at the American house, and notified her waiting true love at Lake City of the fact of her presence. She remained at the hotel three days and then repaired to the residence of her cousin, Mr. Schuler, whom she told of her expected early marriage.

A few nights later the Denver and Bio Grande train from the south brought among its passengers Mr. Sally Bernheim, of Lake City, who took a room at the American. The next day he called upon his promised bride, and their meeting was most affectionate. A speedy marriage was urged by Bernheim and consented to by the lady.

In the course of the forenoon they took a walk about the city, and the confiding Miss Maggie told Bernheim that she had nine new $100 bills, with which she hoped to endow him, a small portion of the legacy to which she had lately come into possession. With a natural and becoming solicitude the groom expectant urged the impropriety of her carrying so large a sum of money with her, and suggested that she entrust the funds to-him, and that he would deposit the money in the Exchange Bank in her name and subject to her check. A thankful consent was given, and leaving the lady at her house, Bernheim went to the bank and deposited the $900—in his own name.

That afternoon at 3 o'clock the pair called at the residence of Bev. J. G. Leist, of the German Methodist church, and the twain were made one flesh. They, now Mr. and Mrs. Sally Bernheim, repaired at once to Brunell's boarding house, then a fashionable place, on Fourteenth street, where the best the house afforded was extended to them. and Sunday was passed in the delectability of the honeymoon. Monday forenoon a man giving his name as H. A. Thompson, who was introduced to Mrs. Bernheim by the husband as a friend from Garland, called on them at Brunell's, the bearer of a letter from Bernheim's partner at Lake City, which stated the necessity of purchasing a bill of groceries at Kansas City. The letter was written in a business-like manner and shown to the bride, who was forced to admit the necessity of a brief separation from her husband, for, of course, the expense and trouble of her accompanying him was not to be thought of. It was decided then than Bernheim was to go East to purchase goods.

For some reason this plan was not acted upon, or rather a new phase in the affair changed the course of the plot, as will be seen. The following day Mr. and Mrs. Bernheim repaired to Dr. Buckingham's office, the lady requiring medical attention. While there a man entered the office, and walking to Bernheim, said loudly:

"How is wife number two?"

Receiving no reply he turned to the horrified bride and asked:

"Are you this man's wife?"

She replied, greatly agitated, "I am, sir."

"Why," said the stranger, "you are not; and this man, if he has married you, is a bigamist, and has a wife and child in this very state. I am a sheriff from his home and have come to arrest him."

Imagine the feelings of the poor woman, her dream of happiness thus rudely brought to a close. But where was the man who had wronged her? While the stranger and the woman had been talking, Bernheim had slipped out of the room and could not be found. The stranger rushed in pursuit, but had no sooner passed out of the office than the husband returned, saying he had simply hidden. He admitted to the weeping woman the truthfulness of the charge. He was married, but was carried into the terrible wrong he had done by his passionate love for her. Now, nothing remained for him but to fly. He left the heartbroken woman swooning in the office and started by the rear entrance to the building for the depot. This was about 3 o'clock in the afternoon.

Dr. Buckingham was informed by the woman of the wretchedness of her condition, and that worthy gentleman hastened at once to the office of the Rocky Mountain Detective Association, where he laid the matter before Chief Cook, bringing that officer and also Sheriff Abe Ellis, of Pueblo, who was in the office, to the room where Mrs. Bernheim was waiting their coming. In broken sentences the woman told them her story. Sheriff Ellis at once recognized from her description of her husband a somewhat noted character of Southern Colorado, named Charles Blume, a fiddler who had furnished music for social parties and dance houses in Garland, Lake City, Las Animas and other towns for the past three or four years. He had married a young woman at Las Animas in 1875, who with their baby was living in Lake City.

The detectives undertook to find Bernheim, or Blume, if possible, although the outlook seemed very gloomy. No one could be found who had seen the rascal since he had disappeared from Dr. Buckingham's office, and there was no trace to be had of him. The next day the man Thompson, who had brought the letter to Bernheim, was arrested at the American house. He denied all knowledge of the affair, except that he bore a letter from Lake City to Denver for Bernheim. But when, upon searching him, a telegram, written to be sent Bernheim at Wallace, was found in his pocket, he confessed that he knew something was wrong, and that he had come to Denver in answer to a telegram from Bernheim, and had received from that worthy the letter he represented as having brought from Lake City. He said, furthermore, that his name was H. A. Morris, and that he took a fictitious name at Bernheim's instigation, as he knew that party had done. Thompson was locked up.

The next morning, November 1, Deputy Smith, at the instigation of Chief Cook, took the east-bound express on the Kansas Pacific in pursuit of Bernheim, or Blume, it being very evident from the dispatch found on Thompson that he was somewhere on that road. At noon of the same day a telegram was received from Deputy Smith to the effect that Bernheim had stolen a ride on the special car carrying Judge Foster to Wallace, and instructing the officers to head the man off by telegraph. The wires were at once clicking, sending word to the agents of the detective association at Junction City, Topeka, Leavenworth and Kansas City, and that night about 9 o'clock word came over the wire from Sheriff D. R. Kiehl at Junction City:

"Your man Bernheim is under arrest."

He was brought back without difficulty, and had to serve out an eight year's sentence in the penitentiary at Cañon City. At last accounts his first wife was still living in Lake City, and the second was still in Denver. Morris was discharged from custody.

TWO OF A KIND

Back in the early days, two of the most noted desperadoes and horse thieves of the Rocky mountain region were George Britt and William Hilligoss, who, like many others, did not come to grief until Gen. Cook got on their track. They had been guilty of many crimes, but no one ever succeeded in overtaking them until Dave Cook was elected city marshal of Denver, and made it his duty to track them down, which he did, almost unaided, and brought them to town in four days after their crime.

When Cook was elected marshal of Denver for the first time, in 1866, he printed a notice, saying that he would agree to find stolen stock when notified twenty-four hours after its disappearance, and that if he did not find it, he would pay for it himself, after such notification. One day in December, 1867, a well-known ranchman named McIntyre came to the city and put up at McNassar's corral, which then stood on the present site of the American House. The next morning the horses had disappeared, and Mr. McIntyre was quite in despair. The animals were very fine ones, and the loss would have been very severe upon him. He had little hope of recovering them, as up to that time the thief who had been able to once get away with stock had generally made good his escape.

However, Cook undertook to find the stock, telling Mr. McIntyre to be of good cheer, as the chances were that he would yet secure his property for him. In looking about, he discovered that Britt and Hilligoss, whom he had already spotted, had disappeared. He at once came to the conclusion that they were the guilty parties. This "pointer" once obtained, he soon added one clue to another, until he was quite thoroughly convinced that his men had gone north. Selecting as an assistant a deputy marshal named Rhodes, he started in pursuit on horseback.

The weather was freezing cold, but the officers traveled forward, notwithstanding this disagreeable circumstance, stopping only to make inquiries for the fugitives and to get their meals. The trail was struck at the Platte bridge and followed by the officers to Boulder, where it was lost.

Two days and nights were spent in the effort of the officers to run their game down, but apparently to no avail. On the third day Gen. Cook returned to Denver, having left Rhodes in Boulder. He had scarcely arrived, and had had no time for rest or recreation, when he received news from Capt. J. W. Barron, of Bijou Basin, a member of the detective association, telling him that two men answering the description which he had sent out of Britt and Hilligoss had passed there acting very strangely. Barron's message stated that the men had applied for something to eat. They had stated that they were traveling to Denver, but after getting a short distance from Bijou had turned, circumventing the settlements and going towards Kansas.

"They are my men," said Cook, "and I'll go for them forthwith."

He had not yet rested since his long ride to the north, but he was off on the next stage, which soon left for the East.

In those days there was no Kansas Pacific railroad to the East, and all the travel was done on coaches—not a very pleasant mode of traveling in cold weather, or when there were Indians about. This was a time when the plains abounded in Indians, and when it was necessary to keep a guard on the outside of the coach to protect passengers from the Sioux and Cheyennes and Arapahoes. It was also very cold weather, and frost-bitten feet and hands and ears were quite the fashion with the travelers of the time. But Mr. Cook started out undaunted. Stopping at Bijou Basin and other points only long enough to get information of the progress of the horse thieves, he pushed on with speed. At Cheyenne Wells he received information which made it quite certain to him that he was on the right track, and he exchanged his ordinary clothing for a stage driver's outfit, so as to avoid detection. After crossing the Kansas line he heard of the fellows more frequently, and while sitting with the driver he espied two men just west of Pond creek, near Fort Wallace, whom he believed to be the men he sought. They had hired out as laborers, and were carrying picks and shovels, with which to begin operations. They were near the road, and as Cook drove closer to them, he established their identity beyond a doubt, so that he instructed the driver to stop after passing them a few feet, and get down and pretend that something had broken about the gearing.

The driver did as instructed. Cook also dismounted and walked carelessly about, while the driver swore at the innate meanness of the stage gear.

Hiligoss and Britt were evidently taken entirely unaware. The two thieves had stopped and gone to work, and did not suspect the shabby looking stranger who was now standing with his back towards them only ten paces away, until he turned upon them with cocked pistol in his left hand and as usual, presented with an aim which they saw would be fatal, and commanded in clear and distinct tones:

"Hands up!"

They hesitated a minute.

Cook drew a finer bead.

"It's no use," said Britt; "he's got us, damn it!" and up their hands went.

Thus were two desperadoes, either one of whom was considered a match for any two ordinary men, taken by Gen. Cook. He even compelled them to disarm themselves by unbuckling their pistol belts and letting their pistols drop to the ground. Then he threw a pair of handcuffs to Britt and told him to put them on.

"I can't," Britt replied.

"Put it on or I'll put a hole through you as big as a bay window."

The fellow snapped the irons on. Both men were served in this way. Both horses were also recovered.

The succeeding night was spent at Fort Wallace waiting for the return stage, and Cook was compelled to stay up with his prisoners all night to guard them. The next day he started back with his men, riding with them in a stage coach, or freight coach, almost as dark as a dungeon even in the day. Cook had not been out for four nights and was naturally exhausted. He sat on the floor of the vehicle, his feet resting against the opposite side, while the two prisoners reversed his position, their feet resting against the same wall which supported his body. They were thus sitting when the officer dropped off to sleep after night came on. While thus situated Cook felt his pistol slowly crawling out of the scabbard by his side. He was awake in an instant, and, slapping his hand upon the weapon, found it half way out, one of the thieves having pulled it out with his feet. Mr. Cook demanded a light from the driver after this pleasant episode, which the driver at first declining to furnish, he told him that he could either give him a candle or carry two dead bodies to Denver, as he would most assuredly kill the two fellows if they were given another opportunity to bother him. The light was furnished.

Cook now set the two men in one end of the vehicle and took a seat himself in the other, telling them that he always slept with one eye open, and that if they even touched him again, he would blow them through. They didn't touch him after this. They afterwards confessed that if they had gotten Cook's pistol they meant either to kill him with it or make him set them free. He had a derringer besides the revolver, however, and would probably have been equal to the emergency if they had gotten his revolver. Still he did not care to risk himself in their power, and hence did not go to sleep again.

The scoundrels were as quiet as mice the rest of the way, and the journey to Denver was devoid of further incident, except that soon after the little matter referred to one of the thieves had complained that his handcuff hurt him. Thinking the fellow had been fooling with it in trying to get it off, Cook reached over and simply tightened it for him.

The officer arrived home on the fifth day out. He was, of course, almost worn out and nearly frozen. Turning the prisoners over to the jailer he went to bed and slept seventeen hours. When he awoke he found the man whose handcuffs he had so kindly tightened suffering great agony, and discovered then that George Hopkins, who was then jailer, had tried in vain to wake him to get the handcuff keys, but had failed utterly, so dead asleep had Cook been. He was sorry, but he couldn't cry, as he had only, though unintentionally, punished a man who would have killed him if he had gotten an opportunity.

Britt and Hilligoss were afterwards tried and sentenced to three years' imprisonment each, but both escaped after serving a year, and neither has ever been, heard of since. The stock were returned to their owner, who, it may be inferred, was quite rejoiced at the success of the officer.

This, take it all in all, was a remarkable exploit—remarkable in the odds against Cook when the men were captured, in the persistence of the pursuit, and in its many details. It has, for these reasons, been chosen to suggest the frontispiece picture of this volume.

HANGED IN A HOG PEN

"Sedalia can not have Schamle. His goose is cooked. Found him hanging over a pig-stye this morning. Saltpetre can't save him. Biggest show of the season."

Such was a telegram received from Georgetown by Gen. Cook, on Saturday, the 15th day of December, 1877. Robert Schamle was a brute of a tramp who murdered an inoffensive man in Georgetown a few weeks previous to his lynching, and who was charged with having committed a rape in Sedalia, Mo., before coming to Colorado, no claimed to be the grandson of Schamyl, the Circassian warrior, who made a big name in his guerrilla warfare upon Russia in the early part of the present century. But the probabilities are that he lied in this matter, and he is believed to have been a native of Switzerland. Whatever his nationality or lineage, he disgraced it.

The murder was committed on the 13th day of October in the year mentioned, the name of the murdered man being Henry Thedie. Thedie was a respectable German butcher employed at G. E. Kettle's slaughter house, about two miles below Georgetown, near which place he resided with his family, consisting of a wife and three small children. The evidence obtained at the coroner's inquest conclusively proved that Schamle was the murderer, and that the crime was one of the most diabolical and cold-blooded outrages that ever stained the annals of a civilized country. The murdered man was known to have had about 80 on his person, immediately prior to his death, and the possession of the money appears to have been the only motive for the perpetration of the hellish act.

Schamle was employed as a helper at the slaughter house at the time, borrowed a pistol at Harvat in Aicher's slaughter house on the afternoon of October 12, and although the shooting was heard, and Schamle seen to flourish a pistol at 5 o'clock that evening, and immediately afterwards leave the place, the result of his bloody work was not known until the following morning, thus giving him a start of over half a day. There was no evidence of a struggle having taken place, or of any ill feeling having existed between the parties, and the position of Thedie's body showed plainly that he had been deliberately shot and almost instantly killed.

The officers of the law started in pursuit of the wretch as soon as the crime was made known, but nothing definite as to the direction he had taken, was discovered at that time. It was suggested in the Georgetown *Miner* that if The Rocky Mountain Detective Association should be employed it would probably result in his capture, but no steps were taken in that direction by the proper authorities. Two weeks later, Mr. G. E. Kettle employed that association, giving a description of Schamle, and promising a reward in case of his arrest. This step, as usual, had the desired effect. The fellow was traced by Gen. Cook's force from Georgetown to Denver, from this place to a point on the divide, from there to Pueblo, and from Pueblo to West Las Animas, where he was arrested December G, by Pat Desmond, a deputy of Abe Ellis, at that time sheriff of Pueblo county, and a member of the detective association.

The case was well worked up by Ellis, who was, during his life, one of the most efficient of Gen. Cook's aids. In this ease he had employed a colored man to track the murderer down, and he proved quite a capable detective. Gen. Cook had informed Mr. Ellis that Schamle was coming in that direction, and by some means Ellis became aware of the fact that the negro man had in days gone by been associated with the murderer and knew him. His sub-detective was stationed about the cattle yards at Pueblo, as that was considered the place at which Schamle would most probably turn up. The inference proved to be a correct one, and the watch had no difficulty in spotting the fellow, who came to the place and remained a day or two. While there he was very non-committal, but did not seem to carry any great weight upon his mind, as a murderer would be supposed to do. For this reason the negro had his doubts about his being the guilty man; and while he was hesitating about furnishing his information, Schamle swung into a freight train and took his departure, stealing a ride to West Las Animas.

Finding his man gone, Mr. Ellis sent his deputy in hot pursuit. Being overtaken, the fellow sullenly surrendered to Mr. Desmond and accompanied him back to Pueblo. He said but little on his way to Pueblo, but when told in Pueblo that a Georgetown man was coming down to identify him, he remarked:

"I wonder if they'll hang me if they get me there," and immediately relapsed into silence.

To Sheriff Ellis he denied ever having been in Northern Colorado.

Photographs were taken and sent to Georgetown for identification, and they were recognized at once; but to make doubly sure, George Chapman, Mr. Kettle's clerk, went to Pueblo to see him personally, and he at once identified him.

When Chapman met Schamle he broke down and acknowledged the crime, he said that he quarreled with Thedie about skinning a beef; that Thedie knocked him down; that he got up and ran, and passing a pistol—which he said was borrowed to shoot some chickens—he seized it, turned and fired, and continued his flight, not knowing whether he had killed him or not. This is his story, while the fact is he murdered Thedie for his money.

VIGILANTES ORGANIZED AND AT WORK

On the 12th of the same month Schamle was taken to Georgetown by Sheriffs Ellis and Easley. It had been discussed on the streets and elsewhere that he was a proper subject for lynch law, but no demonstrations of that nature were made upon his arrival.

On the following day his shackles were removed in the presence of a large but not appreciative crowd. Their remarks on this occasion evinced no particular affection for him, and must have suggested to him the propriety of making arrangements for a trip to a warmer climate than Colorado. On the same day he was taken before J. P. DeMattos, justice of the peace, but waived examination and was committed to jail.

That was all right so far, but the public mind was somewhat agitated over the matter, and did not deem the Clear Creek county jail sufficiently secure for the safe keeping of such a wretch as Schamle. The report of the Sedalia rape case had also reached Georgetown, and this did not raise him any in the estimation of the people. An ominous murmur buzzed around on the streets. For one night he was permitted to slumber undisturbed, if the blessings of repose could lull such a brute, and for a few short hours render him insensible to the misery he had wrought.

On Saturday morning, the 15th, between 3 and 4 o'clock, a number of masked men kicked open the door of the room in which Mr. Sanders, the jailer, and A. IV. Brownell were sleeping, and covered them with the light of a dark lantern and three pistols, at the same time requesting them, in a manner that showed they were not to be trifled with to hold up their hands and make no noise.

Both were thus awakened from a sound, slumber, and they instinctively obeyed orders, well knowing that resistance was in vain. The vigilantes then searched for the keys to the cells, and at length found them between the bed and the mattress where the jailer was sleeping. They then left the room, leaving two men to guard the door, and took Schamle from his cell, sometime after which the keys were thrown on the bed where the men were lying, and the lynchers left.

Here there is a missing link in Schamle's history. It is not known to the general public whether he made any unbecoming demonstrations, or protested his innocence, or said his prayers. At any rate, the body of the murderer was found when the sun rose, hanging by the neck to the frame of a dilapidated building, a few hundred feet from the jail, which Is used as a pig pen. As soon as the deed became generally known, a large crowd of both sexes collected at the spot to gaze upon the ghastly spectacle. His toilet had evidently been hastily and carelessly made, but possibly he was not to blame for this. He was minus his hat, coat and vest, and in spite of the predictions that are usually applied to his ilk, he did not die with his boots on.

Between 8 and 9 o'clock a brief inquest was held over the remains, and a verdict in accordance with the facts was returned. The body was then cut down and laid on the end of a large cask which served as a sleeping apartment for pigs. When it fell down the head was gashed by the rocks. The body remained where it was placed until 11 o'clock a m., and during that time was viewed by hundreds of people who were constantly arriving and leaving, and among all that crowd there was not one pitying eye, or a single expression of sorrow or sympathy.

The action of the Vigilantes was universally applauded in Georgetown; in fact, they were regarded as public benefactors.

A local paper said: "His capture is another demonstration of the effectiveness of The Rocky Mountain Detective Association, and of its great usefulness in bringing criminals to justice."

A TUSSLE WITH THE HABEAS CORPUS

During the month of October, 1877, Gen. Cook received a postal card containing the following:

$500 Reward—The above reward will be paid for the arrest and detention of Charles H. Foulk, who is under indictment for arson, larceny, perjury and subornation of perjury. Description as follows: Age, forty-one years; height, six feet; weight, about one hundred and eighty pounds; has brown hair; had a light colored chin goatee about eight or nine inches long when he left here about the 20th of July, 1877, which covered the chin pretty well; long face, thin cheeks, high cheek bones; blue eyes; scar on right side of upper lip; large shot lodged in back of one of his hands—think it is the left hand; upper front teeth far apart and have conspicuous gold plugs; large feet and very long, and always wears shoes; generally fancy ones; when walking he takes long steps, and has a rolling gait; his shoulders are broad, stooped and of average breadth; gambler by profession; faro dealing is his choice game, and would be found in the association of gamblers. Arrest and notify

SAMUEL J. ANDERSON,

Detective, Harrisburg, Pa.

The card was filed in the book devoted to such literature In the office of the Detective Association. No trace of the man was obtained, however, until in January, 1878, when another postal card from the Pennsylvania detectives stated that they had n heard that the man was in Cheyenne and that $500 reward would be paid for his capture. This turned out to be a false report, but early in March Gen. Cook learned through a member of the Rocky Mountain Detective Association at Little Rock that the man had been seen there, and had only left a few days previous, on a rumor that the marshal of that place was about to arrest him, and that it was believed that he had gone to Colorado, most likely to Leadville.

The next clue bringing the game nearer home was the arrival in Denver, early in May, of a modest looking little woman, who registered at the Went worth house, standing where now the St. James stands, as Mrs. G. M. Curtis, of Marysville, Cal. Soon afterwards Mrs. Curtis left the Wentworth and went to the Inter-

Ocean, where she registered under the same name. The next day, Thursday, a man registering as G. M. Curtis put in an appearance, and claimed to be the husband of the woman. He registered from Marysville, Cal., also, and she acted as if his arrival had been anticipated. After his coming he was seen frequently in company with gamblers and sporting men. Gen. Cook, of the detective association, was then sheriff he caught a passing glimpse of him Saturday afternoon, and at once hurried to the office to look up the description of Foulk. It answered perfectly, and having found the man, the next thing to do was to capture him. To accomplish this, the first officer retired from the field and Deputy Sheriffs Frank Smith and Arnold were detailed to work up the capture. They shadowed the man all day for two or three days and until 6 o'clock of the evening of the 26th, when, being satisfied that he was the party they were after, the two repaired to the Inter-Ocean and waited for Curtis to come in to supper. His wife happened to pass through the office, and seemed to have her suspicions aroused by seeing the two men present. She walked up to the clerk and remarked in a tone loud enough to be heard by the officers, that she would go out and meet her husband, as he seemed to be late.

Thinking that she was trying to mislead them, the officers followed her.

Mr. Smith then motioned to Mr. Arnold to come (meanwhile keeping an eye on Mrs. F.), and said: "Get my horse; she may be going off to get into her carriage." Arnold did as requested, and overtook Smith several squares from the hotel. He then concluded to get back to the hotel as fast as he could, for he believed this to be a game put up on them to follow Madame and allow the husband to get away. Arnold went back to the Inter-Ocean as fast as possible, it being understood that if he should find Foulk there, he should arrest him at once. Smith was to stay with the woman. Meanwhile Detective Smith closely watched Mrs. Foulk, who had entered Mr. Ballin's store, on Larimer street.

Detective Arnold had scarcely time to go back to the hotel when Mr. Smith looked around and saw Arnold coming toward him with Foulk under arrest. He had been "nabbed" with the assistance of

Officer Hudson, and the two came marching up the street with their prisoner between them—each having hold of an arm.

When Arnold entered the Inter-Ocean he saw Foulk standing in the hotel office. As soon as the officer entered, Foulk seated himself on a chair. Arnold walked up as though he intended passing Foulk, and, turning suddenly, grabbed his right arm firmly. Hudson came to his assistance, and seized the other arm, giving Foulk no chance to use his revolver.

Foulk sang out in a rage, "What do you want?"

Arnold replied: "You know something about the Bloodworth murder committed in Leadville?" [This was a ruse to throw Foulk off his guard and to get him away from the hotel quietly as possible.]

Foulk said: "I know nothing about Bloodworth."

Mr. Arnold: "You do; and you must go with us."

Foulk walked along quietly, thinking there was some blunder in the job, and that he could easily prove his innocence of the charge.

When Foulk was searched at the jail a large self-cocking revolver was found upon him. He was here told in response to a question from himself as to what he had been arrested for, the facts in the case, but he denied everything, laying his name was Curtis and not Foulk, and that he was from California instead of Pennsylvania. Considerable money was found upon his person.

The prisoner was then taken to the county jail and examined. There was found in an inside vest pocket $933.55. He was searched again the same night, closely, and there were found carefully sewed up in the lining of his vest two $500 bills in one place and four $100 bills in another place, making the total amount he had on his person $2,383.55, for which amount Sheriff D. J. Cook, of Arapahoe county, gave Foulk a receipt, $5 being handed the prisoner for spending money. On the following morning Foulk's wife visited him in prison, bringing with her W. D. Carlisle, a Denver lawyer. They held a conversation for some time, and going to the sheriff's office demanded the money taken from the prisoner. Sheriff Cook flatly refused to hand it over until it was ascertained whether it justly belonged to Foulk. The prisoner's wife and attorney left the office, and immediately entered suit against the sheriff for the sum taken from Foulk, adding $1,000 for damages.

Although Curtis continued to protest his innocence, there was no doubt left that he was the man wanted.

It is presumed that after leaving Little Rock the fellow came straight through and went to Leadville. It is known that he stopped at Fairplay, at the Bergh house, as the proprietor of that hotel, who was in the city just previous to the time of the arrest, seeing his name and that of his wife registered at the Inter-Ocean, sent up his card, but was told that they were not in. Curtis came to Denver evidently from Leadville. He was there through a portion of March, April and May. He was a part owner in a gambling house there, and the memorandum book showed the receipts of the house for each night in the month. The receipts aggregated $1,500 per month for the first two, and nearly that sum up to the 21st of May.

After his arrest it leaked out that his departure from Leadville was caused by the remark of his brother-in-law, a man named Creek, who was a partner in the gambling house, and who is now wanted for murder in Arkansas. It seems the two fell out over the management of the house, and Creek is said to have remarked in a crowd that he "could send Foulk back to Pennsylvania for firing a house."

After his arrest here, a sporting man who seemed to have known him in Leadville, volunteered to go up there and settle up his business, which was still in operation.

Curtis was a very powerful built man, cool as a cucumber, and is said to have been left severely alone by the thumpers and roughs at Leadville, because of his determined manner and his threat openly expressed to kill any man who interfered with him. His wife showed great distress upon hearing of his arrest, and cried and sobbed at a great rate.

The Pennsylvania authorities being advised of the arrest, dispatched William McKeever, of Harrisburg, as a special officer to take him to that state. The officer arrived here with a requisition, and was soon on his way home with the prisoner, accompanied by Detective Smith. The officers gave it out that they expected to start on a Monday, but fearing a habeas corpus proceeding, left on Sunday, driving to a station with the prisoner a few miles out from the city.

THE POSSESSION OF FOULK

But all was not accomplished, and not by any means the worst of it. The officers, sailed along over the Kansas Pacific [Railroad] quite smoothly. All went well until they reached Topeka, Kan., where the party stopped to get dinner. At this point W. D. Disbrow, the sheriff of Shawnee county, met the officers on the platform on their way to dinner. The sheriff stepped up boldly to the party, handing Mr. McKeever a paper purporting to be a writ of habeas corpus, and laying his hand on Foulk said. "And this is my prisoner!" claiming that a requisition upon the governor of Colorado would not hold good while a prisoner was in Kansas. Here was more of the work of the Denver lawyers.

Quite a scene now ensued, and a crowd soon gathered around the platform. High words followed, and both parties persistently claimed Foulk as their prisoner. Foulk here had an opportunity to display his wrath, and he seized it at once. He appealed to the crowd around him that he was arrested illegally—had been robbed of his money—torn away from his wife—had been given no "show" whatever—was the wrong man, etc.

The prisoner was then taken before Judge Carey, who concluded to postpone the case, as he alleged, "to obtain evidence to prove that the prisoner was not Foulk, but ostensible for the purpose of bringing on a lawyer from Denver to Topeka, with a view of having Foulk released if possible. The sheriff's writ claimed that the prisoner was not C. H. Foulk. Judge Carey decided that the officer who had him in charge was bound to prove that the prisoner was the identical man wanted—C. H. Foulk. But on their part the Topeka crowd had no evidence to offer that the prisoner was Curtis and not Foulk although Mw

McKeever was ready to swear positively to Foulk's identification. Strangely enough, Judge Carey discharged the prisoner in the very face of the fact that Mr. McKeever knew the prisoner well and was ready so to testify.

Mr. McKeever then desired Sheriff Disbrow to re-arrest Foulk, and Detective Smith stepped up to the sheriff and said: "I demand of you to arrest this man (pointing to Foulk), and hold him as a fugitive from justice front the state of Pennsylvania, until we can have time to swear out the necessary papers to hold him."

Sheriff Disbrow, however, persistently refused to interfere. Mr. McKeever then inquired of Judge Carey whether "Sheriff Disbrow had not the right to arrest Foulk without a warrant." The judge shook his head.

Detective Smith: "Judge, won't you order the sheriff to arrest him till we take out the necessary papers?"

Judge Carey: "I have no right to do so."

Foulk's attorneys, Messrs. Drown and Carlisle, together with Sheriff Disbrow and one or two of his deputies, then hurried the prisoner across the street to a blacksmith shop, where Sheriff Disbrow ordered the smith to "take off this man's irons, and do it quickly." Meanwhile a crowd of about forty or fifty persons gathered around the smith shop to witness the proceeding. In the shop stood a horse hitched to a post. The officers expected that Foulk, after his shackles were removed, would spring upon the animal's back and gallop off. "Had the prisoner attempted that move," said Detective Smith, afterwards, "instead of landing him safe in Harrisburg, he perhaps would now be looking from behind the bars of the Topeka prison."

Soon as Foulk started out of the court room, Mr. McKeever repaired to the office of Justice Serrell to procure a warrant. Remaining away rather long, Mr. Smith went after him and pressed the justice for the warrant desired. The justice replied, "I cannot give you a warrant without a complaint." Mr. Smith then made the charge himself, and carrying the document before the justice of the peace, swore to the same and obtained a warrant for the re-arrest of Foulk.

Smith then looked for the sheriff or one of his deputies (there were three or four in all), but found only one of the deputies. He stated to the man that he mow had a warrant for the re-arrest of Foulk, and desired the deputy to go with him and arrest Foulk speedily as possible. The deputy laughed in Mr. Smith's face and said: "Oh, I have not the time to spare!"

After a full half-day's work. Constable Fred Miller was found, and he agreed to serve the warrant. The same afternoon at 3 o'clock Foulk was given a hearing, and held in $1,000 for ten days.

The requisition from Gov. Hartranft to the governor of Kansas arrived on the next Sunday, and on Monday the governor's warrant came to hand. Thus matters rested till 9 o'clock Monday night, when the officers who had Foulk in charge caused it to be reported that they would start East on Tuesday morning. One of Foulk's lawyers repaired to the sheriff's office and told that officer not to deliver up Foulk after night. District Attorney Vance stated to Sheriff Disbrow that he wars in duty bound to hand over the prisoner whenever the officer wanted to go East with him.

The officers then devised the following plan of action in order that there might be no further interference. They made, or rather pretended to make, confidants of a number of Topekans, and stated to them that they would leave Topeka by team: would strike for the Atchison and Nebraska railroad at Brenner's station, fourteen miles northwest of Atchison; that it would take three or four days to get there, and by that time the friends of Foulk would leave the track of them and give them no further trouble. This ruse worked splendidly. Instead of taking the above route, they left North Topeka the same night, driving at a rapid gait three-quarters of a mile; thence headed southward the same distance; then headed due east to Lawrence, distance twenty-eight miles—all after dark. From Lawrence they drove to Plymouth Hill station. Mo., 120 miles from Topeka, traveling with Foulk now as a companion, having no irons on him. The above distance was made from Monday. 9 p m., till Tuesday, 7:55 p m, when they boarded the Missouri Pacific train eastward bound.

McKeever procured the tickets and attended to the baggage while Mr. Smith got Foulk on the train on the side opposite the platform, unobserved. Three tickets were purchased for St. Louis, one of which was placed in Foulk's hands, so that the conductor could obtain it without-exciting suspicion. Smith sat behind the prisoner and McKeever opposite.

Directly afterward a well built, robust man came through the cars, stopping in front of Detective Smith, eyeing him and Foulk sharply. (The man was supposed to be an officer with an official paper.) Eyeing Mr. Smith for a few minutes, he said: "Ain't your name William Johnson?"

"'My name is William Franklin," replied Mr. Smith.

The stranger continued: "I thought I knew you; once knew a man resembling you very much."

"Guess you have struck the wrong man," replied the officer. The stranger walked off and left the train at Sedalia, Mo., at 10:15 a m. Detective Smith had a curiosity to know more about him and stepped out upon the platform, where he observed the man walk up to three others, and handing them a paper, remarked: "They are not on this train."

All hands feeling fatigued after two days' excitement and an all-night drive, they took a sleeping car and retired, Foulk consenting to sleep between them. The officers, however, never closed their eyes. Next morning they reached St. Louis, and from that point to Harrisburg had no further trouble. Foulk denied his name until the party reached St. Louis, where he admitted that he was Foulk and not Curtis. He was met at the depot by* a number of his former friends, who cordially shook him by the hand,

He was taken to Carlisle by Detective Smith, who collected his reward and returned home, the money found upon Foulk being turned over when it became known to whom it belonged. Next to Foulk himself, his Denver attorneys fared worse than anyone else. They fell into great disfavor because of the part they took in the affair, and one of them soon left the city and has not been seen in it since. Of course the damage suit against Cook was soon dismissed.

The charges against Foulk were not proven, and after coming back to Denver and getting his money, he went to Hot Springs, Ark., where in partnership with another man he opened up a big gambling hall. Gen. Cook met him there in 1883 going by the name of Potts. A couple of years after that Foulk was shot by a negro policeman who was trying to halt him for fast driving. The policeman called to him to stop, and he told him to "go to hell." The policeman shot him through the back of the head, killing him instantly.

A DESPERATE RAILROAD CONTRACTOR

Charley Maxwell, a bright-faced and well-dispositioned lad, was shot down in a cold and cruel way by one John Kelly, a contractor on the Union Pacific railroad, near Fort Steele, Wyo. in 1868, while the railroad was building through that country. He was a Colorado boy, and his parents had permitted him to go away from home to secure work, and he had taken a place under Kelly as night herder of the contractor's stock. The boy owned an excellent pony, which was almost his entire property, and he was naturally very fond of it. One day the Cheyenne Indians came along and stole it, and left him quite in despair at his loss. His grief was so intense as to have an effect upon the railroad workmen, and their sympathy grew to be so strong that they determined to buy him another pony, and raised sufficient money for this purpose by clubbing together. The animal being procured, young Maxwell decided one day to return to Colorado, and demanded a settlement with his employer. Kelly was a rich man, worth perhaps no less than a hundred thousand dollars, but he was about as small a specimen of manhood as was ever permitted to live in this western country, where such characters as a rule are not tolerated long at a time when the boy asked to be paid for his services Kelly coolly handed him the amount due, less the cost of the pony—with the purchase of which he had had nothing to do, mind you—saying that he would deduct the amount paid for the animal from the boy's pay. Maxwell was indignant, but helpless. He could only appeal for his just dues. This he did when opportunity offered, and seeing Kelly in a bank one day, went in and asked him for the balance which he thought should be to his credit. Kelly turned upon him with wrath and poured a stream of profanity upon him, exclaiming as he went out of the bank:

"I'll teach you, you damned little son of a bitch, to ask me for money!"

He passed out of sight for the time, and Maxwell thought no more of the matter until he saw Kelly coming down the street with a rifle thrown across his shoulder. He was then uncertain as to the man's purpose and made no attempt to get away. Passing down the street on the opposite side from the boy, he said nothing until directly across from him, when he threw his gun across the wheel of a wagon for a rest, and, taking deliberate aim at Maxwell, shot him down in his tracks. The boy fell bleeding, crying:

"O Mr. Kelly, you have shot me; please let me live. I will not bother you again."

Kelly loaded his gun and walked across the street, saying in response to the lad's utterances:

"I don't think you will," responded Kelly as he placed the muzzle of the weapon to the boy's ear; "not if I know what I am about. No, you won't ask me for any more money in a public bank. I'll warrant you don't."

As he spoke the last words the trigger was pulled, and the top of the writhing boy's head was blown almost off by the bullet which went crashing through it.

The men around were most of them employees of Kelly's, to which fact alone is doubtless due his escape from lynching at the time. He was arrested and imprisoned at Fort Steele, but soon escaped from there and disappeared. Kelly's home was in Council Bluffs, Iowa, and thitherward he wended his way. In Omaha He was arrested, but contrived to get out of jail, whether by the use of money is not known. In Council Bluffs the programme was repeated, and the fellow after that was allowed to go free for over two years.

In 1870 Maxwell's father decided to make a last effort to have his son's murder avenged, and he placed the matter before Mr. N. K. Boswell, of the Rocky Mountain Detective Association of Laramie City, to whom he related the facts, saying he was poor and able to pay but little, and appealing to Mr. Boswell's humanity. Mr. Boswell undertook the case, and never did a detective work more assiduously, or with more skill, or display greater tenacity of purpose or more downright courage than did Boswell on this case. The story would, indeed, be told except for the detective's work; but as it is, it is just beginning.

Mr. Boswell soon learned the place of residence of his man, and going to Council Bluffs, there ascertained that Kelly was still contracting, and that at that time he was engaged near Red Oak on the line of the Burlington and Missouri road, which was then being built in that section.

In looking over the ground, Mr. Boswell found that his man was engaged three miles from Bed Oak, but that to get a train it would be necessary to drive forty miles, to the junction of the Missouri Pacific railroad, through a thinly inhabited region. Mr. Boswell, however, arranged his programme perfectly in advance, ascertained the time at which trains passed the junction, and secured the services of a faithful man, the sheriff of the county in which Kelly was at work, and together they drove out to the point where Kelly was supposed to be engaged.

Mr. Boswell had never seen Kelly, but he carried such a complete description of him that he knew he would recognize him at first glance. Fortunately the officers came upon the fugitive alone. As they drove along by the side of a railroad cut, they recognized him standing on the other side of the cut. After observing the movements of the officers for a few minutes, Kitty apparently decided in his own mind that they could bode no good to him, and started to walk away from them. When they cried to him to stop he only walked the faster, and soon he started to run, evidently intending to reach a wagon and span of horses standing half a mile away across the prairie. The officers then left their horses standing and crossed the cut, finding Kelly at a dead run by the time they came up on his side of the track. They again shouted to him to stop, and as he did not obey the command. Boswell had his man send a shot after the fugitive. With this he ran the faster.

Boswell again warned Kelly that if he did not stop he would shoot him dead; but the fellow paid no heed, and only continued his run. He was fast gaining upon the officers, and was evidently determined not to surrender. Boswell decided to make a grand effort to bring his man down. The fellow was running rapidly and the distance was great. Boswell is ordinarily a dead shot, but at this time the great distance, and the fact that he had only his pistol, were odds against him. He, however, stopped, and deliberately squatting, placed his pistol on his knee. Almost simultaneously with the report of the pistol Kelly stopped, threw up his hands and exclaimed:

"My God, stop! You have wounded me. I will surrender!"

Going up they found Kelly lying upon the ground with a bullet hole through his body, entering at the small of the back and passing out near the navel. Seriously wounded as one would have supposed the fellow to be, shot as he was, he scarcely bled at all, and he did not appear to be materially disabled. The officers compelled him to go back with them. One of them stepped the distance as they returned, and found that Boswell had shot two hundred and twenty yards when he struck Kelly. They found their man desperate, but apparently helpless. He swore with violent rage when first taken, and asserted that he had been murdered in cold blood, saying that he would not have been taken at all if his captors had not taken a miserable advantage of him.

The officers were soon permitted to see for themselves how difficult, if not impossible, it would have been for them to secure their man had they come upon him at a less fortunate time than they did. The firing of the pistols had attracted the attention of Kelly's workhands, who were engaged near the scene of the shooting, and the officers had not gotten Kelly to the carriage, when the laborers began to swarm around them. There were no fewer than sixty of them, led by a brother of Kelly, who came marching towards them, armed with sticks and stones, and swearing that Kelly could not be taken away.

"We'll show you about that," responded Boswell. "We came for him and we will take him. Keep your distance!"

As Boswell talked, the two officers leveled their guns at the crowd and ordered them to not make a move. Kelly was told to get in the buggy, but he declared that he was unable to do so. Boswell, still keeping his pistol leveled at the crowd, told his fellow officer to shoot Kelly down on the spot if he did not step into the vehicle immediately. The order had its desired effect. Kelly stepped into the buggy and the officers drove off, covering the mob with their pistols until well out of their range, leaving them gnashing their teeth and swearing but in vain.

A fine prospect the officers had before them—very fine, indeed! A wounded man to take care of, and how badly wounded they did not know; a howling mob, headed by the brother of the prisoner, to follow them, and forty miles to the nearest railroad station, through a wild country, to them comparatively unknown. But Boswell is a man who never knew fear, who newer shirked a duty, however gloomy the outlook or dangerous the path to be trod he felt that his safety depended on the celerity of his movements, and he decided to "'get up and dust." His captive complained a great deal at first at the pain occasioned by the jolting of the vehicle; but finding that his groans occasioned no apparent compassion in the breast of his captor, that it certainly did not cause him to slacken his speed, he at last settled town into grim and sullen endurance, and the party drove on, no one saying anything. Boswell's companion held the reins, Boswell kept his arms in readiness to meet any sudden attack, and the prisoner continually glanced about him for the friends which he felt confident would come to his relief sooner or later.

AN ARMY OF DESPERATE CHARACTERS

The arrest of Kelly had been made early in the morning, and it was not late in the day when Red Oak was reached. A brief stop was made at this point to consult a physician as to Kelly's wound. The man of medicine said the prisoner had been dangerously shot; that the ball had passed through the abdomen, and the chances were two to one that he would die, but that his prospects would be in no wise injured by taking him on to Pacific Junction. Much against Kelly's will the officers mounted the vehicle, and with a "go long there." were off on the long and dangerous journey.

On they went, as fast as the rough roads and the speed of their animals would permit, feeling that every step they went was putting danger all the further from them. They began to feel somewhat secure from attack when they passed the half-wav point on their road lint their exultation was only short-lived. They were jogging along over a corduroy road through heavily shaded bottom land, when, glancing back, they beheld a small and motley army advancing upon them. Kelly's brother had' gotten about twenty men together, armed them with revolvers, shot guns, shovels, pitchforks, and mounted them on mules and "old plugs" of horses, and had come in pursuit. They were galloping along over the rough road strung out for a hundred yards, making quite a formidable appearance, indeed.

"Well, I guess we'll just give them the best we've got in the shop, anyhow," says Boswell. "Let them come if they want to," in a general way, and to his companion officer, "Put your pistol to Kelly's ear and blow the top of his head off if he makes a move, or if his friends do," at the same time nudging the officer as a warning not to take him literally at his word. The command was intended for Kelly's ear and not for the officer's. We shall soon see whether the stratagem had its desired effect.

In the meantime the horses had been stopped, and Boswell remarking. "I guess we'll face the music right here," had jumped out of the wagon, leaving his companion to take care of Kelly while he should face the mob. They rushed on even after Boswell had stepped out. When the infuriated crowd had come within hailing distance, Boswell raised his pistol and ordered them to stop. But they did not stop. He drew a bead on the leader and shouted to him:

"Move another step and I'll shoot you dead as you come." This had its effect and the mob drew the reins on their animals and came to an unwilling standstill.

"Now, what do you want?" he asked.

'We want Kelly, and mean to take him."

"Oh, you do, eh? Well, if that is all, come on and get him." It was now Kelly's time to speak. The muzzle of a cocked revolver was jammed into his ear and a firm officer's forefinger almost touched a trigger so that a move of it would have sent him into eternity in the twinkling of an eye. He fancied that he could almost hear the crush of the hammer, and he trembled like an aspen bough as he shouted to his rash friends:

"For God's sake, boys, don't make a move; they will kill me."

This had its effect, and a brief parley resulted in a promise from the crowd to not further molest the officers. They were told that if they should again attempt to come upon them, Kelly would be killed outright and that the officers were prepared to kill at least twelve of their assailants before being taken.

The mob were true to their word, and did not put in an appearance during the remainder of the entire drive, which w-as made as hurriedly as possible. The captive and captors reached the junction a few minutes before train time, as Mr. Boswell had calculated to do. They found, somewhat to their surprise, that Kelly's brother and his party had taken another road and had gotten in ahead of them and had rallied a mob of two hundred to their support, who swore vehemently that Kelly should never be taken on the cars. Boswell managed to rush his party into the hotel unobserved, but they had no sooner settled there than the mob began to beat at the door and demand admission. This was denied them, and they were stood off until the train came up. It proved to be a freight, but Boswell determined to take it.

Now was the trying time. The mob had congregated on the platform between the hotel and the railroad track and was so dense that it looked impossible to force a way through it. But Boswell was equal to this occasion as he had been to others. "Now is our time, boys," he said, and they prepared to move out. He had procured the assistance of another well-armed and faithful man, and he placed him and the Missouri sheriff on either side of the arrested murderers, while he cocked two revolvers, holding one in each hand. The hotel door was opened as soon as the train stopped, and the party walked outside. They were met with a wild yell, and then became apparent a disposition to move upon the little party. Again the pistols were leveled and the crowd was told to divide so as to make a passage.

Slowly it rolled into two walls as the Red Sea did of old. The two assistants were placed in front while Boswell brought up the rear with his pistols in hand, and they passed through the jeering and swearing crowd. As they were nearing the cars a piece of cordwood struck Boswell in the rear, but did not hurt him badly. Quick as thought he turned his back to the cars and fired both of his pistols over the heads of the crowd. Such a scattering was never seen. The platform covered a marshy piece of ground and all around was a shallow pond. Two-thirds of the gallant two hundred were sent sprawling into the water—presenting a scene which was quite sufficient to excite Mr. Boswell's idea of the ridiculous, notwithstanding his serious surroundings. Adjoining this pond was a cornfield, and through this the frightened creatures flew like Texas steers.

There were, however, still a few left, and they seemed more disposed to fight than ever. Kelly's brother jumped upon a fence and was preparing to shoot when Boswell leveled upon him and brought him down with a bullet through the thigh, producing a yell which acted as a potent quietus upon the crowd, and the battle was over.

Some of the roughs made an effort to board the train, on which Kelly had been placed during the melee, but were knocked off, and * soon the party was on the way to the Bluffs. The journey was without incident.

But all was not yet over. Kelly was so badly wounded that it was found impossible to proceed further, without absolutely endangering his life. He was placed in the Council Bluffs jail and a physician sent for. Strange as it may seem, it was discovered that, although the ball had passed entirely through him, he had hardly bled enough to color his shirt, and the doctor stated that with ordinary care and rest he would soon recover. He was kept in the jail there two weeks while the physician was attending him, recovering rapidly all the time. Boswell remained close with his prisoner and slept with him every night. Not aware of this fact, Kelly's friends came one night in force and began an effort to break the doors of the jail down. But being met by this man of eternal vigilance and an ugly Winchester rifle, they retired in some disorder, heaping imprecations upon his head.

The next assault was upon Boswell's cupidity, and consisted in an offer of $40,000 in clean cash to him if he would allow Kelly to escape. But this was met as all other efforts of a different character had been, and failed of its object, as it was refused, though Boswell allowed it to be understood that probably it would, be accepted, thinking that he might the more easily get his prisoner away when he should desire to remove him.

It was while they were resting in this doubt as to Boswell's intention that he stealthily took his now well-recovered captive out of the Council Bluffs jail and crossed the Missouri river to Omaha on his way to Wyoming. The ruse was, soon after the departure, discovered, and while the officer was at Omaha another effort was made to recapture him. This was a well-laid plan and came very near succeeding. Boswell had stopped at the Cozzens house for the night, and Kelly had gone to bed. A young man named Day had been employed as a guard while the detective was out making arrangements for transportation. Kelly suddenly claimed to have a call of nature, which demanded that he should retire to the water closet in the back yard. Day stooped down to get the prisoner's boots for him, and as he did so, Kelly snatched the guard's revolver and shot him through the breast, though, fortunately, not dangerously. A struggle ensued between the two men and soon a large crowd of the guests of the house came to the rescue of the guard and assisted him to disarm the now thoroughly enraged criminal.

Someone rushed over to the railroad office and informed Boswell of what was transpiring. Hurrying back to the hotel he concluded to go in the back way to avoid interference. Then another feature of the plot was revealed. A carriage stood backed up against the rear fence and a mob of forty friends of Kelly's were demanding admission to the hotel, while the proprietor of the house, a courageous old man named Ramsey, stood at the head of the stairs, up which they sought to go, brandishing an old saber and defying them. Boswell's appearance was sufficient to disperse the crowd, as his character had already become known to Kelly and his friends. Kelly was after this episode placed in jail.

Boswell feared still another effort at rescue, and took precautions to frustrate it. He employed a railroad man named Thomas McCarthy to join the mob and keep him informed of their movements. Through this means he discovered that a plot had been set on foot to wreck the train six miles out. Obstructions were placed on the track at a point where the train would have been thrown from the track before it could have been stopped. But Mr. Mead, then superintendent of the Union Pacific, sent out a fiat car carrying forty armed men, who removed the obstructions and allowed the passenger train carrying Boswell and his man to pass without further molestation.

The seven or eight hundred miles across the plains to Laramie City were traversed without incident, and the desperado was fudged at last in jail—another feather in Mr. Boswell's cap and that of the Rocky Mountain detective force.

Let it be said to the shame of the courts that after all this effort to capture Kelly, and after his terrible crime had become known throughout the West, he was allowed to go scot free, after remaining in jail a few months. He succeeded in buying off the witnesses against him and at last got off, though at a cost of not less than $37,000.

Of course, such a man would be expected to die with his boots on, and he did, having been shot dead some years ago in Texas while in a row there.

DEALING WITH STRIKERS

As a rule, the work of detectives and detective associations during strikes has been such as to incur the bitterest hatred from the strikers, and in many cases the condemnation of all disinterested citizens. We opine that this has been caused in the main by the various associations employing for strike purposes the very worst thugs and blacklegs that could be found—men who desired to see a strike prolonged indefinitely that they might have a job, and men who would not hesitate to do anything that would increase the bitterness existing between the employers and the employed.

As an illustration of this fact, we might call attention to the great engineers' strike on the "Q." several years ago. Two or three engines had been blown up and much other damage had been done, so the officials of the company were led to believe, by the strikers. The labor unions of Denver denied this, and to completely refute the charges and clear themselves, they resolved to employ Gen. D. J. Cook and the Rocky Mountain Detective Association, in whom they had implicit confidence, to ferret out the real criminals. In a few days Gen. Cook was able to report to the unions that they were rigid, and that the deviltry was being done by miscreants in no way connected with the strikers. But the greatest services Gen. Cook and the association have ever rendered for labor anions was done during the great Leadville strike in June, 1880.

How they saved the state of Colorado from eternal disgrace, and several hundred of the foremost citizens of Leadville from eternal infamy, by nipping in the bud the conspiracy to lynch six of the leaders of the Miners' Union, has never been told; but it deserves publication as one of the most brilliant achievements of Gen. Cook's career.

It is not our purpose to give here a history of the strike in detail, but merely to relate the part played by Gen. Cook, and some of his most trusted lieutenants. The Miners' Union, consisting of several hundred miners, with Michael Mooney at their head, had declared a strike about the last of May, and by persuasions and threats soon had nearly every miner in the Leadville district out. The bitterness increased from day to day, and by the 10th of June the excitement had risen to such a pitch that nearly everybody in the city had arrayed himself with either the union or with those who sympathized with the mine owners.

Leadville was in a condition of anarchy. There were organizations of mine owners and citizens, and organizations of miners which were intensely hostile to each other. The bummers of the city had attached themselves to one party or the other, hoping for plunder. It was generally believed that a vigilance committee had been organized to deal with the leaders of the strike. It was known that mine owners had received notices from unknown sources threatening their lives. The most intelligent portion of the community believed that a deadly collision was imminent,

In this condition of affairs the sheriff of the county officially notified the governor that he could no longer preserve the peace, and called upon him to declare martial law as the only means of preventing bloodshed. Gov. F. W. Pitkin at once responded by ordering Gen. Cook to take command, at the same time declaring the city and county under martial law, which step was immediately taken. Gen. Cook at once summoned ex-Sheriff Peter Pecker and Lieut. Matt. Hickman, both of whom are now dead, but who were then trusted members of the Rocky Mountain Detective Association, together with two other members, and detailed them to circulate through all the crowds and obtain definite information as to what the "Committee of 115" was doing. These men soon discovered that there was a plot on foot to cause the arrest of Mooney and live other leaders of the strikers, place them under a guard of militia friendly to the committee, and then to take them away and lynch them.

Gen. Cook at once conferred with Brig. Gen. James, whom he knew to be opposed to the proposed lynching, and they agreed that at least half of the militia could not he trusted in the matter. Gen. Cook then directed Gen. James to choose three companies that were all right to scour the town and arrest every suspicious party. Gen. James chose about 300 out of the 600 men in the command, taking only the companies that he felt could be relied upon, but a large number of whose members, as the detectives found out, were members of the committee of safety themselves! They went on duty at 8 o'clock, but as a matter of course, they failed to find any riotous assemblages. After midnight Gen. Cook's detectives reported these facts to him, adding that the mob was only waiting for him to retire, when they would have their victims placed under arrest, and placed in charge of militiamen who were in full sympathy with the mob. Then, of course, they were to be taken after a slight show of resistance and hanged. As soon as Gen. Cook found that he could not depend upon the other men he sent for Capt. Murphy and Lieut. Duggan, of the Tabor Tigers, a company formed principally of sporting men, who were opposed to hanging on general principles, arguing that it was something that might happen to anybody. On being questioned as to whether their men could be trusted to round up the "stranglers" or not, Murphy replied: "Now you're shoutin'. If there's anything in the world these boys are dead sore on its stranglers." Gen. Cook at once ordered the company to report at his headquarters, on the double-quick, and upon their arrival directed Capt. Murphy to divide them into small squads and at once scour the tow n, arresting any group of three or more men they might find, no matter, militiamen or civilians. The men departed in all directions with a whoop, and in less than an hour the detectives reported to Gen. Cook that he could go to bed without the least fear of anymore trouble, nor was there any.

As soon as the "Committee of 115" found that Gen. Cook had detected their conspiracy, they knew in a minute that the "stuff was off." and the idea of lynching the strike leaders was given up. Gen. Cook soon convinced everybody that he had no entangling alliances with either mine owners, citizens or miners. He went under instructions to protect all classes from violence and to prevent bloodshed. His actions were so impartial and his protection to the community was so complete, that when on the third day after martial law was declared, the governor proposed to revoke the order, every class of the community appealed to him to continue the order in force. More than a hundred of the citizens telegraphed imploring him to continue the protection for a few days longer. A majority of the city council, with the city treasurer, city 'clerk and city marshal, united in the same request. The Miners' Union sent him this dispatch:

"Leadville, Colorado, June 17.

"Governor F. W. Pitkin:

"We request you to leave the matter of military law in this county in the hands of Major General Cook. It is for the best interest of all concerned.

"JAMES T. BLACK,
"Secretary *pro tem.*
"P. J. LAWLESS,
"TIM GOODWIN,
"JOHN CRELLY,
"Vice Presidents, Union."

Thus was the danger averted. Dave Cook's cool head and strong determination had prevented the riot, and ruin, and bloodshed that must certainly have followed the lynching of the strike leaders by the infuriated citizens' committee. He had won the respect of all classes, and the Miners' Union, seeing that their cause was already lost, appealed to him to devise some means of settling the strike. He consented, and in a few hours had arranged a conference between the miners and their employers, at which their differences were satisfactorily adjusted, and the great strike was over.

When Gen. Cook was first appointed to the command of the military forces around Leadville, a local paper, the Carbonate *Chronicle*, said, editorially:

"The man whom Gov. Witkin has selected to take command of the state forces in this county during the reign of martial law, needs no introduction to any Coloradoan. Sheriff of the capital county for years, he became the best known and most prominent official in the state by reason of his able administration of his duties, his wonderful detective achievements, and the fact that his arrests were made in every quarter. For the past ten or fifteen years criminals have felt that if Dave Cook was on their trail their escape was hopeless and their fears have proven well founded.

"As an executive officer, Gen. Cook possesses the highest ability. His iron will, level head and perfect coolness mark him as the one man for chief in this emergency. No matter where you see him—at table, desk, on promenade, in the saddle, confronting Utes or criminals—he is the same calm, quiet, nervy man.

"The memorable ride over the range into Middle Park, and prompt action in the Ute campaign of last summer, have passed into history, and Gen. Cook will ever be remembered with deepest gratitude by the settlers whom he succored so quickly.

"Leadville may well congratulate herself that the presence of such a man has been secured in the commander's saddle in this most trying and important ordeal."

Subsequent events proved that the confidence of the people in Gen. Cook's ability was not misplaced, and the prompt and decisive settlement of the troubles, added fresh laurels to his fame and that of the Rocky Mountain Detective Association.

A VICTIM OF DRAW POKER

John A. Bemis is the name of a young man who must figure in this narrative because of his weakness—because he allowed himself to fall into bad habits when he was entrusted with money belonging to other people. When the crime was committed in the summer of 1877, Bemis was, and is yet if he is still living, a young man of good family. His people resided in Syracuse, N. Y., whence Bemis started out on one of the New York railroads as an agent for the American Express company, running into New York. As agent for a big carrying enterprise running into the nation's financial metropolis, he became the custodian of large sums of money, often carrying a million dollars on a single trip. He was implicitly trusted by the company, being a young man whose life was supposed to be singularly exemplary, and backed by family connections of the very highest order. There were many times that he might have made a big haul without taking more than the ordinary risk which thieves take. But he seems to have resisted all the more luring bait which was thrown out to him, and to have at last been tempted by a comparatively small sum.

As was learned after his arrest by the Rocky Mountain Detective Association, he fell into loose company one clay while carrying $3,600 for his company. He was lured into a game of penny-ante poker, which assumed, before the game was finished, extensive proportions. Having exhausted his own pile, and feeling chagrined at being beaten, he drew upon the money which he held in trust. He did not draw upon the pile very extensively, but sufficiently to create a deficit which he was unable to make good. Finding himself in a corner, fearing to explain his breach of trust, and being unable to supply the missing sum himself, he decided in an evil moment upon flight, and also concluded to carry the residue of the company's money in his possession with him.

This decision once formed, he left his express car at a way station, and jumping upon a train coming westward, was off before the theft was discovered.

The company was thunderstruck when the crime was discovered. The New York papers were full of the details a few days afterwards, and the wires carried the report to all sections of the country, dwelling upon the young man's family connections, the trust which had been reposed in him, and filled with surmises as to what could have induced him to take the foolish step which he had taken. Soon followed other telegrams and posters, the latter carrying portraits of the young fellow, offering a reward of $800 for his apprehension. The express company determined upon close pursuit and the capture and punishment of the defaulter, not because they did not respect the feelings of his family, but because they felt that he should be made an example of. Detectives throughout the eastern states and as far west as the Mississippi river were put to work on the case. They sought in vain for the fugitive. He was not to be found by the most vigilant of the officers who took the trail.

A month after the robbery, Gen. Cook received a letter from Mr. Fargo, president of the [Wells Fargo] express company, giving a description of the robber, renewing his offer of a reward of $800 for his apprehension, and saying there were reasons to believe that Bemis had come to Denver. The principal reason urged was that Bemis had a cousin here, whose name was given.

The case was placed in the hands of Detective Arnold by Gen. Cook, who was relied upon to do his best work on It. Mr. Arnold worked a long time without a due. The hotel registers for I month hack were scanned with the keenest scrutiny. They were dumb. Not a shadow of a clue was presented. No one going by the name of Bemis had registered at any of the hotels since the time of the robbery. The cousin was sought out and skillfully pumped he knew nothing, or professed to know nothing, of his relative. He declared that the young man had not been in Denver to his knowledge. This to Mr. Arnold. But Arnold soon came to the conclusion that he was not the best man to talk with the cousin. Arnold is one of the men who believe that there are more ways to accomplish a purpose than one. He made himself acquainted with the associates of Bemis' coming in Denver and set some of them quietly after him. Not only the man's male friends, but some of his female friends were set to work. This ruse was at last successful. The cousin at last told one of these sub-detectives that his cousin had been in Denver; that while here he had gone by the name of James Walker, by which name he had registered at the American house, but that he had taken his departure sometime previous. The kinsman professed to know nothing of the course Bemis had taken, leaving the detectives almost as much in the dark as they were before.

Having the Denver name of the man, they were enabled to ascertain something of las conduct while in Denver, to pick up information as to his habits, and to get a minute description of him. They found that he had been "one of the boys;" inclined to be a little loose and reckless, and considerably addicted to card playing. While still looking about for information as to the direction the man had taken, they received a note one day from Mr. Nat Hickman, who at that time was a confidential agent of the association, dated at Santa Fe, N. M., and telling them that there was a young stranger in that city going by the name of John L. Jerome, whose actions were quite mysterious. Hickman was a shrewd observer of human nature. He knew of no charges against the man concerning whom he had written to headquarters, but merely inferred from the fellows conduct that he was a fugitive from justice, and considered it probable that if he was such, Gen. Cook would know something about him.

After reading the letter, Mr. Cook handed it over to Mr. Arnold, with the remark:

"There's your man"

To which Arnold replied, more forcibly than elegantly:

"Bemis, begad."

After taking some preliminary steps, such as the procuring of a requisition for the arrest of the man, Arnold was off for Santa Fe. There was no doubt of his identity after getting Hickman's description of the party.

In those days a trip to Santa Fe was not so easily made as now. Trains ran only to Trinidad, in Colorado, rendering it necessary that the traveler should make the rest of the journey of over two hundred miles on stage coach, which was not a very pleasant undertaking, considering that the roads were bad; that almost the entire population was Mexican, and road agents were both numerous and persistent. But these were obstacles which did not stand in the way of the Rocky Mountain Detective Association. So Mr. Arnold was off for Santa Fe, the ancient capital of New Mexico, in search of John A. Bemis, *alias* James Walker, *alias* John L. Jerome.

The southward trip was devoid of incident. There was a long and hard ride. Santa Fe was then further from Denver, considering the time necessary for the trip, than Chicago, and the ride was a far more trying one. But Joe Arnold is not very delicately organized, and he landed in Santa Fe "right side up with care."

Arriving late in the evening, he went to the principal hotel—the Exchange—and was soon in possession of evidence which made it absolutely certain that the John L. Jerome, of Santa Fe, was the John A. Bemis, of Syracuse. Arnold had registered as "W. F. Smith, Salt Lake City," that his arrival might create no suspicion in Bemis' mind in case he should glance over the hotel register.

Being sure of the presence of his man, Mr. Arnold next went to work to find the governor, and to get him to honor his inquisition. This was a work Minch consumed a greater part of the night after Arnold's arrival, and morning came on soon after he had finished the preparation for the arrest. Having everything in readiness to spring his trap, he set put to find his game. It began now to look as if the detective had had all his trouble for nothing. He waited patiently about the hotel for Bemis to put in an appearance. He watched the breakfast hall carefully, supposing that his man would come in to get something to eat. Breakfast finally being over, Arnold wandered about the town during the forenoon, with the hope of getting a glimpse of his man. But his vigilance was not rewarded by the least trace of him. He was not to be seen anywhere. Going back to the hotel when the dinner hour approached, he again kept close watch upon the dining room. This time, as before, no Bemis made his appearance. Arnold was beginning to fear that the fellow had spotted him and given him the slip. But he resolved to put in the day in his search. Accordingly his investigations were continued during the afternoon. But still no Bemis.

The supper hour had come on and had nearly passed. Arnold had kept an eagle eye upon the room. His man had not gone in. Finally he wandered into the billiard hall, which was then but dimly lighted, and was unoccupied except by Arnold. Throwing himself down in a chair, the detective was preparing for a little meditative spell to decide what course to pursue, when a footstep fell upon his ear. Looking up he saw that a man had entered the door, opposite him. A second glance told him that the newcomer was none other than Bemis. Sitting still until the stranger approached quite close to him, Arnold then got up and advanced to meet the man, speaking to him when he had approached very near him:

"Mr. Bemis, I believe?"

The man did not appear startled or especially confused. He seemed to have been expecting to be overtaken.

"Bemis—yes, that's my name, and you are an officer come for me?"

Mr. Arnold told him that he had made a very good guess.

"I knew it. I am glad of it. I am ready and anxious to go with you. I want to get out of this hole, and I am tired of skulking about. I would rather a thousand times over go back home and meet all my old-time friends, explain all to them and go to prison, than to go hiding about the country all my life. I could not stand it much longer. So I am glad that you have come. You need fear no resistance from me."

Arnold took his prisoner to his own room, where the fellow continued his talk in the above strain for some time. It was not long before the detective discovered another interesting feature of the story. In answer to Arnold's inquiries as to where Bemis had been during the day, he stated that when he had gone to Santa Fe he still retained the bulk of the money which he had stolen, and believing that he had found a place to which detective vigilance would not extend, he had decided to settle down and go into business. He had determined to buy a cigar store, and had closed the contract, nothing remaining to be done but to pay over the money. He had, soon after going to his hotel, left his money for deposit in the safe, the proprietor of the house being aware of the amount which he had. This same individual, it seems, had become anxious to possess the roll himself, and while he was not courageous enough to steal it outright, as Bemis had done, he hit upon another plan, which was just as effectual and far more safe. He had discovered Bemis' propensity for cards, and finding that the money was about to slip out of his grasp into the hands of the then owner of the cigar store, he proposed to Bemis that they have a quiet game of poker.

Nothing was more to the liking of the Syracuse mam He was willing. These two men and a pair of accomplices of the hotel proprietor were playing poker while Arnold was getting his requisition papers into shape on the night of his arrival. The game at first ran along very smoothly. There was little excitement for a long while. There was plenty to drink, and there was a supply of good cigars. The game appeared to be purely social. The bets were small. There was a general good time, and the entire crowd appeared to be quite "mellow" when the wee small hours came on. It was not a matter of appearance with Bemis. He drank too much. Finding the young man in good shape, his "friends" began to tighten the screws. They had determined to get his money before the night should pass, and about 2 o'clock in the morning prepared to put their plans into execution.

It was the landlord's deal. As he pushed out the ante, one of his accomplices said to Bemis:

"Go a dollar blind."

"All right," said the now thoroughly excited voting man, and shoved out the chip representing that amount.

The cards were dealt slowly. The first that fell to Bemis was an ace, and a gleam of gratification passed over his face. His countenance fell as a ten followed, but when another ten, and another, dropped, it was easily seen how much pleasure he took in the contemplation of the little pieces of cardboard. The landlord saw the blind and raised it five dollars. Bemis followed with a raise of ten dollars, which was promptly responded to by a raise of a like sum on the part of the

284

landlord. Bemis raised it twenty dollars, and the landlord simply covered the raise.

"I'll take two cards," said Bemis.

"That's about what I want, myself," responded the landlord.

The cards were dealt, and after a careless glance at the draw, Bemis laid his hand down on the fable and bet fifty dollars.

"I'll raise you fifty," was the response.

"That lets me out," said one of the other players.

"Here, too," said the second accomplice.

"See your fifty and go a hundred better," exclaimed Bemis.

"We'll play for two hundred," exclaimed the landlord.

Bemis was now thoroughly excited, and the bystanders, accustomed as they were to high play, began to draw hearer to the contestants, and display an unusual interest in the game.

"Will you stand a raise?" asked Bemis, with an air of confident good humor.

"Try it and find out," replied the landlord, while a close observer could not have failed to note the air of conscious triumph in his manner, so outwardly imperturbable.

"I'll raise you five hundred dollars, then," said Bemis.

"I'll go you another five hundred," was the answer.

"See here," said Bemis; "I've got the boss hand, but I don't want to win your money. I'll raise it a thousand dollars."

I'll see that and raise it another thousand," same in the coolest terms from his antagonist; but immediately added, as he remembered the fact that Bemis' bets now covered nearly all his capital: "No, I won't either. It would be robbery to keep on betting with you. I'll call you."

"Four Tens!" called Bemis, stretching out his hand to take in the stakes, with a smile.

"Hold on a minute," exclaimed the landlord. "That's a boss hand, ordinarily, but it don't win this time;" and he laid down four kings.

"Four Kings!" exclaimed Bemis. "My God!"

Thus Bemis, a fugitive from justice and a long way from home, was "dead broke." The game was abruptly ended. He had no more money, could borrow none, and must quit. He wandered out into the dark shadows of the adobe houses, and the thoughts which came to him were quite strong enough to sober him off. Here was, indeed, a pretty kettle of fish, and Bemis told Arnold that so great was his anguish that he had almost determined to free himself from it by committing suicide. Better counsel, however, prevailed, and he decided not only not to take his own life, but to make; an effort to get back home, and when once arrived there, to surrender himself to the authorities.

He went to the hotel determined to go to bed and try to sleep the remainder of the night. But he was met at the counter by a refusal on the part of the clerk to turn over the keys of his room. He was then informed that he had not paid his bill, and that as he had no money he could get no further accommodations there. Thus was he robbed and turned loose penniless and to be persecuted by the man who had robbed him. He spent the remainder of the night walking about and thinking over his situation. He had not gone to the hotel for breakfast, because he had been forbidden to again enter the house. For the same reason he had gone without his dinner; but finding himself very hungry when supper time came on, ho had decided to make an effort to steal in and get something to eat. This resolve he was trying to put into execution when he met Arnold and was arrested.

The fellow a as really suffering from a fear that his life was not safe. In those days they could arrest and imprison a man for debt in Sew Mexico. He was satisfied that his late "host" would be only too glad to dispose of him in that way to get his mouth closed, and so informed Arnold.

Of course the officer promised every protection, and the promise had hardly been made before he was afforded an opportunity to fulfill it. The door of the room had been locked by the officer when he had entered with his prisoner. The story above related had hardly been finished when there came a loud rap on the door, in response to which Arnold demanded to know who was there.

"The proprietor of the house," was the response.

"What do you want?"

"I want Jerome," giving the name by which Bemis had gone in Santa Fe.

"Well, you can't have him."

A long parley ensued, but Arnold steadfastly declined to allow the hotel man to enter or to surrender Bemis to him. The fellow went away swearing vengeance. When he was well gone, Arnold began barring the door more securely than had been done before, and handing Bemis a pistol, told him to defend himself with it in case it should become necessary for him to do so, saying as he did so:

"He will come back with reinforcements, and if they get you I would not give much for your hide."

Sure enough, the man did return, and with a body of men. They began to pound upon the door, but were met by Arnold with the assurance that the first man that entered would be shot down in his tracks. This defiance had the effect of cooling the ardor of the besiegers. They remained about the door all night, however, so that Arnold and Bemis were compelled to remain awake with their weapons in hand during the long night that followed, for it was a long night to both of them. Both had been exposed to great hardships and were fatigued. Arnold had been a night in the stage coming down. The next night he had devoted to his papers. Bemis' experience has been described.

But they had another night before them, and nothing was left to them but to make the best of it.

At last morning came. The stage was to start a 6 o'clock. They must get off on that stage or all was lost. Accordingly a few minutes before 6 the two men unbarred the door of their prison and walked out with their pistols in their hands.

The besiegers had disappeared. The stage was in waiting near the hotel. Arnold and his prisoner jumped in. As they did so, the landlord came up, and as he demanded his pay, struck at Bemis.

The stage driver had seen the row coming on, and having exclaimed, "Jerusalem! it's after 6, and I am off!" had made a sudden start, which left the irate poker player standing alone, while Arnold and his prisoner were off for Denver.

This was a triumph, to be sure, but all was not yet over. The stage passed rapidly on to Las Vegas without incident. Arriving at that place it was stopped by a well-armed Mexican, who was followed by a dozen determined looking fellows, all evidently well heeled. Arnold had taken a seat by the driver's side. The Mexican stated that he was the sheriff of the county, and said he had received a dispatch from Santa Fe, directing him to arrest one John Jerome, who was on the stage in charge of an officer named Smith, from Salt Lake City, on a capias. Arnold at once came to the front, and making himself spokesman for the stage party passed the question around to every passenger on the coach:

"Is your name Smith?"

"Your name Jerome?" etc.

All answered no. "Must be a mistake," said Joe. "My name is Arnold; I am an officer from Denver, and I have a prisoner here named Bemis, but of course we are not the people you want." He then showed his papers, which confirmed his statement.

"Oh, naw," replied the sheriff in broken English; 've vant Smeet— no vant you."

Mr. Arnold then volunteered the information that he had heard in Santa Fe of some trouble of tube character described about a prisoner, but thought: it probable that the fellow had evaded the officers and would be along on the next coach, which the sheriff also considered a plausible theory, and allowed Arnold and Bemis to pass on. The reader will see that the wrong names had been telegraphed. The Santa Fe officials had consulted the hotel register and not the territorial books for the names.

At Cimarron, the next station of importance, Arnold expected to have trouble, and determined to avoid it this time by not meeting it. Consequently he bought a quart bottle of whisky at Bayada, a few miles south of Cimarron, and presenting it to the driver, got off the coach with Bemis before the town was reached, requesting the driver in case they were asked for to state that they had left the coach, and promising to join the stage after the town should be passed. The Jehu promised compliance, but there was no demand for either the officer or his man. They jumped the coach per agreement, and were landed in Trinidad without further incident.

Bemis was sent back to Syracuse, where he pleaded guilty and threw himself upon the mercy of the court. Even the express company officials pleaded for clemency. Hence he was let off with a sentence of but eighteen months in the penitentiary. He should long remember Detective Arnold as his best friend a

A HORSE THIEF'S FOLLY

As a rule officers of the law are careful of the lives and general safety of their prisoners, often taking great risk upon themselves to protect the unfortunates who may chance to fall into their hands. Yet they are occasionally compelled to resort to violence to protect themselves or to prevent the escape of criminals from their custody. Sometimes the officer brings his man down, and occasionally death is the result.

A man giving the name of John Doen became a victim to a fate of this kind in Cheyenne, in the summer of 1876. Doen was a deserter from the army, who had for several years been engaged in herding cattle on the plains, and he had accumulated some cattle of his own. He appears to have been naturally predisposed to rascality, and one night he happened along by the premises of Rufus Clark, residing near Denver, and seeing a good looking horse, he laid his hands upon him and rode him off. Mr. Clark brought the information of the disappearance of the animal to Detective Cook, and asked him to bring the skill of his association to bear in returning the animal to him. He was able to give no clue, either as to the appearance of the thief, or the route he had taken. After brief investigation of the matter, Gen. Cook decided in his own mind that the horse and the thief had gone in the direction of Cheyenne, and he determined to notify his assistant superintendent at that place, Mr. T. Jeff Carr, to be on the lookout for the pair. There was not a long waiting. Carr received the notification at 9 o'clock in the morn- mg, and at 10 the same forenoon the thief rode into town with the animal, as Carr learned by a visit to the livery stable kept by a Mr. Jeffrey. Doen had put the horse up at the stable, and had stated that he meant to have him sold at auction that afternoon. The animal answered the description which Cook had sent, to perfection, and Carr determined to lose no time in taking possession of him and in getting the thief. Hence he procured the services of an assistant detective, Mr. Clark Devoe, also of the Rocky Mountain Association, and they laid a plan to capture the thief at the same time that they should take the horse. This was to lure Doen to the stable, and this project was accomplished by getting the liveryman to send for Doen

and tell him that there was a man who wanted to buy his horse immediately, and that' it would be well for him to repair to the stable and put the animal up for sale.

The plan worked. Doen soon put in an appearance. He found Carr and Devoe awaiting his arrival. The animal was accordingly put up, and a mock auction was gone through with. The horse was knocked down to Carr, and he requested a bill of sale, which was made out and signed by Doen, giving a description of the horse. Having procured this, Carr said:

"I think the description you have just given me corresponds exactly with the one I received this morning of a horse stolen from Denver."

Doen seemed confused, and his confusion increased as Carr read the description from Denver, and his attempted explanations were a series of contradictions. Noticing the fellows embarrassment, Devoe stepped up, and, laying his hand upon Doen's shoulder, said: "I guess this thing has gone about far enough. You are in possession of a stolen horse, and I think you are the thief. I arrest you."

Doen made no resistance and said nothing. He seemed inclined to make the best of a bad job, and the officers began to congratulate themselves that they had disposed of a disagreeable duty with but little trouble. They started off to the city jail with their man, and were proceeding leisurely along Eddy street, the prisoner being some eight or ten feet in advance of them.

Having gained so much upon the detectives, the fellow stalled to run, and broke out suddenly for liberty. The officers started in pursuit, crying to the man to stop or be shot. But he paid no heed to their warning. Two shots were then fired into the air to frighten him into a surrender, but they had no more effect than the volley of words. Doen only ran the faster, and was gaining upon his pursuers all the time. It became apparent that he was in a fair way to make an effectual escape, and the officers increased their speed. Still the thief kept in advance. When he reached a point back of Recreation hall he placed his hands upon a high board fence and began to clamber over. When he reached the top of the fence he drew a pistol and leveled it at the officers. "Shoot him," said Carr to Devoe. The officer sent a bullet whizzing through the air just as the fugitive fired. When the smoke cleared away Doen had disappeared from the fence. He was supposed to have continued his flight, and the officers had begun to fear that they had lost their prize. But in this supposition they were mistaken. When they came up to the fence they heard moans on the opposite side, and glancing over saw their prisoner lying on the ground, and the blood running from his wounds he still held his pistol firmly, and showed more disposition to fight than ever.

"Throw away your pistol," said Carr to him.

"I won't," was the reply. "I will fight to the last."

"Throw that pistol down, I tell you," again Carr commanded, as he drew a bead on the fellow's forehead. "Will you put it down now?"

The thief relinquished the weapon reluctantly.

While Carr was examining the wounds, Devoe came up, and not noticing the pistol as it lay on the ground, stepped upon it and caused it to explode, creating a report which startled both prisoner and detectives but did no other damage.

Doen was taken to the jail and his wounds examined. They were at first pronounced not necessarily mortal, but a closer examination revealed the fact that the bullet had entered the small of the back and passed into the abdomen, causing internal hemorrhage, which resulted in death about ten hours after the shooting.

Before he died, Doen stated that he was a native of Pennsylvania, and that his real name was Edward W. Myers. He made no confession, however, and continued to the last to tell conflicting stories about the affair. He was a desperate man, and would undoubtedly have killed the officers if he could have done so. The Cheyenne *Sun* the next morning said:

> "The unanimous sentiment of the community, so far as we are able to learn, is that Officer Devoe was perfectly justifiable, under the circumstances, and that he didn't shoot the fellow a minute too soon. Nine out of ten men would not have exhibited half the leniency that

these officers did on that occasion. This arrest is one more of the many evidences of the efficiency of the Rocky Mountain Detective Association. Within ninety minutes after receiving Sheriff Cook's letter the criminal was in the county jail. Doen is said to be a deserter from the regular army, and he has visited Cheyenne several times before, and always as a dealer in horse flesh. That he belongs to a regularly organized band of horse thieves there is little doubt."

PUEBLO VENGEANCE

Bill White's career in Colorado was brief. It was cut short by an accident which he could not control. Bill made his advent in Denver in the spring of 1872, and he might have been here yet it he had behaved himself properly, and to the fact that he did not deport himself well is the origin of the pictures herewith presented due, and if used as a pair of chromes might be called, and not inaptly, "Before and After Taking." He came from Chicago to Denver, but was originally from Montreal and was a well-known Canada crook.

A great many of the Denver people were away from home when White made his advent into our society. They were attending a jollification at Pueblo which followed the completion of the Denver and Rio Grande road to that point. Many of the officers were absent, and White conceived it an excellent opportunity to get in his work. He had come to Denver from Canada, and was accompanied by a Kansas City man named Larnigan, who was known throughout the Missouri valley as "Handsome" Larnigan. They put up at the Broadwell house, a hotel kept in what is now known simply as the Broadwell block, on Larimer street, back of the Tabor block, and there began to ply their game. White's role was that of the invalid. He put plasters and liver pads all over him, and affected the Camille cough. He was a man of good appearance, and never had the least difficulty in winning the good will of people with whom he came in contact. Hence it was that when it came to be known that, on the night when so many were absent at Pueblo on pleasure, a boarder at the hotel had been robbed of a very line watch valued at $700 and $300 in currency, no one suspected White, until Gen. D. J. Cook, of the Rocky Mountain Detective Agency, was consulted, and had spotted him and Larnigan as the thieves.

When the case was put in Cook's hands he went to work without a clue, but in less than a day had satisfied himself that the guilt lay with these men. He accordingly proceeded to arrest the pair and to lock them up. But they had observed the attention that the detective was paying to their movements, and had "unloaded" when they were taken. The crime could not be proved against them, although Gen.

Cook was satisfied of their guilt, and he was compelled to let them go. He, however, warned them that they must get out of town "I know you are crooks," he said to them, "and although I have failed now, it is only a matter of time when I shall get you if you stay here. So you had better skip." They were liberated after this warning. White concluded to take Gen. Cook's advice and to leave town, but Larnigan remained behind.

White went from Denver to Pueblo, and was not long in justifying Gen. Cook's prophesy that he would get into trouble. Arriving in Pueblo, White took rooms at the National, the best hotel of the place, and was soon as familiar with the people there as he had been with those in Denver. He was a man of slight stature, and he played the invalid dodge there just as he had done in Denver. He put himself on good terms with the ladies, many of whom about the hotel had been anxious to do whatever they could do for "the poor fellow." He was invited to the rooms of individuals in the hotel, and in fact was the pet of the house. Mr. White was thought to be anything else besides a thief. He had told the good people that his father had been a minister of the gospel in Canada, and he carried a gilt-edged Bible, the parting gift of his dear mother, he said.

When out with the boys, however. White was a very different sort of fellow. He was one of them. He appeared to be of a very affectionate and confiding disposition, but the most striking peculiarity about the young man wots that he always appeared to be thoroughly and completely drunk. We say appeared to be, for with all our inquiries, we have vet to find the first one who actually saw him take a drink, he this as it may to the outsider the young man went to bed drunk at night, and got up drunk in the morning he staggered at 9 o'clock. He clung to the telegraph pole at 10 o'clock he rolled in the gutter at 12, and would be carted off to his room, blubbering meanwhile to those who towed along his worthless carcass, and telling how much he loved them. After the Pueblo robbery it was suspected that the young man had been "playing it on the boys." It was then believed that he was not as drunk as he had pretended to be.

One morning it was discovered that during the previous night several rooms in the hotel had been entered and robbed of sums of money ranging all the way from five cents to $300, and of numerous watches and other valuable articles. It was ascertained that at about 2 o'clock the night previous some audacious thief had entered a bedroom containing two beds, in which reposed Gen. R. M. Stevenson, P . C. Leonard, one of the proprietors of the hotel, George Schick, and another man sleeping with Stevenson, whose name is unknown. In accordance with the usual custom, the door of the room had been left unlocked, and the burglar had an easy job, going through the sleepers in detail. Schick upon retiring had placed his clothes under the pillow. In his pocket ticked a gold repeater of exquisite workmanship, worth, with the chain, at least $300, while in the fob pocket of his pantaloons were two $100 bills. When he awoke in the morning he found his clothes precisely as he had placed them, not disturbed in the least, but his watch and money wore gone. His exclamation of surprise awoke the others, and they commenced searching with varying results. Leonard found himself out a five-cent nickel and a few pool checks. Gen. Stevenson missed between four and five dollars in currency, while his roommate bewailed the loss of $15. Messrs. John and Cal. Peabody, who occupied a room over Jordan's store, in the Conley block, were the next victims. The door of their room was locked, with the key inside, but the cracksmen turned this by means of nippers and walked in. Cal's pocketbook, containing $112 in cash, was soon rifled, and a watch and chain, belonging to John Peabody, of no great value, taken. The pocketbook was found on the street corner in the morning, with nothing inside but a few papers. The room adjoining Mr. Peabody's was occupied by Mrs. Snyder, a milliner, and the thief was ungallant enough to enter this and rob the slumbering lady of her gold watch and chain, valued at $125. Mr. George Perkins, a furniture dealer, was also visited and robbed of a watch and $300 in money.

Of course, the town was in an uproar, for Pueblo was not then so pretentious a place as it now is, and it did not take so long for news to travel all over the city. Officers were put to work. In a few hours the fact was developed that White, the popular invalid, was nowhere to be found. Zach Allen—who has since been killed, poor fellow!—was then sheriff of Pueblo county, and he became convinced that White had been guilty of the robbery. When he let a few words drop to that effect the announcement was met with loud protestations on the part of the ladies. They pooh-poohed the idea. Yet evidence accumulated to fasten the guilt upon White, and Allen determined to arrest him. But where to find him? That was the important question. He was not in Pueblo; that was certain. Mr. Allen decided to send the following telegram:

To D. J. Cook, Superintendent Rocky Mountain Detective Association, Denver:

Be on lookout for man named White, who has stolen watches and other valuables. Has a friend in Denver named Larnigan.

(Signed) ALLEN, Sheriff.

The telegram quoted at the close of the last chapter was. "nuts" for Cook, he knew his man. Taking W. A. Smith—then an honored member and assistant superintendent of the-association-—with him, they started out in their search. They learned at the depot that a freight train had come in from Pueblo an hour before, and that it carried a passenger bearing the description- of White. They had from the first kept close track of Larnigan, and knew his haunts. They knew further that White was most likely to join his pal immediately upon his arrival: in Denver, and they started forthwith to search for them both at a joint ten-pin alley and saloon on Holladay street kept by one Green, which Larnigan was known to frequent. Thither they went, and throwing open the door to the establishment suddenly, they walked in. Sure enough, there stood their men* before them. The room contained some half a dozen other men, but these two were nearest the door, and they were engaged in earnest conversation when the officers entered. White was standing with his back to the door which Larnigan was facing. Before the latter had had time to notify his pal of the entrance of the officers, which he had observed. Cook had stepped rapidly forward and laid a heavy hand upon the shoulder of White, pulling him around so as to face him.

As may be imagined, a scene followed. Everybody was astonished, and all in the room rushed forward to the assistance of A Lite. The officers had stirred up a hornet's nest. All was buzz and bustle.

"What is wanted?" demanded White.

"You."

"Me?"

"Yes."

"Guess you are mistaken; I am not your man."

"We'll see about that."

"Where's your warrant?"

298

Just then Larnigan jumped forward and thrust his hand into White's pocket, where it was to be naturally supposed White carried a pistol.

"Draw on him!" said Cook to Smith.

Promptly as clockwork out came Bill Smith's revolver. "Shall I shoot the son of a bitch?" he asked.

"Yes, shoot him dead if he makes a move."

Cook himself wore a tight-lacing military jacket at that time over his pistol pocket and was delayed in getting out his own gun. The crowd was disposed to take advantage of this state of affairs and to assist White and Larnigan out of their awkward predicament. The barkeeper started for his pistol which was lying on a convenient shelf, and the crowd rushed forward for the purpose of cutting off the retreat of the officers with their prisoner. Dave Cook's blood was thoroughly aroused at this spectacle, and Bill Smith stood with teeth set as if to defy the entire gang. Still holding his prisoner with his right hand, Dave tore his coat open with his left, sending his military buttons flying with a bound in all directions. In an instant the barkeeper was covered by Dave, who still held on to his prisoner with his right hand. The crowd was still in an instant.

"Throw up your hands!" commanded Gen. Cook. "Every one of you!"

When Dave Cook gives a command under such circumstances as these, those who hear it obey it. A dozen hands flew instantaneously into the air. The victory was complete. The capture was made.

"Now search him," he said to Smith, while he himself held his pistol over the thoroughly awed crowd. The first pocket into which Smith thrust his hand yielded up a pair of burglar's nippers and live stolen watches.

"Do you want to see our warrant mow?" demanded Cook.

"No," replied White quite demurely, "I guess you've got proof enough. But," he added, "don't take me to Pueblo; they'll hang me sure."

With this the officers marched out of the saloon with their prisoner, and he was soon securely locked up in jail and all the stolen property recovered in less than an hour's time after the first information of the Pueblo burglaries was received.

The next morning Gen. Cook started to Pueblo with his prisoner, who was greatly frightened at the idea of going back to face the wrath of those whose confidence he had so grossly abused.

"They'll hang me; they'll hang me. I know they will." Thus he pleaded.

"Well," replied Cook, "you'll doubtless deserve it. Didn't I tell you if you didn't get out of this country, and keep out, I would overtake you? Haven't I been as good as my word? There is nothing left for you but to go back and stand trial. I'll protect you while you are in my keeping. Of that you may rest assured."

Engaged in such conversation as this they journeyed on down the narrow gauge—then the baby road, indeed—to Pueblo. They met only a slight demonstration there, and officer and prisoner were encouraged to believe that all apprehensions of violence had been unfounded. White was turned over to the jailer and was locked up. No unusual demonstrations were made, and after remaining at the prison for a little while and observing that all was quiet, Gen. Cook withdrew.

The next day the preliminary examination of the prisoner took place before Justice Hart, and resulted in his being bound over, on seven separate indictments, for burglary, larceny, etc., in the sum of $8,500, to appear for trial. He was remanded back to jail.

Gen. Cook was detained as a witness, and was thus compelled to remain over two nights in Pueblo.

The evening of the second night he spent with several friends, including Sheriff Allen.

He was absent from his hotel until about 12 o'clock, and was just returning to it in company with Allen, when the somewhat notorious "Hoodoo" Brown rushed up, with the exclamation:

"There's hell to pay at the jail!"

Gathering an idea of the situation in an instant, Cook and Allen were off for the jail. That institution was half a mile distant, but they ran every step of the way, and rushed in just in time to find one of the guards at the jail untying the other.

"Just got loose," he muttered. "They came in, about twenty of 'em, with guns and pistols, overpowered us, took us completely by surprise, tied us here, got the keys, marched into White's room. There was one big man in the crowd. He looked seven feet high. Why, he just went up to White—White's a little fellow, you know—and he seemed to be moaning and crying, and he just picked him right up—he had gone to bed—and said: 'Come to me arms, me baby,' and carried him out, his bare feet dangling down to the big man's knees. Oh, it was awful, sir. I guess they hung him."

Recovering himself somewhat, the speaker explained briefly all he knew about the transaction. He said that his name was Redfield, and that he was the jailer, and that he was sleeping in the jail, having retired about 10 o'clock p m. He was awakened by the assistant jailer, A. W. Briggs, who told him there was a mob outside. Redfield went to the door and asked, "Who's there?" when a voice replied, "Zach Allen, the sheriff; let us in." Not doubting but that the voice he had heard was Mr. Allen's, and supposing that he had a prisoner, Mr. Redfield turned the key of the door and opened it, when a number of men rushed in dressed in calico and masked, and in a moment the jail was in possession of the mob. Their first act was to bind Redfield and his assistant, hand and foot; leaving them gagged and helpless on the floor. One of the men stooped over and hissed in the ear of Briggs:

"Lie still and you shan't be hurt, but give the alarm and I'll blow your brains out!"

After leaving Redfield and Briggs, the mob started for White's cell, the key of which they seemed to find without any trouble. They walked White out with his shackles on. When the miserable man reached the front entrance, and fully comprehended the terrible fate soon to be visited upon him, he turned around and desired time to pray, but ibis request was sternly denied. He was picked up by one of the party and taken out in the darkness, the stern avengers closed around him in a solid mass, the word "forward*' was given, and that was the last ever seen of White alive.

The officers listened to this narrative with impatience, and when it had been finished, asked to know the way the mob had gone. The man pointed in the direction of a telegraph pole a hundred yards away, and Cook and Allen started towards it.

The gentleman who hangs limp from the telegraph pole, with his bare toes reaching for *terra firma*, is the late Mr. White. The vigilantes have done their work and have departed. They are nowhere to be seen. White is gone beyond the hope of recovery, and nothings left but to cut him down and bury him.

But White was not unaccompanied to his last resting place. His jail guard, Briggs, followed close upon his heels. He had lived to confirm Mr. Redfield's story of the jail delivery, as above related. He was subject to heart disease. The excitement had been too much for him, and the next morning he fell to the floor a corpse.

So there were two burials in Pueblo the next day, and people said of one death, "It was deserved;" of the other, "It was an accident; poor fellow!" Such, in brief, were the public funeral orations passed upon the two. There was a sigh for one. There was no sigh for the other. So passes the world away. It is the fortune of the detective to see death as well as life sharply contrasted at times.

When Cook returned to Denver he found that Larnigan had disappeared. He had received the news from Pueblo. He took the hint and left, and has never since been seen in Colorado.

THE RETRIBUTION OF FATE

The murder of August Gallinger, *alias* "Cheap John," created a sensation in Denver in the latter part of the year 1866, which for a long while engaged the public attention. Mr. Gallinger kept a small store on the corner of Twelfth and Blake streets, and lived alone over the store in a small room. He had been a member of the Third Colorado regiment, enlisted for a hundred days, and had taken part in the Sand Creek fight. He was quite popular, and although a street peddler, he did a thriving business. He lived in plain style, and was supposed by some to be a miser. This impression it was which led to his murder.

The assault occurred on the night of December 15, 1866. Gen. Cook had been elected city marshal of Denver for the first time a few months previous. On the night of the occurrence he was passing across the Blake street bridge from Denver to West Denver, accompanied by another officer. They were walking leisurely along, when they heard something fall, creating a loud noise. Cook immediately formed the conclusion that something wrong had happened, and he and his companion started in the direction of the point from which the noise had come, and it appeared to be in John's house. There was no one below, hence the officers rushed upstairs. It was about 9 o'clock in the evening, and as there were no artificial lights in the house, they found the place quite dark. As they went up the front steps they thought they heard someone descending the rear steps, but as they at that time did not know what had happened, they passed on into John's room, and did not pursue the party who was leaving the house.

Reaching Mr. Gallinger's room, their ears were greeted by moans from a man sitting on a lounge. Gen. Cook went up to where the man—who proved to be Gallinger—sat and assisted him to his feet, demanding to know what had occurred and how it had all come about. He found Gallinger covered with blood, and when the officer pulled him up the poor fellow clutched the lapel of Cook's coat with his bloody hands. The blood was flowing from a deep wound four inches long in the head. When questioned, John replied in German, and was evidently demented. But it did not require any speech to explain that murder had been attempted. The wound was of a nature that precluded the possibility of suicide; and, besides, the instrument with which it had been inflicted was nowhere to be seen. It was evident from the appearance of the wound that it had been made with a hatchet, the murderer coming upon the victim while sitting, and striking with the edge of the tool. Dr. F. J. Bancroft was summoned. Upon examination he found that the skull had been seriously fractured, and pronounced the wound necessarily fatal. It may as well be stated here, as elsewhere, that the doctor's prediction was verified, and that the old man died a week afterwards. He was never conscious after the night of the assault, and hence could throw no light whatever upon the affair.

Leaving the wounded man in care of others, Gen. Cook immediately began a search for the murderer. He found the tracks of a man leading out from the rear of the building, and made an exact measurement of them. He also found a woman who stated that she had seen a man go out of the building at the rear at about the time of the attack, but she had not been able to get a good look at him on account of the darkness, and thought she would be unable to recognize him.

Here was a dilemma. A crime had been committed only a few minutes before, but the criminal seemed to have escaped as effectually as if he had had a month's start of the officers.

But Cook is not the man to lose time in hesitation. He spent the night in searching for some clue which would lead to the detection of the villain, whoever he might be.

He learned enough during the night to decide him in a determination to raid a house which stood nearby. This house was occupied by several persons, all of them of loose character. Among others who occupied it was a worthless individual named George Corman who was the "solid man" of another inmate of the dwelling, a low prostitute called Mrs. Foster. The fellow did not work for a living, but depended upon the earnings of this woman for support. He was known to be none too good to steal, and it was believed that he would commit murder if there was hope of reward. Cook knew enough about this man to lead him to believe that the chances were good for his being the murderer of Cheap John. He decided to investigate, at any rate. Accordingly, in company with H. B. Haskell, then a special officer in Denver, he repaired to the Corman residence early in the morning succeeding the murderous assault, ne found the front of the building occupied by Corman and his woman, while in the rear premises resided a Mrs. Mary Kerwin with her family.

The officers decided to investigate while the inmates of the house were still asleep. They entered the yard by a back entrance, and as they came up to the door found a hatchet lying upon the ground thoroughly besmeared with blood. Here was certainly a pointer—the first important one found—and it bid fair to lead to speedy results. The officers felt that they had made a big discovery, and without further ado walked into the house, where they met Mrs. Kerwin, of whom they demanded to know the name of the owner of the hatchet. Her reply was that it was the property of Corman.

Corman and the Foster woman were next approached. They did not deny the ownership of the hatchet.

"Where did this blood come from?" demanded Cook.

The woman became the spokesman. "I killed a chicken last night," she said, "and cut its head off with the hatchet."

"Chicken! chicken!" replied Cook. "Chickens are worth a dollar and a half apiece in this country now and I know you can't afford chickens. Sowbelly is good enough for you."

The woman replied that she put on style occasionally herself.

When Cook asked where the feathers were she declared that they had been thrown into the privy vault, while the bones had been burned in the stove.

A close search of the vault and of the ashes in the stove failed to reveal any trace of the remains of the alleged chicken. Here were other strong pointers. The arrest of Corman was decided upon. There seemed to be a pretty fair case against him already developed, and Mr. Cook had confidence in finding a great deal more testimony. Consequently he took Corman into custody and locked him up.

George Hopkins was at that time an officer in Denver, and he was called upon to aid in working up the case. He was sent to see Mrs. Kerwin and to ascertain, if possible, whether she did not know more about it than had so far been developed. Gen. Cook, himself, believed that she could tell the entire story if she would. In this case as in most others, he Hit the nail square on the head. The woman knew a great deal, and Hopkins was able to prevail upon her to tell her story. Her revelation was startling enough.

Mrs. Ker win's sleeping apartments adjoined those of Corman and Mrs. Foster, and there was only a thin board partition between the two rooms, there being many cracks in the boards. On the night of the assault she had heard Corman come in. She had already retired, and was supposed by him and the Foster woman to be asleep, though she was not ne had appeared to be considerably hurried, and had said to Mrs. Foster:

"Well, I hit the damned old Jewy and I hit him hard, but I did not get anything—not a cent. The officers came so quick that I couldn't move a wheel, and had to run like the devil to get away."

As may be supposed his disclosure had aroused the curiosity of the listening woman. She was now wide awake, and was determined to hear all that was to be said. She put her ear to an open crack, and then heard the man tell his woman how he had come upon the Jew and struck him with his hatchet. This he had no sooner done than John clutched him, the blood spurting out of his fresh wound and covering his shirt. The garment, he said, was then bloody. An examination by the two which Mrs. Kerwin witnessed, continued his statement. It was then decided between them that the tell-tale garment must be disposed of. Corman accordingly took the shirt off, and they stowed it away in a cooking vessel which they found in the room, which Corman took to the back yard and buried, returning and going to bed.

The officers having this story in their possession, began to look for the hidden shirt. A snow had fallen in the early morning after it had been buried, and they were compelled to look over almost the entire yard for it before uncovering it, but they at last came upon the hidden article. It was found snugly buried some eight inches below the surface, and when brought out it was discovered to be pretty well bespattered with the crimson fluid.

Thus the case was worked up by Gen. Cook. He had not rested until he had probed the mystery to its foundation. It would seem that there could have hardly been the least chance for Corman to escape the gallows. Strange as it may appear to the reader, he not only was not hanged, but he was allowed to go scot free.

There was then but one term of the district court held each year in Denver, and it came in January. The trial of Corman came on in January, 1867. The crime was then fresh in the minds of the people, and the proceedings were watched with very great interest. The people were represented by Hon. V. D. Markham, then prosecuting attorney, while Messrs. M. Benedict, G. W. Chamberlain and— Bostwick appeared for the defense. The case was ably presented on both sides, the defense relying principally upon impeaching the testimony of Mrs. Kerwin, who was the most important witness for the prosecution. They succeeded in making suck an impression upon the mind of one of the jurors as to cause him to hold out for acquittal against the other eleven, who favored a verdict of murder in the first degree, the penalty for which would have been hanging. The obstinacy of this one man resulted in the bringing in a report of disagreement by the jury. The case was thus continued until the next term of court. By the time this term convened Mrs. Kerwin had died, and Mr. Haskell had left the city, and their testimony could not be obtained. Hence the case was dismissed, and the murderer of Cheap John became a free man in 1868.

When Corman was turned out of jail he found Denver a very disagreeable place of residence, as everybody believed him guilty of murder. He went to Georgetown, where he soon became known as one of the worst sots of the town, earning a scanty living by scrubbing out barrooms. Even his woman deserted him.

Gen. Cook saw him in Georgetown in 1874 and asked why he did not tell all about the murder of Cheap John.

"If I should do so," he replied, "they couldn't prove it on me."

Poor fellow! he met with a worse fate than death on the scaffold. There was in those days an unused tunnel in the side of a mountain near Georgetown, extending in about a hundred feet. The people of the town were startled one quiet afternoon by a report of an explosion coming from the direction of this tunnel, which seemed to them to be loud enough for the bursting loose of a volcano. Almost the whole city was shocked.

The temporary bewilderment having subsided, an investigating committee was organized to explore the tunnel. They went in with lights, and soon discovered to their dismay that there was fresh flesh sticking to some of the rocks of the wall. Other pieces of flesh, and some clothing and fragments of bones were found scattered about. There was enough of the clothes left to identify them as those of old Corman. He had gone into the tunnel—for what purpose no one will probably ever know—and had found a five-pound can of nitro-glycerine lying on the ground, and had evidently picked it up to examine it, and, finding that it was nothing that he wanted, had thrown it down, creating the explosion which had shocked the town, and which tore his carcass into shreds.

People said it was Fate that did it. Who knows?

And this is the end of the story which began eight or nine years before, with Gen. Cook's hearing a strange noise while crossing the Cherry creek bridge. Strange, isn't it, how all these scoundrels meet their just deserts? There are other laws than those which the courts deal with, and superior to them. One of these prescribes punishment for the murderer. It always comes sooner or later.

A TOWNFUL OF THIEVES

The month of January, 1877, was devoted by the Rocky Mountain Detective Association to the ferreting out of a gang of thieves who made their headquarters at Kit Carson, on the Kansas Pacific railroad in this state, and who earned a living by stealing from the railroad cars.

The case was one of prolonged and bold stealing, in which a large number of the citizens around Carson took a high hand. They carried on with great success a scheme for the robbery of the Kansas Pacific Railroad Company and those who entrusted their freights to the care of this corporation. Carson is situated about a hundred and fifty miles from Denver, and was then the point at which the Arkansas Valley branch of this road left the main stem. It is also at the foot of a heavy grade, and was* then used as a place for leaving cars. On account of the grade, it was often the case that the most heavily laden of the cars were laid over there. The plan with the rascals who carried out this scheme was to help themselves to a portion of whatever articles they might find themselves in need of.

The watchman, whose name was Frank E. Williamson, it seems took part in these plunderings, and was well paid for his trouble. They did not confine themselves to merely laying in groceries, dry goods, etc., but actually broke into the live-stock cars and secured good prizes in the shape of horses and mules. At first but little notice was taken of these depredations, as they were, for a time, on a very small scale, but the losses being continually reported, aroused a suspicion in the minds of the officials of the road that the goods were more than one man could comfortably get away with, and hence they reasonably concluded that a gang was engaged in the business. The reports constantly coming in, it was by some means ascertained that Carson was the point at which they were taken, and accordingly the matter was placed in the hands of Gen. D. J. Cook, the superintendent of the Rocky Mountain Detective Association. Not, however, until the railroad company had made an effort to make one of its own detectives useful.

Having convinced themselves that the goods which shippers complained of finding missing were being stolen at Carson, the company sent one of their "fly" men to the place to work up the case, that evidence might be obtained and the parties arrested. After spending a few days about Carson, he decided to take some action, thinking that he had sufficient facts to justify arrests. He accordingly went before the magistrate of the place, whose name was Pat Shanley, and who was also proprietor of the hotel there. The warrant being sworn out against a few men, Shanley told the detective that he would take him around and introduce him to the constable, whose name was Worth Keene, and who was also proprietor of a saloon, intimating that it might be a good opportunity to kill two birds with one stone by getting a drink at the same time the paper was handed over to the constable. The drink was taken, and the two enjoyed a laugh at the expense of the fellows who were so soon to be in the hands of the minions of the law. But the detective probably did not see the sly wink which passed from the justice when he handed over the warrant, or if he did, did not understand its import. He must have thought it rather strange, however, when after going out Constable Keene did not return, and the men whom he knew to be offenders against the law began to disappear. It may be that he was given a hint of the intention of the citizens of the place, which was to lynch him that evening.

Census records show that Worth Keene was born on May 8, 1848 in Kentucky. He married his wife, Nancy Emaline Young, in 1876. They later moved to Los Angeles, where Keene died in 1907.—Ed. 2016

Whether his suspicions were aroused or not, when the train came along bound for Kansas City, the detective quietly stepped aboard and was seen no more in those parts. He departed with but little more information than he had possessed when he went in, and convinced that the ways of the people of Carson were peculiar, quite peculiar, and past finding out.

It was then that the case was placed in the hands of Gen. Cook to have it worked up. The job was a delicate one. There were but about twenty-five people, women and children included, residing at Carson, so that a man who should go there would be open to immediate inspection, and if he should go as a detective, the chances were that he would be found out before he could find out anything. Yet Cook decided to chance it. He concluded to send a man down to the place, who should stop there for awhile and play the role of a deserter from the army. Alex MacLean, at present a resident of Denver, was commissioned to perform this delicate task. All went well with him for awhile—almost to the end, in fact. He got along quite swimmingly for many days. His story was accepted, and as he displayed a considerable sum of money and used it freely, he was made at home with the boys.

Alex MacLean is listed in the Denver city directory in 1876 as a driver and in 1879 as a "checkman."—Ed. 2016

At last, however, the thieves began to suspect MacLean and made a strong endeavor to catch him. One of them prevailed upon MacLean to sleep with him one night, and during the night undertook to draw him out, telling him that there was a splendid opportunity there for a detective, and entering at some length into the scheme of robbery which had been carried on at the place. MacLean listened with eagerness, though he did not, by words at least, betray himself. He, however, agreed with his friend that they could make a great deal of money together by exposing the thieving, and that the man should show MacLean the next morning, where the goods were hidden. This was done according to programme.

It now became apparent to the thieves that MacLean was a detective, and they arranged their plans to put him out of the way, in other words, to quietly kill him on the following night. This programme would most likely have been carried into effect had the thieves not been so indiscreet as to whisper their intentions to someone, who dropped the information far down the Kansas Pacific [Railroad], beyond Carson, to a party who telegraphed Gen. Cook the peril that his man was in. With this Cook decided to recall MacLean and ordered him home that very day, and thus were the plans of the murder frustrated.

A previous train the same day brought in Williamson, the watchman, who, concluding chat he had been found out or soon would be, was preparing to skip the country, and came in with his baggage checked for Montana. Being informed through MacLean that Williamson was on the train and that he probably knew a great deal, Cook proceeded to the depot in Denver, met the train and quietly took Williamson into custody. He at first made an effort to bluff the officers, but failing in this, agreed to make a full confession on the condition that he should be released from custody. The officers agreed to this proposition, especially as they had already taken precautions to prevent his capture being known or telegraphed to his friends at Carson, Being placed in a close carriage he was driven to a place of safety and then told the entire story of the thievery to the detective.

It appeared from this story that the entire town of Kit Carson, with the exception of two men who were too old for action, had been engaged in the thievery, which he said had been going on for nearly two years, beginning by small stealings and increasing them as time went on until some big holes were made in the shipments which passed through. Shanley, the justice of the peace, was the head of the gang, and he accumulated quite a fortune in carrying on the work. His hotel was supplied from the proceeds of his robbery. He purchased herds of cattle, and before he was discovered had stolen sufficient stock to start a line of teams between Carson and Del Norte, thus procuring a market for the stealings of the gang in the San Juan country, and hauling them away at the expense of others. Keene, the constable, was also a leader in the gang. With the magistrate and the constable, the state's only officers in the district, and the cooperation of the railroad watchman, the stealing was made easy. It was now, alas, about to be brought to an end forever.

It was on the 1st of February, 1877, that Williamson was arrested and that MacLean arrived at home. Gen. Cook decided that the gang must be taken without delay, and as soon as MacLean arrived and he heard his story, he decided upon a *coup d'etat*. Procuring a special train, he organized an expedition under the leadership of Assistant Frank Smith, and sent them down to make the arrest of the parties implicated. The party consisted of Smith, MacLean, Major Sam Logan, John Copeland, Tom Chandler, and Tom Porter.

The special left Denver in the evening and ran leisurely down the track, timing itself so as to reach Carson about daylight. All worked well, and the train drew up a few hundred feet west of the station just as the gray dawn was beginning to make itself visible on the eastern knolls of the plains. But little time was lost in preliminaries. Most of the men belonged at the hotel, and it was determined to surprise them first. The officers crept cautiously behind a protecting house, and finding that a majority of the rogues were already out of bed and standing in front of the hotel, marched boldly out before their startled gaze, and with arms presented and ready for instant use, commanded the scoundrels to hold up their hands.

It was all over in a minute. Nothing was left for them to do but to throw their hands into the air and quietly surrender.

This party being in the possession of the officers, the few others scattered in various directions were soon taken, there being eight in all namely: William Kelly, Worth Keene. Mike Fitzpatrick, William Tally, Thomas Rasbaugh. J. Ratliff, C. W. Lindsley (Texas Bill), and Pat Shanley. A hurried search was made in the vicinity and large quantities of stolen goods were found hidden from Kit Carson down the railroad for four miles, as well as two miles east, on the Big Sandy, and some on Horse creek, north of Kit Carson. Nearly all the articles were buried in the ground. Among the miscellaneous assortment of articles stolen were hats, caps, laces, silks, groceries, boots, ladies' shoes, raisins, feather beds, beef, beef tongues, apple butter, bacon, ham, tea, coffee, laid, a quantity of coal, tobacco, powder and butter. The goods were mostly taken from the original packages, and where they were not so filched, most of the marks were erased, except in the case of the butter.

When these men were removed from Carson to West Las Animas, the county seat of Bent county, in which the stealing was conducted, there were but two men left at the station to take care of the horde of women and children who cried after them as they moved away in their shackles.

One more arrest made in Denver completes the list. While the posse was down the road Col. C. W. Fisher, division superintendent, telegraphed to Gen. Cook to arrest a brakeman named Adam Ehls, for complicity with the gang. He was discovered late in the evening at 520 Arapahoe street, in full dress for an engineers' ball.

The 1877 Denver city directory lists Ehls as a brakeman.—Ed. 2016

But the appearance of Detective Arnold convinced him that a change of programme was unavoidable, and that Turner hah must dispense with his presence. When informed that Col. Fisher had ordered his arrest, he seemed to perfectly comprehend the whole affair. The officer accompanied him to his own house, where were found a trunk and valise containing a large quantity of fancy goods, ladies' shoes, silver plated pistols, and several boxes of cheap jewelry. Forty pocket knives had been placed on sale at Tierney's hardware store, but were recovered several days before.

Thus was this well organized and extensive gang of thieves brought to justice in a way so effective that the road never since had a trouble of this kind of half so extensive a scale to deal with.

The association received, as it certainly deserved, the warmest thanks from the railroad company, as well as liberal pay for their services.

At the preliminary examination of this band of thieves, which was held at West Las Animas soon after their capture, several of the men were released upon bail, in sums ranging between $1,000 and $5,000 bail each. Shanley's bail was fixed at $5,000, Keene's at $2,500, and Ehls' at $1,000. Three of the men were sent to the penitentiary for long terms, and the other four escaped upon technicalities. Shanley, Keene and Ehls forfeited their bonds and disappeared from the state, never having been seen in Colorado since.

The town of Kit Carson was broken up by the raid, and is now little more than a water tank on the Kansas Pacific.

RAGSDALE GATES

Ragsdale Gates was a "bad" man. He hailed from Mississippi, and came away from that state under circumstances which did not speak well for his character. He left his country for his country good and to save his own neck, which was in jeopardy. Mr. Gates was one of those numerous southern "gentlemen" who drink too freely, and who, when in liquor, are apt to do many rash acts, which, when they are once sober, they are sorry for. Mr. Gates had lived for many years prior to 1879 at Friar's Point, where he killed three white men while drinking. He is also said to have been a famous "nigger hunter" ["slave catcher" in less offensive terms] in the Mississippi swamps, and had been a leader of one of the famous Ku Klux clans back in the days succeeding the close of the war. He had the reputation of having laid several colored men to rest. But it was not an act of this kind that got him into trouble. It was the killing of a fellow white man under circumstances peculiarly aggravated. He was arrested and escaped jail.

Gates was born in Mississippi in 1850 and married Marina Victoria Pittman in 1873.—Ed. 2016

Having gotten out of prison, Gates left Mississippi, and it was some time before his whereabouts became known to anyone. In some way the Friar's Point officers obtained an inkling that the fugitive had come to Colorado. They did not know to what point he had come, or, indeed, whether he was in the state at all, but merely surmised that he was. Being desirous that Gates should be apprehended, they wrote to Gen. Cook, chief of the Rocky Mountain Detective Association, of their surmises, and offered a reward of $500 for the capture of the man sending a description of him. The matter was turned over to Mr. William Wise. Mr. Wise was then and had been for years previous, one of the leading members of the detective association, and one of the most astute and discreet detectives in the state.

Mr. Wise took the case in hand and worked it up with his customary energy and caution. He was not long in learning that a man giving the name of J. J. Reed, and answering to the description of Gates, was figuring in the southern part of the state. He learned of him at Silver Cliff, and learned that the man had been accused of horse stealing, not for any innate love of horse flesh, but merely that he might gain time in his movements. Mr. Wise opened a correspondence with persons at Silver Cliff after learning of the presence of Gates at that point, and had the fellow arrested. Hearing that his man had been taken and locked up, Mr. Wise prepared to start for Silver Cliff. He had not gotten away from Denver when he learned to his surprise and regret that Mr. Gates had taken his departure before the officer's arrival. He had again broken jail.

Mr. Wise did not, however, cease his pursuit of the criminal. "Hilly" is not the man to let up easily when he once gets well started. He was determined that Gates should be taken. He accordingly kept on the lookout. He learned that after getting out of the prison at Silver Cliff, the man had stolen a horse to escape on. He tracked him to Dodge City, Kan. But the restless southerner did not remain long at any point, and joining a cattle drive from that point to Dakota, was soon off for the far north, going now by the name of Warren. He was tracked across the plains by Wise, all the way to Camp Robinson, where he was heard of in in drunken row, as usual, which ended up in his seriously injuring a man. He was again thrown into prison, and again escaped, the military being unable to cope with him.

Gates then escaped to Wyoming, where he again got into a fight and shot a man. This fracas resulted in the re-arrest of the fellow and of his being taken to Sidney, Neb., where Wise heard of him, and where he determined to go after him with a requisition. He had, however, not started, when he heard that his man had again stolen away. The information of the escape was soon, however, followed by that of his recapture, and after hearing this, Hilly was soon off for Sidney, determined this time to lose no time, that he might be sure of coming upon his man before he should have another opportunity to get away.

Accordingly Mr. Wise went down to Sidney. He found his prize this time, and had no difficulty' in getting him away, starting immediately for Denver. On the way from Sidney the man's propensity to escape asserted itself, but it was not given an opportunity to develop fully, and was in fact nipped in the bud at a very aggravating moment. Gates remonstrated while on the train with the officer for exposing him as a prisoner, and requested the officer to allow him to cover up his hands with a robe, saying that he was a gentleman, and pleading that his pride was wounded in the exhibition which he was compelled to make of himself. Mil Wise at last consented to give the man an opportunity to hide his shame and his hands, and threw the robe over the latter.

Billy sat by the side of his prisoner and appeared to be looking through the floor, when, in fact, his full gaze was directed through the corner of his eye towards the prisoner. Soon he saw the robe lying across Gates' folded arms begin to move. He sat as stolid as a block while the fellow worked at his handcuffs for half an hour. At last he saw the two hands separate, and watched the fellow quietly lay the irons under him on the seat. He had succeeded in getting the irons off. His scheme was to replace his hands under the covering until the light moment should come, when he would take the cuffs from his seat, strike the officer over the head with them, grab his pistol, jump from the car and be a free man.

That moment never came. The irons were hardly laid down when Mr. Ragsdale Gates found the muzzle of Billy Wise's big pistol thrust half way up into his ear. All was over with him. The officer had played with him as a cat with a mouse. He promised if the officer would allow him to live, he would make no further effort to get away while In the custody of Mr. Wise. The promise was kept, and Gates was soon landed in Denver.

Mr. Wise took Gates from Denver to St. Louis, where he met a sheriff from Friar's Point, turned the prisoner over to him, received his reward, and returned home after receiving a warm compliment for both himself and the Rocky Mountain Detective Association, from the officer.

Gates being taken back to Mississippi was confined for nearly a year awaiting trial he escaped from jail again on the 25th of June, 1880, and was still at last accounts at liberty. It is safe to say, however, that he will keep away from Colorado in his wanderings.

Daniel Ragsdale Gates died in 1882 Quitman, Mississippi.—Ed. 2016

TAKEN BY.SUKPKISE

Sometime in the spring of 1878, Ed McGrand, the murderer, and the subject of this sketch, came up over the trail from Texas as a herder or employ of Bosler Brothers, of Sidney, Neb. (who for several years had the contract of supplying several Indian agencies, from Red Cloud agency, near Sidney, to the agencies up the Missouri river, with beef cattle). They were driving a herd of cattle to some of the Indian agencies on the upper Missouri, and McGrand had just returned from the trip and was at or around Bosler Brothers' range, near Sidney bridge, across the North Platte river, about fifty miles north of Sidney.

One D. J. McCann also had a cattle range near there, and it seems McGrand had some ill-feeling or prejudice toward McCann, Bruce Powers, and the outfit in general, over some trivial matter.

On June 25, 1878, McGrand came to McCann's camp, near Platte bridge, feeling very hostile, and with the intention of killing McCann and probably some of his men, being well-armed and under the influence of "bug juice." He attempted to shoot and kill McCann, and would have done so but for the intervention of McCann's men and friends. Among the friends of McCann who had interceded for him, to prevent McGrand's murdering him without cause, and had spoken in favor of McCann, was the victim, John Wright, a young man of twenty or twenty-one years of age, though a mere boy in stature and looks—a quiet, inoffensive cowboy, who had done nothing more than anyone naturally would do to persuade McGrand not to insist on murdering McCann and others.

As soon as the row had apparently quieted down, this boy mounted his pony and rode away, crossing to the other side of the river unarmed, and with no weapons of any kind about him, doubtless not dreaming of danger. But he was followed by McGrand still with murder in his heart. McGrand was mounted on a good horse, which did not belong to him and which he stole to escape on, and armed with a Sharp's carbine and two Colt's large size army revolvers. Thus prepared he followed Wright and overtook him soon after he had crossed the river, and shot him two or three times in the

319

head, killing him instantly, and undoubtedly without any cause, only that he was a friend of McCann's outfit.

After murdering the boy, McGrand immediately disappeared, going up the North Platte river, and was not heard of until his arrest on June 30, 1878, at a freighter's camp, at Sloan's lake, near Cheyenne, Wyo., by T. Jeff Carr, agent of the Rocky Mountain Detective Association at Cheyenne.

Immediately after the murder the authorities at Sidney offered a reward for the arrest of the murderer, and also sent out descriptions all over the country, but through some oversight had failed to notify Carr of the murder, and it was by accident and a streak of luck that he heard of the murder in time to head off the murderer, who was making south and was ready to start. In a few hours he would have been out of reach and danger, when arrested.

It was about June 29, 1878, when a teamster, driving a team in a mule freight train coming from Fort Laramie to Cheyenne, which had gone into camp near Cheyenne, on the banks of Sloan's lake, came to Carr and stated "that a suspicious acting, bad looking man on horseback, well-armed with gun and revolvers, had joined their outfit near Fort Laramie, on the North Platte, and had traveled and camped with them all the way that the man acted as though he had committed some serious crime and was afraid of capture. He kept out of the way quietly when strangers came around, always keeping his horse, gun and arms alongside of him; slept with gun and revolvers at his head, and would awake at night and grab them." He described the man as tall, with the left eye out, and when in camp near town he would be, the teamster said, always at camp "on guard apparently, and had said to him that if any one came to take him, "he would not be taken, as he would be hung."

Carr did not know of such a man's being wanted, but thought something was wrong or he would not act so, and at once set to work to find out if a crime had been committed lately by a man answering this description, and on Sunday, June 30, 1878, he met a cattleman from Sidney, on arrival of the train from the east, and asked him if he knew of a tall, one-eyed man being wanted at Sidney, or around his part of the country. The cattleman replied that such a looking man, named Ed McGrand, had murdered a boy at Platte bridge some two weeks before, and a reward was offered for him, and was surprised that Carr had not been notified. He said, also, that McGrand was a desperate man, and advised Carr to go well prepared, and be careful about taking him, as he was a dangerous man to fool with, "and would surely show fight." Carr immediately telegraphed to Sidney, asking the sheriff for particulars, and at once received answer that Ed. McGrand, a tall, one-eyed man, was "badly wanted for murder, and if around Cheyenne, to get him at all hazards." Carr at once called to his aid Deputies W. C. Lykins and E. H. Ingalls. He detailed Lykins on horseback with a rifle to approach the camp on the lake from the northeast, while he and Ingalls in a buggy would approach the lake from southwest, as though all were out for a "Sunday ride," and carelessly approach McGrand's camp and take him unawares. On arriving near the lake and camp, they saw our "solitary guard" standing alone near his horse, against a wagon tongue, his gun leaned against the wagon wheel and his revolvers in his belt around him. They gradually and in an apparently earless manner rode nearer the camp, not apparently noticing him or the camp, until they were in speaking distance. Carr then carelessly engaged McGrand in conversation about the teams, expressing a desire to buy some of them and to know where the boss was, etc., still driving nearer until close to McGrand, when Carr jumped out of his buggy, grasping the murderer's two hands or wrists, immediately followed by Deputy Ingalls, who took his revolvers out of his belt, Deputy Lykins all the time covering him with his gun.

Thus McGrand was taken completely by surprise by means of the strategy used, and no one hurt. Otherwise, he would undoubtedly have given the officers a warm reception. After he was taken he gritted his teeth and cursed himself for being such a fool as never to suspect they were officers, and told them if he had suspected they were after him, they could not have taken him, as he could have and would have killed all of them and got away on his horse. "He was the maddest and worst fooled man you ever saw," says Carr. He said he killed the boy, "but whisky done it," and "he knew he would be hung." etc.

McGrand was then taken by Sheriff Carr and placed in the county jail at Cheyenne, until the next day, July 1, when he was taken to Sidney, and on December 16, 1878, he was indicted by the grand jury for murder in the first degree, and on the 17th he was arraigned and placed on trial at Sidney for his life, and through some technicality of law, he saved his neck and was allowed to plead guilty of murder in the second degree, and was sentenced to imprisonment for life in the state penitentiary at Lincoln, Neb., and is now serving out his time.

McGrand's history is not known any more than that general report says he had to skip from Texas for murder committed there, and that he was a murderous and desperate man, and thought nothing of killing. He was then about forty or forty-five years of age; six feet tall; slender build; blind in the left eye; spare, thin, long face, high cheek bones, and a very muscular man; a typical Texas cowboy, with white slouch hat, etc.

Ed McGrand was born in Texas around 1852 and was of Native American heritage.—Ed. 2016

A RACE FOR LIFE

It was on Saturday, during the last days of February, 1875, that the then deputy United States marshal and Deputy Sheriff Charley Wilcox, of Arapahoe county, was shot down, and it was then believed fatally injured, at Island station, while making an effort to arrest one John W. Johnson on the charge of an improper use of the mails. The affair was, take it all in all, one of the most thrilling of the kind which ever happened in this vicinity, and created intense excitement at the time—a time, by the way, when excitements were rare in Denver.

Charles F. Wilcox is still listed in the Denver city directory for some years after the date of his shooting, so apparently he survived.—Ed. 2016

The facts leading up to the tragedy are these: For a long time a "confidence" game had been carried on by principals, who had their headquarters in or about Denver. As early as August, 1874, the fact became known to the post office department that the mails were being freely used by these swindlers and knaves to accomplish their purposes, and at once steps were taken to bring them to justice. Several months afterwards sufficient evidence was obtained to satisfy any ordinary mind of the guilt of a certain party, but not to render conviction by a jury a certainty. Consequently a plan was arranged to capture the fellow with sufficient evidence on his person to admit of no "reasonable doubt."

The game practiced by the villains was to send circulars to different parties living in this and adjoining territories, and even in the states, agreeing to furnish a good watch on the receipt of three dollars, or to deliver the same C. O. D. by express.

Stones, sawdust and other worthless articles were wrapped up very carefully in paper and sent to those who were so foolish as thus to be caught. The extent of the swindling thus carried on is not known, as hundreds would feel too "cheap" to acknowledge that they had been duped in such a ridiculous manner.

This man Johnson, who made his headquarters at Island Station, was spotted as the individual who was responsible for the swindle, through the exertions of the Denver post office officials and the Rocky Mountain detectives, and Deputy Sheriff Wilcox was sent to arrest him, being first deputized as a United States marshal, as the offense was one against the national government.

Wilcox reached the station before the arrival of the mail on that day, and waited the arrival of Johnson in the post office. When he came in he was accompanied by another man, by the name of Ike Clodfelter.

As soon as Johnson had received a registered letter, sent to trap him, he was arrested by the deputy sheriff. Upon being commanded to hand over whatever weapons he might have about him, Johnson promptly turned over a pistol to the officer, who naturally supposed the man to be disarmed after this, and permitted him in accordance with a request which he had made, to go to the door to give some directions about having his horse cared for.

The man was no sooner in the door than he sprang out like a pursued deer, and was off with the wind. He drew another revolver from his bootleg as he passed out, and was prepared to defend himself. The officer gave chase, attempting to draw his revolver. As he did this, the weapon fell, but rather than lose time, he pushed on, not having yet discovered that Johnson had drawn a second time, and believing that it would be one unarmed man against another when he should come up with his man, as he thought he would be able to do. Hence he concluded to waste no time, but to push forward in pursuit of his game. The result shows that the counted without his host, and that he did not half appreciate the cunning and the desperation of the man, or men, with whom he was dealing.

Johnson struck out at full speed, and was followed by the officer at a dead run. Finding that he was gained upon constantly, Johnson cocked his pistol as he ran and, without stopping, threw it back over his shoulder with the barrel pointing towards the pursuer, sending a streak of smoke and fire and lead after him as he flew over the ground. The ball went sizzing by Wilcox's head, but left him unharmed.

Wilcox was, of course, slightly astonished to find the man whom he considered unarmed firing at him, but did not stop at discovering this odds against himself. On the contrary, his pluck was fully aroused, and he determined to have his man whatever the cost, now that he had been fired upon by him, and he pushed on with more speed than before. Of course, if Johnson had known that Wilcox had dropped his pistol, he could have turned upon and defied him, and the officer shrewdly counted upon his man's ignorance of this fact to aid and save him. The fellow continued to fire over his shoulder, but as he took no aim—did not even see the object which he wished to strike—there was no danger except from accident. Five shots were discharged in rapid succession, the balls passing uncomfortably near, but none of them striking the officer.

Not dreaming that Johnson carried anything more than a five-shooter, the officer now pushed forward with still greater speed, supposing that he had his man safe. Here he learned a second lesson as to the character of the man with whom he had to deal. The fellow had reserved one load. The deputy was allowed to approach within a foot or two, when the gun was suddenly thrust back so close as to allow the muzzle to almost touch Wilcox, when to that gentleman's great amazement, "bang" it went again.

He felt the hard lead crashing through the flesh of his thigh and saw the blood spurt out, but he grappled with his man, determined to get him now or die in the effort. Wilcox then feeling that he was safe, collared Johnson who struck him a violent blow over the head with the empty revolver, which indented but did not fracture the skull. The officer began to push his man as best he could towards the housed calling out for Postmaster Fowler to come and assist him. Fowler started out, but Clodfelter, who was standing by, drew a revolver, and told him to "git" or he would shoot him. Fowler preferred the former alternative, and left Wilcox to his fate. By this time Johnson had begun to call on his confederate to shoot Wilcox, which Clodfelter refused to do, especially as Wilcox told him he did not believe he was coward enough to shoot an unarmed officer while trying to do his duty. Wilcox had yet to learn that this base villain was more than simply a friend of Johnson's.

Upon being repeatedly urged to shoot, Clodfelter finally gave his revolver to Johnson, with the remark:

"Shoot the son of a bitch yourself."

The instant Wilcox saw the weapon in Johnson's hand he so wrenched the fellows arm that the weapon was useless, and Johnson immediately called on his confederate to take it back and shoot. This Clodfelter refused to do, but as the bitter, angry words:

"God damn you! don't you remember what I did for you once?"

Were uttered, Clodfelter reached for the pistol, and Wilcox for the first time realized that he had to deal with a confederate as well as the principal. Feeling that he would probably be shot, the thought occurred to Wilcox to at least so "mark" Johnson that he could not escape. He was engaged in a tremendous struggle to throw Johnson, intending to stamp his head with his boot, then Clodfelter stepped about four feet off and fired. Instantly Wilcox dropped, and the two villains mounted their horses, which Clodfelter had brought close by, and made off.

Wilcox was discovered to have been shot by Johnson in the thigh, the ball entering the groin and passing out half way down to the knee, while Clodfelter had planted his lead in the poor fellows back.

Sheriff Willoughby, Postmaster Cheaver, Assistant Postmaster Maj. Lander, Dr. Charles Denison, and Gen. Cook, of the Rocky Mountain Detective Agency, were summoned to the scene as quickly as possible. They found "Wilcox in a precarious condition and likely to die at any moment. They decided to take him to Denver where he could have good care and the best of medical aid.

OFF FOR THE SOUTH

While the valiant officer is lying at the point of death, there are other scenes enacting elsewhere. Johnson and Clodfelter are off for their lives, and the officials are hunting them down with all the avidity and keenness of scent of bloodhounds. The community was greatly enraged, and excitement was intense in Denver, as well as in other portions of the state. There were loud cries for vengeance, and the demand was made on all hands that the would-be murderers should be hunted down. On account of their well-known skill, the Rocky Mountain Detective Association were called upon to take the matter in hand. They were ready to respond to this call, as they have always been ready to respond to any call made upon them.

Saturday, the day of the killing, was spent in looking after the wounded man, but Sunday the detectives put in in preparation for the work that was before them. They began the ball by offering $250 [about $5,400 in 2015] for the apprehension of the desperadoes, and by sending out circulars informing the country at large of what had been done, and describing the culprits.

On Tuesday night, a Mr. Wakeman, who lived then on Spring creek, about twenty-one miles from Denver, saw one of the posters and immediately remembered that the parties described therein had been at his place and were inquiring the way to Pueblo without passing through Colorado Springs.

This was clue enough, and immediately Gen. D. J. Cook, accompanied by Frank Smith, took the trail of the fleeing scoundrels.

Additional rewards had now been offered by the state, the county and the postal service, swelling the aggregate to $1,700 [nearly $37,000 in 2015], affording in itself a temptation to the utmost endeavor.

The pursuit was one of the most memorable ever recorded in the history of detective work. The officers left Denver on Tuesday morning, taking the Denver and Rio Grande train. As they traveled down the road they inquired at every station in regard to the men.

At Larkspur they met a men who said that the fugitives had taken supper at 6 o'clock the evening before at the house of Mr. Thompson, only a short distance away. At Kelly's Switch the officers received a note from a Mr. Waterbury, stating that the men who stopped at Wakeman's were the ones they were after, and that they had gone south. No other word was received by telegram or in any other way by these diligent men until after the men were seen to enter Pueblo. Thompson, at whose house the fugitives had taken supper the night before, directed them by the Templeton Pass road, which comes into the southern road along the Fountaine at Stubb's which is twelve miles below Colorado Springs.

At the Springs the officer found Mr. Rickerman, a miller, whom they engaged to go over to the Fountaine road and fob low it down, while they would go to Stubb's on the train, procure horses, and travel up the road to meet him, thus cutting off the pursued. At Stubb's they could not procure horses, and while deliberating over the matter Rickerman rode in. He had learned that the fleeing men had crossed the Fountaine two miles above Stubb's about 9:30 o'clock that morning. As no horses could be procured, Cook and Smith footed it to Fountaine, live miles, while Rickerman went on ahead on horseback.

By this time night had come on, and a severe March snowstorm, accompanied by strong winds and occasional sleet, was setting in. Still no horses were to be procured, and the prospect for progress was exceedingly gloomy for the officers. They not only seemed in a fair way not to be able to procure means of pursuing the men, but there was a chance of being compelled to remain out all night without adequate protection from the storm. Just as the outlook seemed the darkest a ray of hope broke upon the scene.

A second Colorado Springs party of five, well mounted on the very best livery horses, and armed with carbines and pistols, and headed by a deputy sheriff, rode up. Cook and Smith had no doubt that they would be able to make terms with these men, and thus be able to proceed with their work. Consequently they made a proposition to the leader of this party to leave two of his men at the place at which they were then stopping, and to let Cook and Smith have two of the horses, agreeing to divide the reward in case the criminals should be overtaken and captured. This proposition caused the Colorado Springs officers to hold a consultation, which resulted in a decision on their part to reject it.

"We can get the men as well as you can," said the leader. "We have their description. None of our men want to stay here, and we will not make the arrangement you suggest. We will pursue the men ourselves, and will not give up our horses. You are out of luck, boys. Hope you will do better next time."

This was a crusher. Another hope was blasted.

But Cook and Smith kept their own counsel and did not lose temper. They took supper at the same place with the Colorado Springs officers.

After supper the party of six, Rickerman having joined them, had their horses prepared for the go, and had mounted, when the leader approached Cook thus:

"Say, old fellow, which way do you think they went?"

It was Cook's time now to get in his lick.

"Gives us two horses and I will tell you; without the horses I don't know a damned thing."

"All right," replied the leader, laughingly, we'll get'em," with which the well mounted party rode off, going in the direction of Cañon City, much to the delight of the Denver men, who, though still afoot, had a great advantage in their experience of years and in the knowledge which they possessed. They determined to press forward, notwithstanding the snow was falling at a blinding rate and night had well set in.

Cook and Smith prevailed upon a ranchman to take them to Mason's ranch, six miles below, in an express wagon. Here they ascertained that the two men had passed between 3 and 4 o'clock in the afternoon. Cook and Smith then went over to the railroad station and endeavored to persuade three men, by an offer of $30, to take them to Pueblo on a hand-car. This the railroad men refused to do, as it was against orders to put a hand-car on the track at night.

"If you don't put it on we will," said Cook to the boss. "We must have it."

"That would make no difference; we cannot disobey orders."

"You can't, eh?" said Dave, as he pulled his revolver around so as to show it to the astonished Mike. "Now we've got to have the car; we're officers and must have it. If you don't give it to us we shall have to take it, and compel some of your men to go along with us."

This was an argument of more force than had yet been used, and resulted in the boss's agreeing to take the officers to a point seven miles below, which would be only fourteen from Pueblo, where he was sure transportation could be obtained.

In the face of the most disagreeable snow storm of the season the indomitable detectives, aided by three of the section men, propelled the car, the officers and men alternately working the lever and holding brooms to sweep the snow from the rails so as to allow the car to move. So they worked their way along for several miles until they reached Mr. John Irvine's ranch. There they hired a wagon and team for $20, and with that went into Pueblo, where they arrived at 3 o'clock on Thursday morning. As may be imagined, they were pretty well used up. They had put in about as hard a night as ever falls to the lot of mortals, walking at times, as they had to do, through slush and snow; riding on rough wagons, working the lever of the hand-car, and all the time going through the dark and facing the wind and sleet. Besides this, they had been compelled to bulldoze everybody, ranchmen and railroad men. A hard night it had been. No wonder that when they got into Pueblo they were well-nigh exhausted. Their clothes were wet through and hung limp on their limbs like clothes on a pole.

There were but a few hours left till morning, and the officers decided, after stationing two guards at the bridge over the Arkansas, between Pueblo and South Pueblo, to get a little rest. They, accordingly, after instructing the guards as to what to do in case Clodfelter and Johnson should come up, as they were confidently expected to do, repaired to a hotel, where they stretched themselves out upon cots before the fire with their clothes still unremoved, with the hope of drying their garments while they should rest their weary bodies.

A THIRTEEN-MILE RACE ACROSS THE PLAINS

Rising about 6 o'clock in the morning, the officers started to engage horses, but bad much difficulty. Finally they secured two, one of them a very fine animals. They then went back to the hotel, and started up the Fountaine to strike the trail of Clodfelter and Johnson. Cook had a Colt's forty-four calibre pistol, with only six loads, and a Henry rifle, borrowed at Pueblo. Smith was armed only with a. Colt's breech-loading pistol.

They had proceeded about two hundred yards from the hotel when they heard a shout, and looking back saw one of their guards—Officer Bilby—on the hotel steps, waving his hat. The officers glanced over the town and saw the two men they sought riding through. Instantly they let their horses out, and endeavored to cut off their exit across the bridge. In this they were not successful. Then both rode up behind a building and then into the street, down which the men were riding, about a hundred yards behind them. The men had discovered they were being pursued, and had thrown away their blankets, drawn their revolvers, and put spurs to their horses.

As Cook and Smith rode into the street, Cook called upon the men to halt, but the demand was not heeded.

"If you don't halt, you are dead men." But in vain. The scoundrels pushed on with all the greater vim. Their horses were flying over the ground, and the officers were following with the speed of the wind.

"Let them have one just to scare them." said Dave to Frank, and the two officers sent two shots into the air. These had no effect. The horsemen rode on without noticing the shots.

There were a few people in the street at this early hour, early and cold as it was, but they all scampered indoors when the bullets began to whiz in the air. The horsemen rode on regardless of surroundings. The pursued pair now swung around in a circle and came up on the mesa near the bridge above the officers, and riding abreast and as fast as their horses would carry them. Cook stopped his horse, cocked his gun, threw it to his shoulder, and drew a bead, while both men were riding side by side, sixty yards from him. They saw the action, and realizing their imminent danger, started to drop behind their horses just as the detective's linger touched the trigger of his Henry rifle.

The long and hard chase seemed about to be finished, as it was almost certain that Cook, being a dead shot, would either kill or seriously wound both of his men. His bead is perfect. The finger goes to the trigger; there is a quack, nervous pull—down goes the hammer and—"clack" goes the gun. It is a misfire, and the two men ride triumphantly on into the plains.

The real chase is only begun, for over the plains fly the swift steeds, pursuers and pursued. There are few parallel cases on record. For a distance of thirteen miles across the open country the two detectives chased the two criminals. At times the escape of the culprits seemed inevitable; at times their death or capture seemed certain.

After the effort above described to shoot the criminals, Smith at once seized his revolver and poured six shots after them. One of these shots just grazed Johnson's leg, cutting through the cuticle. As they rode through the town Cook left word for Sheriff Ellis to follow with a posse of men.

Across the country the chase continued, and up a small hill. Both pursuers threw away overcoat, gloves, scarf and pistol scabbards. Cook carried the gun, while Smith, having the fleetest horse, would ride ahead, stop, get off the horse, and be ready to take the gun and fire while Cook held the reins, or to hold the reins white Cook should fire.

But time and again the gun refused to go off. Finally, Cook turned over his revolver to Smith and tried to fix the gun, while on they ran. He endeavored to take it to pieces, but failed. He pulled one cartridge, and while putting in another it stuck fast. By main strength it was finally forced into the gun. Just before this Cook's horse, while attempting to jump a high sage brush, landed with his hind feet in a prairie dog hole, and he was thrown forward on the pommel of his saddle and was painfully hurt. After the cartridge had been forced home the officers rode up within range and gave two shots, both missing the mark. They again went after the men, who now left the road and turned into the prairie, and slightly towards Cañon City, moving over the country, jumping over the tall sagebrush and plunging into embankments of snow, over which the sun, which had now risen, gleamed as on the crest of ocean waves, almost blinding men and beast, but yet failing to take the edge off the March air, which was bitter cold.

Thus the chase went on until both parties gave evident signs of weakening. The fugitives had ridden their horses hard, and they were visibly weakening. The poor animals could not be whipped out of a trot. The officers came up to within sixty yards, and Cook being so near, shouted to them:

"'See here, boys, this thing has gone about far enough. Your horses are broken down. We are well heeled, and if you don't stop we'll kill you. You may count on it."

But the precious pair paid no heed to this warning, and went on as rapidly as their weary nags could carry them. Two more shots were sent after them,

A few feet further on the fugitives were seen to slacken their pace, and one of them to reel in his saddle and fall off his horse into the snow. This was Clodfelter, and he said to Johnson, as he stopped:

"We must surrender. It's no use. I'm shot."

He tried to brace himself with his right hand, but that had been disabled by a bullet which had struck the palm of the hand and plowed through it and up the fellows arm, breaking his pistol into smithereens. It was then that the officers discovered that they had "winged" one of their men. They had at first supposed that the men had determined to stop and make an even fight of it for their lives and liberty, but they now began to appreciate that they were preparing for a surrender, especially an Johnson also threw himself out of his saddle and threw his hands into the air, tossing his pistol away from him.

The officers dismounted and walked up to within twenty feet of the men. Johnson was standing with his hands up, and Clodfelter lay on the ground by the side of his horse, which was blowing so loud that he could have been heard a distance of two hundred yards, as were all the others, in fact. There was a momentary silence, when Cook, addressing Johnson, said:

"You surrender, do you?"

"We do," was the reply.

"Have you got another pistol?"

"I have just thrown it away."

"But have you another one? You don't come any Wilcox business on us. I will have you searched, and if another weapon is found upon you I will kill you where you stand. Do you understand?"

Slowly Johnson put his hand into an inside pocket and pulled out a revolver with his thumb and forefinger, and threw it upon the ground at his feet.

Clodfelter replied to questions that he had been so badly wounded as to be unable to get his pistol, which was in his pocket. Cook then covered the men with his gun while Smith searched them. Clodfelter was found to be quite seriously wounded, and faint from the loss of blood. He fainted away when the search was completed, and did not recover until a liberal supply of fresh snow had been dashed into his face.

The two men were then mounted upon their horses, and the party of four, officers and prisoners, started into Pueblo.

Looking far off towards the city, they saw a string of horsemen coming towards them, numbering apparently about twenty, and some of them five miles away. These were Sheriff Ellis and his posse, coming to the rescue of the two officers. The first of them had been encountered about half a mile from the scene of the capture, and soon after the sheriff himself was met. Mr. Ellis had started out gallantly at the head of his party. Put it must be remembered that the hour was early. The sheriff was a man of regular habits. He had started out very soon after getting his breakfast. He had ridden along for ten miles far in advance of the remainder of his party. He was fast gaining on Cook and Smith, and might eventually have passed them in the chase and have been the first to come up with the flyers. But he was compelled to stop to see other and slower members of his party pass him one by one, and to hear their jeers and hoots. In brief, the same circumstance which prevented the proverbial dog from catching the proverbial rabbit, stepped in to prevent Sheriff Ellis from overtaking the fugitive criminals. Poor fellow! no one enjoyed the joke more than he did. He was a good soul, and loved his fun and his fellow mortals too.

Almost the entire town of Pueblo met the party upon its return, and a cavalcade of fully two hundred men rode into town with them. Johnson was full of bravado, and swore that he and his "pard" would never have been captured had Clodfelter not been shot. As for Clodfelter, he sang another tune entirely. He professed to deeply regret his part in the affair, and time and time again said: "I'm sorry; I only hope they will not hang me." The tears would start and roll down his face when any one spoke of Charley Wilcox and his wounds, and he often asserted: "I had no enmity to Wilcox; I did it under excitement." Indeed, he seemed anything but a desperado, and was evidently deeply sensible of the grievous wrong he committed, and suffered as much as anyone.

Once on the train after leaving Pueblo, the two men told the story of their flight after the shooting of Wilcox, at Island Station, immediately after which they mounted their horses and rode to Brantner's. Johnson remained on his horse*, while Clodfelter went in and obtained a pair of blankets, and a cap and a coat for Johnson. Clodfelter told Brantner that there had got into trouble, but did not tell him the whole story. They then rode directly to Richard Morris' ranch, on the Platte, and about a mile from Brantners, and inquired for Morris. Not finding him in, they rode on to Jackson farm, about two miles and a half from Morris', up the Platte, and from there they went to Sopris' old ranch, at the junction of the Platte and Clear creek.

Here they endeavored to obtain pistols, and then bullets and powder and shot, but did not succeed. They did obtain food.

Their course was then straight for the mountains, intending to strike them south of Golden. They reached the foothills about sunrise Sunday morning, about eight miles, as they think, above Platte cañon. They spent most of the day in the mountains, but late in the afternoon came out, went to a ranch about three miles below and obtained feed for the horses and provisions for themselves. They then struck south, and a little before sundown crossed the Platte about a mile below the cañon, intending to strike the southern road. They traveled until about 12 o'clock that night, and after tying their horses laid down on the prairie and slept until morning. They were then on Willow (South Plum) creek, about a mile above Wakeman's. About 7 o'clock Monday morning they rode to Wakeman's and got coffee. From there they made south, in a direct line for the foothills, and struck the road running south to Colorado Springs about 3 o'clock in the afternoon. They followed the road for an hour, and then stopped at a house and got supper. They continued along the road, passing Monument and other stations. About 4 o'clock in the morning (Tuesday) they passed through Colorado Springs, and took the road south. Soon they became bewildered, and were uncertain about being on the right road. They descried a ranch and went to a hay-stack and fed their ponies, and discovered the railroad. This assured them, and crossing over to the west side of the track they continued their journey south, crossing the Fountaine about live miles below the ranch, and afterwards crossed back. About twelve miles from Colorado Springs they obtained a dinner and oats for their horses. As they pursued their southerly course, the snow began to fall and impede them. When about one mile from Pueblo, they put up at a ranch for the night, about 10 o'clock in the evening. About 7 o'clock in the morning (Wednesday) they started for Pueblo, and rode down one of the principal streets, when they were discovered. Not until they were close to the bridge did they imagine they were pursued, and then only from the peculiar action of two men on foot and two others on horseback.

Both men denied that Johnson said, "You know what I did for you once." They declared all that was said was, "You know what I've done" meaning the shooting at Wilcox, and hence requesting Clodfelter to help him out of the scrape.

There was great interest in the prisoners and their successful pursuers at all stations along the road, and especially at Colorado Springs, whose pursuing party had "marched up the hill and then marched down again;" or, in other words, had slept out all night after leaving Cook and Smith at Fountaine, and returned the next day to Colorado Springs, hungry, fatigued, sleepy, almost frozen and without their booty. Colorado Springs really enjoyed the chagrin of its light brigade, and gave Cook and his party a royal reception on their return through that place as the train halted at the depot.

There was another reception in Denver. The officers came in the third day after starting out, and brought their game with them. There was talk of lynching when the party arrived. Continually after it was announced that Johnson and Clodfelter had been captured and would arrive on the evening train, the probability of a "hanging bee" was discussed on the street and in every store. The sentiment of the community was, however, strongly against Judge Lynch, and certain incentives to the gathering of a mob were generally and severely denounced. Still curiosity and excitement among a certain class had reached such a pitch that measures were taken to prevent and thwart any action of the kind.

About the time of the arrival of the train, men and boys could be seen wending their way towards the Larimer and Fifteenth street crossings, and also to the depot, as rumor had named each place for the transfer of the prisoners to carriages. The largest crowd collected at the depot, where the train did unload its burden. It is said that there were those in the crowd who openly carried ropes for halters.

As soon as the train arrived at the depot the prisoners were transferred to a bus, their persons being protected by a sufficient number of good men to overawe any crowd who did not care to receive cold lead. The bus was occupied by two travelers, Gen. Cook and Frank Smith, of the Rocky Mountain Detective Association, by Johnson and Clodfelter and Sheriff Ellis, of Pueblo county. On top of the bus rode Sheriff Willoughby and aides. In the rear was a mounted policeman. As the bus moved up the street it was surrounded by a number of wagons and carriages, filled with people anxious to get a sight at the noted criminals, while still others followed on horseback.

On arrival at the jail, about three or four hundred persons were found collected at the entrance, who seemed indisposed to give back for the horses to pass. As soon as the bus came to a standstill, however, the crowd were parted by Sheriff Willoughby and his deputies, who arrived on the bus, and by still others at the jail. This passage was guarded by these men with drawn revolvers, and if any eff ort had been made to take the prisoners from the officers of the law, it would have resulted in terrible execution on the crowd. In the presence of such a display of armed men no disorder was observed, and in safety the prisoners were lodged in Arapahoe County jail.

From the time the procession of carriages left the depot until the prisoners were landed in the jail, hundreds of eyes peered from houses, stores and business blocks upon the unusual spectacle, and pedestrians paused in their walk to gaze upon the vehicle containing the men about whom so much had been written and said.

During this hurried trip through the city the prisoners were evidently uneasy and fearful of being lynched. When landed in jail and the doors were closed against the crowd, upon a remark being made to Clodfelter that he was safe, he replied:

"Yes, but the worst is to come hereafter."

Previous to being put in a cell, the shackles, which were riveted to their ankles, were cut off, and then the men were placed in confinement.

They were soon afterwards tried in Denver, but as Wilcox's wound did not prove fatal, they were only sent to the penitentiary for three and a half years each. They are both at liberty now, and their whereabouts has been lost sight of. Mr. Wilcox is still a resident of Denver, and now a member of the police force, and Gen. Cook carries a scar on his wrist which was caused by a slight wound created in attempting to remove the cartridge from his gun during the pursuit of the men.

The case was so thoroughly worked up by the detectives, and a due once obtained was followed with such skill, perseverance and pluck, that the praise of the entire state was justly awarded them. The press was full of commendation, but we shall let one example speak for all. The Pueblo *Chieftain* said the day after the capture:

> "Detectives D. J. Cook and Frank Smith have won fresh laurels for themselves by the excellent manner in which they have managed this case. Notwithstanding the fact that even the elements were arrayed against them, they have managed to follow up and arrest these scoundrels in a manner highly creditable to themselves and the association to which they belong."

A DREAM OF DEATH

Detectives, as a rule, are devoid of superstition. They-have sufficient offer of assistance from mediums and fortune tellers, and of other persons who profess to read the future, but they find that they do better, as a rule, when they depend solely upon the material facts which form their staple. They rely generally upon their own eyes and ears and shrewdness of mind to accomplish their work. As a rule, in fact, they are disbelievers in all that is supernatural or that comes from so-called second sight. But occasionally they see occurrences which they consider strange, to say the least. Gen. Cook does not call to mind any story in which clairvoyance or spiritualism has played any important part in the capture of a criminal, but he relates a reminiscence concerning the death of a fellow detective and member of the Rocky Mountain Detective Association, which is so very, very strange as to deserve a place in this record, especially as the circumstances are thoroughly authenticated. The story, regardless of this feature, is sufficiently thrilling to justify its publication here, but when this is added, the interest is increased tenfold. Indeed, there are few occurrences related in history which combine to such an extent the thrilling elements of official life with the mysterious features of the spiritual realm.

The story deals with Alex Ramsey and his wife, and is located at Hayes City, Kan., the time being the fall of 1875. Ramsey was at that time a man about thirty-three years of age, and was as fine a specimen of manhood as is met with in a day's journey. He was a thoroughly western man in all things—in manners, frankness and courage, as well as in stature. He was ever a hail fellow, genial with his friends, liberal to a fault, and as brave as a lion when duty called him to action. He was a good detective, excelling especially in his dealings with desperate characters. He had, a few years before the date of this story, married a confiding, impressionable little woman down in the Missouri valley, who loved him with all the strength of a woman's nature. She depended upon him implicitly, believed in his prowess in all matters, and realty worshiped him. Soon after their marriage they removed to Hayes City, near the Colorado line and then the terminus of the Kansas Pacific railroad—a live, bustling town, full of life and abounding in the rough characters who accompany the building of railroads in the West.

Ramsey had not long been in Hayes when his courage as well as his many manly qualities came to be known to the people of the place, as he frequently had occasion to aid in handling the violent spirits who congregated there. Hence it came about that when the people of that place came to want an executive officer in whom they could trust, they selected Ramsey. Gen Cook, as chief of the Rocky Mountain Detective Agency, heard of this man, and in 1871 invited him to become a member of his association. The offer was accepted, and Ramsey became one of the most active of the officers of the organization, always conducting himself so as to win the approbation and maintain the confidence of his chief. Ramsey had served one term as sheriff of his county, and in the summer of 1875 was reelected, virtually without opposition. Being in Denver soon after the reelection, he told Gen. Cook that he was the first sheriff who had ever lived to be elected to a second term in Hayes City, his three predecessors having been killed before the expiration of their respective terms of office. To have gone through one siege," he said, "and I am going to try it again. The chances are that I shall be killed, but I will take the chances."

It was in October following his visit to Denver that Mr. Ramsey was called upon to go in pursuit of a couple of horse thieves. A character well-known on the frontier in those days as "Dutch Pete," and known by no other name, accompanied by a pal whose name is not known at all, one night made a raid upon a band of horses belonging to a man living in Colorado, and stampeded thirty-five head of them. When the owner awoke the next morning he found his animals gone, and was able to ascertain that the thieves had taken their booty in the direction of Smoky Hill or the Republican river. His first impulse, as he afterwards explained, was to pursue them himself, but remembering the skill and courage of Ramsey in running down such characters, he changed his mind, and went to Hayes City and put the case in his hands.

Mr. Ramsey cheerfully took charge of the matter, securing Frank Shepherd, a friend in whom he had confidence, as an assistant in the work before him, and kissing his wife an affectionate farewell, he rode off in company with Shepherd, going towards Smoky Hill with the intention of cutting off the retreat of the thieves. The two officers started off thoroughly armed and well mounted. Their horses galloped away in spirit, has if anxious to lessen the distance between the officers and their game.

Mrs. Ramsey watched the horsemen as long as she could see them, gazing even into the blank horizon after they had disappeared as if to feast her eyes as long as possible upon the manly form of her husband, so full of life and hardy manhood. She had been used to having him placed in positions of danger, and so great was her confidence in her husband's superiority over other people in courage and coolness, that she had come to have but little fear for his personal welfare when out on an expedition like this upon which he was now starting. But, somehow, she seemed to feel an unusual desire on this occasion to have Mr. Ramsey not go, although she did not say so to him, for she knew that he would attend to his duty in spite of any forebodings of hers, which he would consider foolish, womanish fear. But she gazed longer and earnestly after him, and at last when she knew that he had gone for good, had turned to go in the house, exclaiming, "Oh pshaw! this is foolish. I know he will come back. He always does, doesn't he?"

She thus dismissed the matter from her mind as completely as she could, and went about her household duties, making herself as busy as possible during the day and as far into the night as she could find anything to do. As a consequence of this over exertion Mrs. Ramsey slept soundly upon going to bed. Everybody about the house had retired either before or at the time that she did, and all were by-midnight busy with their dreams. They were, however, at this hour startled into a thorough state of wakefulness by a scream which rent the air, and which came from the direction of the room of Mrs. Ramsey.

The entire household was astir in a moment, and all rushed pell-mell into Mrs. Ramsey's apartments. They found her out of bed in her night clothes, and her two children, one of them a mere baby, clinging to her. She was talking in an incoherent manner at the top of her voice and the children, thoroughly frightened at their mother's manner, were crying loudly. The inmates of the house succeeded in a few moments in quieting the woman down, and at last procured an explanation from her. "Such a horrid—horrid dream!" she explained. "Oh, I know it's true! I saw it—just as plain as day—plainer than I see you—just as real and terrible as if I had been there. I just know that Alex is dead. I didn't want him to go. I tried to the last to see him. I never in my life so longed to beg him not to go. I wish I had. I believe he would have stayed with me. But poor, poor fellow, I shall never see him again, except in death."

A TWO AND TWO FIGHT

Mrs. Ramsey, after this raving narrative, became more quiet and told the people standing about her that she had dreamed that she had seen Mr. Ramsey and Mr. Shepherd come upon the horse thieves and attack them; that the thieves had started to dee on their horses; that the officers had followed and fired upon them, the thieves returning the tire. Three men had fallen almost simultaneously from their horses, two of them being the fugitives and the third her husband, who had been fatally shot. Her dream had continued so as to take her out to search for her husband with the hope of meeting him upon his return. Instead of meeting him alive and well she had encountered a covered wagon, which she described, bringing in his dead body, seeing which she had screamed so loud as to awaken herself and others asleep near her.

This was the dream as Mrs. Ramsey told it. It had been so real to her and the occurrences so tangible that she felt that a tragedy such as she had described had occurred, and refused to be comforted by the argument that it was foolish to pay any heed to a dream. Such she agreed was usually the case, but in this instance she felt that she had really been present at the hilling of her husband. The conviction seemed to take complete possession of her. No reasoning would shake her belief that she had been a real witness to a tragedy which had resulted in her beloved husband's death.

Mrs. Ramsey refused to again attempt to sleep or even to retire again that night. The only comfort which she seemed to receive was in the assurance that as soon as day should break she should be driven out in the direction which her husband had taken. "I know I shall meet that covered wagon," she said, "I just know it, but I want to go, anyhow, and to know the worst."

According to promise she was allowed to start out from Hayes at a very early hour the succeeding morning, a friend accompanying her in a carriage. They had driven out a distance of fourteen miles without meeting any one, when there began to dawn a ray of hope that the dreadful vision of the dream would prove to have been merely a hallucination, caused by the imperfect action of the brain while asleep. But the poor woman looked eagerly forward for the purpose of getting the first view of that which she most dreaded to see.

Long as it was in coming, the wagon came in sight all too soon. Rising up over the summit of an elevation in the plains and looking down the descending grade she saw slowly coming towards her and her companion a covered wagon drawn by two horses. Throwing up her hands so as to cover her eyes she exclaimed with all the force of positive conviction:

"My God! there's the wagon."

She could not have been more positive if she had seen the vehicle only the day before. After this sight she refused to be comforted and only urged her driver to increase his speed, sobbing as if heartbroken as they pushed on.

The woman's dream had been more than a dream. It had been a real vision. There had been no deception. The vehicle was just as she had described it and in it lay the lifeless body of her husband, just as his wife had said would be found to be the case.

Very strange all this is, to be sure, and yet true to the letter. Let who can explain it.

Inquiry revealed the fact that the shooting had occurred just as it had appeared to Mrs. Ramsey and just as she described it to half a dozen witnesses before leaving Hayes City. The officers had come upon the thieves in the afternoon of the first day out, thirty-five miles from Hayes, just as they were concluding their dinners and preparing to continue their journey. They had mounted when they discovered the officers riding down upon them. The thieves knew Ramsey, and their first thought was to escape from him at all hazards. They accordingly put spurs to their horses which they rode, leaving the others which they had stolen behind. The officers spurred up their horses also, and were soon chasing the thieves across the plains. The two parties were not less than sixty yards apart when Ramsey said to Shepherd, after having summoned the fugitives to halt:

346

"Well, I don't see that there is anything to do but to bring them down. You take the one on your side and I'll take the fellow on my side."

This speech had hardly been spoken when the two thieves turned in their saddles with pistols presented. It was plain to be seen that there must be a deadly duel then and there.

"Won't you surrender?" shouted Ramsey.

"Never!" was the reply.

"Then we will kill you."

"Fire away."

"Give it to'em." Thus to Shepherd.

There were four pistol shots coming so close together as to sound like a volley.

One of the thieves, the one at whom Ramsey had shot, reeled and tumbled from his horse dead. The other reeled but did not fall, and Shepherd spurred on after him, not noticing that Ramsey did not follow. After galloping a short distance the second man fell from his saddle mortally wounded...

Turning then for the first time, Shepherd, who was unhurt, discovered that Ramsey had been knocked from his horse. He had been shot through and through, the ball passing near his heart. There was a ranch a few miles distant and Shepherd determined to make an effort to get his friend to it and to leave the thieves where they had fallen. "Dutch Pete" proved to be the man at whom Ramsey had directed his aim. He it was who had shot Ramsey. But Ramsey's shot had gone straight home, passing through Pete's heart. The other thief was also mortally wounded, and soon died. Their bodies were covered with stones and left where they had fallen. The stolen horses were gathered together and returned to their owner.

As for Ramsey, he was taken to the ranch referred to and given every possible attention. But after lingering on in great pain he died at 12 o'clock of the night succeeding the shooting—at the exact hour at which Mrs. Ramsey had had her startling and strange dream.

The body was then placed in the ranchman's covered wagon, and the cortege started for Hayes City, meeting Mrs. Ramsey on the road.

It is useless to attempt to further describe the anguish of the poor woman. She refused to be comforted after her husband's death, and two weeks after his funeral she was a raving maniac. Four months afterwards her unhappy spirit deserted the flesh and she joined her husband in the world beyond this.

A MEXICAN BANDIT

Candado Costello, a nephew of the famous murderer, Espinoza, although the blood of the ancient Castilian nobility flowed through his veins, was a bad, bad Mexican.

And, although we have neither the space nor the inclination to moralize at any length, it might be well to remark, for the benefit of the boys who feast upon blood-and-thunder novels of the yellow-back variety, that bad men invariably come to grief. For a time they may rob and kill and plunder, and swagger around saloons on the proceeds of their crimes, terrorizing peaceable and defenseless people, yet sooner or later justice will overtake them, and they must pay the penalty of their crimes. This is the inexorable law of fate, and though they may be able for a time to evade its penalties, they are only enjoying a respite—their days are numbered, and the number is never large. But to return to our subject.

Costillo was a murderer as well as a thief, there being no less than four cold-blooded murders that have been directly traced to his bloodstained hand. But the particular case which we wish to relate here, is that of the killing of a wealthy Mexican cattleman near Bernallilo, N. M., in 1886, for which he was brought to justice by two members of the Rocky Mountain Detective Association—Frank A. Hyatt, and Walter O'Malley, of Walsenburg.

Costillo, with his brother Juan and a number of other relatives and friends, made their homes in the almost Inaccessible Huerfano cañon, about twelve miles north of Walsenburg, Colo. From this stronghold they sallied forth on many a raid after cattle and horses, which they generally managed to escape back into the Cañon within safety. In the raid on Romero's ranch, he and his brother secured a line bunch of cattle and were driving them toward home, when they were overtaken near Espanola by Romero and his son. They turned and fired upon their pursuers, and the elder Romero fell dead. The son escaped back home and tried to persuade their neighbors and friends to organize a posse and follow his father's murderers, but they were all afraid to follow the desperado.

Mrs. Romero offered a reward of $5,000 for the capture of Candado Costillo, Juan having escaped to old Mexico. Gov. Shelton offered $500, and an uncle of Mrs. Romero $100 more. All these rewards did not tempt the local officials to capture, him, and the sheriff of Huerfano county, for some reason or other, did not make any effort to apprehend the criminal.

Finally, Senator Barilla, of Walsenburg, a friend of Romero, the murdered man, wrote to Dr. Gale, of Alamosa, asking him to interest Frank Hyatt in the case, as he knew of no one else that would undertake the difficult job.

Hyatt commenced work on the case about the 1st of May, 1887. He went up to Walsenburg and had a consultation with O'Malley as to the best means of securing their man. O'Malley said that it would be almost useless to attempt to take the murderer at his home, but added that Costillo was subpoenaed as a witness in a civil case that was to be called up for trial in about a month, and that would tie the best time to effect his capture. So they agreed to wait, and Hyatt returned to Alamosa.

On the 2d of June he received a message from O'Malley, saying: "Man O. K. Come at once." He went to Walsenburg that evening, and the next morning, O'Malley came to his room at the hotel with the information that Costillo was then in the court room. They both went over to the court house, and Hyatt stepped into the office of Treasurer Nolan to wait while O'Malley hunted up Costillo. When O'Malley entered the room with Costillo, Hyatt was pretending to read a paper, and paid no attention to them until O'Malley introduced the Mexican, who stepped forward, with his right hand extended, to shake hands. Hyatt seized the Mexican's right hand with his own left, and held it as in a vice, at the same time leveling his revolver with his right. Realizing that he had been neatly trapped, Costillo did not make a struggle, and O'Malley quickly slipped the first pair of "dead cinch" handcuffs ever placed on a murderer's wrists on tin' prisoner.

Hyatt and O'Malley, with their prisoner, hurried out of town toward La Veta, to take the train for Santa Fe. At La Veta they were overtaken by a deputy sheriff and a posse, with a writ of habeas corpus for Costillo, and a warrant for the arrest of Hyatt, on a charge of kidnapping. This necessitated a return to Walsenburg but as soon as the case could be called up, Hyatt was discharged, and allowed to proceed with his prisoner, whom he landed safely at Santa Fe.

Gov. Sheldon promptly paid the $500 reward offered by him, as did the uncle of Mrs. Romero, but the widow declined to pay the $5,000 she had offered, or any part of it, and Hyatt finally decided to let her go. Costillo was found guilty and sentenced to eight years in the territorial penitentiary.

Costillo was a model prisoner and in consequence a large portion of his sentence was deducted for good behavior. This was due not to any good qualities of the brute nor to a desire to reform, but was simply a cunning design to obtain freedom that he might the sooner wreak the vengeance his blood-thirsty appetite desired. He was afraid to attack the plucky officer who had sent him over the road, so he contented himself with the murder of inoffensive travelers, by his own confession in a letter to a friend, having killed no less than four white men after his release.

The crime for which he was finally shot to death was the murder of two Swede miners at Red Hill pass, in South park, in 1891. He, with a younger Mexican, killed the Swedes while they were camped at night, and dragged their bodies away from the road so that they were not found for several days. Finally they were discovered, and the sheriff of Park county with two deputies, started after the Mexicans, who they learned had gone to Costillo's old retreat in the Huerfano cañon. They seem to have killed the two miners simply for revenge, as neither of them had any money or other property sufficient to tempt the cupidity of even a Mexican.

When the sheriffs had them surrounded in their cabin the young Mexican surrendered, but old Costillo refused to give up, and stood the officers off for two or three days. Finally he made a desperate dash for liberty and was shot all to pieces by the officers, and no one mourned his loss. It is doubtful if he was even given decent burial, as his neighbors, who were nearly all Mexicans, despised him so thoroughly that they would have nothing to do with him.

The young Mexican was convicted of murder and sentenced to the penitentiary for life, and is now probably serving out his time.

CONCLUSION

Just a word with the reader in finishing this book. Not by way of apology or explanation, but as a general adieu. Certainly we feel that the stories as here given explain themselves, and we believe that the reader, will agree with the writer, after perusing the volume from beginning to end, that he has gotten the worth of his money. Hence no apology is necessary. It is true that the cases here related have not been drawn out as is the custom with some detectives who write books, but this neglect, if such it may be termed, has been intentional. It is not believed that the western reader has time to pore over small details, or that he cares to know of every step of the detectives, whose personal conduct outside of their real accomplishments in the line in which they may be operating is of no consequence to anyone but themselves. Hence this book has not dealt with all the little operations of the detectives who figure in its pages. Its aim has been to present the material and important facts, and to picture the criminal as well as the officer.

The criminal of the Far West is a man who displays himself most thoroughly in times of emergency. It is when he comes face to face with the officer that he is desperate and difficult to deal with. He will always fight, and the officer who hunts him down may in four cases out of five count upon having to take his man at the muzzle of his revolver. It is this fact which makes the western narrative of more thrilling interest than that of the more conservative eastern localities. It is also this fact which increases the danger and hardship of a detective's life in the West. The detective of the Rocky mountains, and of the plains which stretch out to the great rivers in the middle of the continent, must be a man possessed not alone of a keen capacity for hunting down criminals, but must have the courage to face such criminal when taken, and to risk his life in hand-to-hand combat when his man is come upon. But it would seem unnecessary to dwell upon this fact for the benefit of the reader of this volume. It speaks for itself. There is hardly a story of the number told which does not bear out this assertion. There are very few captures here reported which have not been made by officers who risked their own lives in making them. There are some cases in which men made such resistance as to require that they be shot down in their tracks and in some cases it has been the sad duty to chronicle the killing of efficient and faithful officers by these desperadoes. As a class, however, Gen. Cook's men have proved quite capable of taking care of themselves, while his own escape from the desperado's bullet, during his thirty-five years of active detective life on the border, has been little less than marvelous. It can be accounted for only upon the ground that he is shrewd enough to detect many difficulties before they arise, courageous enough to meet them promptly when they do come, and cool and skillful enough to give them better than they send when the emergency arises. It thus happens that he is alive and prosperous, after serving thirty-five years of detective life on the border, when nearly all of his old-time companions are dead. He has also trained his men so thoroughly that they have learned to protect themselves.

But the record here presented is not merely one of daring and adventure. It is one of hardships and great personal sacrifice as well. It will appear in many of the stories told that the events related occurred at a time when there were no railroads in the country. Gen. Cook and his officers have, since the time when he first settled in Colorado, traversed almost the entire barren plains and Rocky mountains from Northern Dakota to Southwestern Texas, climbing precipices, stage-coaching, horseback riding and walking; sleeping out for several nights in succession, subsisting for days on the scantiest supply of food, and often going from sixty to seventy-two hours without sleep; facing the worst of storms, and, indeed, enduring all the privations of frontier life, where there are few people, fewer accommodations and much that is trying upon mind and body. Any one of the trips, such as those recorded of Gen. Cook in the Britt and Hilligoss or Clodfelter and Johnson story, would be sufficient to use up an ordinary individual, and many would be entirely unable to endure it. Yet Gen. Cook has put in thirty-five years in just such service, ever mindful of the public welfare and forgetful of his own comfort and quiet; ever anxious to bring the guilty to punishment and to free the country of the human vultures who prey upon it, regardless of his own private well-being, and in many cases without hope of reward or appreciation. That he has in his day done a grand service for the people of the state in making it a place disagreeable and dangerous to evil-doers is a truth which many appreciate. His services have ever been at the command of the people among whom he lives, and the stories here told—only a portion of those which might be related—best attest that when he has acted he has done so in a way to make the work count.

THE END

Discover more lost history from BIG BYTE BOOKS